Collins easy learning

French
Grammar
& Practice

J'espère te voir
la semaine prochaine.

Qui a fait ça?

Published by Collins
An imprint of HarperCollins Publishers
Westerhill Road
Bishopbriggs
Glasgow G64 2QT

HarperCollins*Publishers*
1st Floor, Watermarque Building,
Ringsend Road, Dublin 4, Ireland

Second edition 2016

ISBN 978-0-00-814163-9

10 9

www.collinsdictionary.com
www.collins.co.uk/languagesupport

Typeset by Davidson Publishing
Solutions, Glasgow

Printed by Martins the Printers

If you would like to comment on any
aspect of this book, please contact us at the
given address or online.
E-mail: dictionaries@harpercollins.co.uk
 www.facebook.com/collinsdictionary
 @collinsdict

Acknowledgements
We would like to thank those authors and
publishers who kindly gave permission
for copyright material to be used in the
Collins Corpus. We would also like to
thank Times Newspapers Ltd for providing
valuable data.

MANAGING EDITOR
Maree Airlie

CONTRIBUTORS
Laurence Larroche
Maggie Seaton

FOR THE PUBLISHER
Gerry Breslin
Craig Balfour

Contents

Foreword for language teachers

The *Easy Learning French Grammar & Practice* is designed to be used with both young and adult learners, as a group revision and practice book to complement your course book during classes, or as a recommended text for self-study and homework/coursework.

The text specifically targets learners from beginner to intermediate or GCSE level, and therefore its structural content and vocabulary have been matched to the relevant specifications up to and including Higher GCSE.

The approach aims to develop knowledge and understanding of grammar and your learners' ability to apply it by:

- defining parts of speech at the start of each major section with examples in English to clarify concepts
- minimizing the use of grammar terminology and providing clear explanations of terms both within the text and in the **Glossary**
- illustrating all points with examples (and their translations) based on topics and contexts which are relevant to beginner and intermediate course content
- providing exercises which allow learners to practice grammar points

The text helps you develop positive attitudes to grammar learning in your classes by:

- giving clear, easy-to-follow explanations
- highlighting useful **Tips** to deal with common difficulties
- summarizing **Key points** at the end of sections to consolidate learning
- illustrating **Key points** with practice examples

Introduction for students

Whether you are starting to learn French for the very first time, brushing up on topics you have studied in class, or revising for your GCSE exams, the *Easy Learning French Grammar & Practice* is here to help. This easy-to-use revision and practice guide takes you through all the basics you will need to speak and understand modern, everyday French.

Newcomers can sometimes struggle with the technical terms they come across when they start to explore the grammar of a new language. The *Easy Learning French Grammar & Practice* explains how to get to grips with all the parts of speech you will need to know, using simple language and cutting out jargon.

The text is divided into sections, each dealing with a particular area of grammar. Each section can be studied individually, as numerous cross-references in the text point you to relevant points in other sections of the book for further information.

Every major section begins with an explanation of the area of grammar covered on the following pages. For quick reference, these definitions are also collected together on pages viii–xii in a glossary of essential grammar terms.

What is a verb?

A **verb** is a 'doing' word which describes what someone or something does, what someone or something is, or what happens to them, for example, *be, sing, live*.

Each grammar point in the text is followed by simple examples of real French, complete with English translations, to help you understand the rules. Underlining has been used in examples throughout the text to highlight the grammatical point being explained.

➤ If you are talking about a part of your body, you usually use a word like *my* or *his* in English, but in French you usually use the definite article.

Tourne <u>la</u> tête à gauche.	Turn your head to the left.
Il s'est cassé <u>le</u> bras.	He's broken his arm.
J'ai mal à <u>la</u> gorge.	My throat hurts.

In French, as with any foreign language, there are certain pitfalls which have to be avoided. **Tips** and **Information** notes throughout the text are useful reminders of the things that often trip learners up.

Tip

If you are in doubt as to which form of *you* to use, it is safest to use **vous** so you will not offend anybody.

Key points sum up all the important facts about a particular area of grammar, to save you time when you are revising and help you focus on the main grammatical points.

> ### KEY POINTS
> ✔ With masculine singular nouns use **un**.
> ✔ With feminine singular nouns use **une**.
> ✔ With plural nouns use **des**.
> ✔ **un**, **une** and **des** change to **de** or **d'** in negative sentences.
> ✔ The indefinite article is not usually used when you say what jobs people do, or in exclamations with **quel**.

After each Key point you can find a number of exercises to help you practice all the important grammatical points. You can find the answer to each exercise on pages 260–276.

If you think you would like to continue with your French studies to a higher level, check out the **Grammar Extra** sections. These are intended for advanced students who are interested in knowing a little more about the structures they will come across beyond GCSE.

Grammar Extra!
If you want to use an adjective after **quelque chose**, **rien**, **quelqu'un** and **personne**, you link the words with **de**.

quelqu'un <u>d</u>'important	someone important
quelque chose <u>d</u>'intéressant	something interesting
rien <u>d</u>'amusant	nothing funny

Finally, the supplement at the end of the book contains **Verb Tables**, where 21 important French verbs (both regular and irregular) are declined in full. Examples show you how to use these verbs in your own work.

We hope that you will enjoy using the *Easy Learning French Grammar & Practice* and find it useful in the course of your studies.

Glossary of Grammar Terms

ABSTRACT NOUN a word used to refer to a quality, idea, feeling or experience, rather than a physical object, for example, *size*, *reason*, *happiness*. Compare with **concrete noun**.

ADJECTIVE a 'describing' word that tells you more about a person or thing, such as their appearance, colour, size or other qualities, for example, *pretty*, *blue*, *big*.

ADVERB a word usually used with verbs, adjectives or other adverbs that gives more information about when, where, how or in what circumstances something happens, for example, *quickly*, *happily*, *now*.

AGREE (to) to change word endings according to whether you are referring to masculine, feminine, singular or plural people or things.

AGREEMENT changing word endings according to whether you are referring to masculine, feminine, singular or plural people or things.

APOSTROPHE S an ending ('s) added to a noun to show who or what someone or something belongs to, for example, *Danielle's dog*, *the doctor's wife*, *the book's cover*.

ARTICLE a word like *the*, *a* and *an*, which is used in front of a noun. See also **definite article, indefinite article** and **partitive article**.

AUXILIARY VERB a verb such as *be*, *have* and *do* when it is used with a main verb to form tenses and questions.

BASE FORM the form of the verb without any endings added to it, for example, *walk*, *have*, *be*, *go*. Compare with **infinitive**.

CARDINAL NUMBER a number used in counting, for example, *one*, *seven*, *ninety*. Compare with **ordinal number**.

CLAUSE a group of words containing a verb.

COMPARATIVE an adjective or adverb with *-er* on the end of it, or *more* or *less* in front of it, that is used to compare people, things or actions, for example, *slower*, *less important*, *more carefully*.

COMPOUND NOUN a word for a living being, thing or idea, which is made up of two or more words, for example, *tin-opener*, *railway station*.

CONCRETE NOUN a word that refers to an object you can touch with your hand, rather than to a quality or idea, for example, *ball*, *map*, *apples*. Compare with **abstract noun**.

CONDITIONAL a verb form used to talk about things that would happen or would be true under certain conditions, for example, *I would help you if I could*. It is also used to say what you would like or need, for example, *Could you give me the bill?*

CONJUGATE (to) to give a verb different endings according to whether you are referring to *I*, *you*, *they* and so on, and according to whether you are referring to past, present or future, for example, *I have*, *she has*, *he had*.

CONJUGATION a group of verbs which have the same endings as each other or change according to the same pattern.

CONJUNCTION a word such as *and*, *because* or *but* that links two words or phrases of a similar type, or two parts of a sentence, for example, *Diane and I have been friends for years*.; *I left because I was bored*.

CONSONANT a letter of the alphabet which is not a vowel, for example, *b*, *f*, *m*, *s*, *v*. Compare with **vowel**.

CONSTRUCTION an arrangement of words together in a phrase or sentence.

DEFINITE ARTICLE the word *the*. Compare with **indefinite article.**

DEMONSTRATIVE ADJECTIVE one of the words *this*, *that*, *these* and *those* used with a noun to point out a particular person or thing, for example, <u>*this*</u> *woman*, <u>*that*</u> *dog*.

DEMONSTRATIVE PRONOUN one of the words *this*, *that*, *these* and *those* used instead of a noun to point out people or things, for example, <u>*That*</u> *looks fun*.

DIRECT OBJECT a noun referring to the person or thing affected by the action described by a verb, for example, *She wrote* <u>*her name*</u>*.; I shut* <u>*the window*</u>. Compare with **indirect object**.

DIRECT OBJECT PRONOUN a word such as *me*, *him*, *us* and *them* which is used instead of a noun to stand in for the person or thing most directly affected by the action described by the verb. Compare with **indirect object pronoun**.

EMPHATIC PRONOUN a word used instead of a noun when you want to emphasize something, for example, *Is this for* <u>*me*</u>*?; 'Who broke the window?' — 'He did.'* Also called **stressed pronoun**.

ENDING a form added to a verb, for example, *go* → <u>*goes*</u>, and to adjectives and nouns depending on whether they refer to masculine, feminine, singular or plural things.

EXCLAMATION a word, phrase or sentence that you use to show you are surprised, shocked, angry and so on, for example, *Wow!; How dare you!; What a surprise!*

FEMININE a form of noun, pronoun or adjective that is used to refer to a living being, thing or idea that is not classed as masculine.

FUTURE a verb tense used to talk about something that will happen or will be true.

GENDER whether a noun, pronoun or adjective is feminine or masculine.

IMPERATIVE the form of a verb used when giving orders and instructions, for example, *Shut the door!; Sit down!; Don't go!*

IMPERFECT one of the verb tenses used to talk about the past, especially in descriptions, and to say what was happening or used to happen, for example, *I used to walk to school; It was sunny at the weekend*. Compare with **perfect**.

IMPERSONAL VERB one which does not refer to a real person or thing, and where the subject is represented by *it*, for example, *It's going to rain; It's 10 o'clock*.

INDEFINITE ADJECTIVE one of a small group of adjectives used to talk about people or things in a general way, without saying who or what they are, for example, *several, all, every*.

INDEFINITE ARTICLE the words *a* and *an*. Compare with **definite article**.

INDEFINITE PRONOUN a small group of pronouns such as *everything*, *nobody* and *something*, which are used to refer to people or things in a general way, without saying exactly who or what they are.

INDIRECT OBJECT a noun used with verbs that take two objects. For example, in *I gave the carrot to the rabbit*, *the rabbit* is the indirect object and *carrot* is the direct object. Compare with **direct object**.

INDIRECT OBJECT PRONOUN a pronoun used instead of a noun to show the person or the thing the action is intended to benefit or harm, for example, *me* in *He gave* <u>*me*</u> *a book* and *Can you get* <u>*me*</u> *a towel?* Compare with **direct object pronoun**.

INDIRECT QUESTION used to tell someone else about a question and introduced by a verb such as *ask*, *tell* or *wonder*, for example, *He asked me what the time was*; *I wonder who he is*.

INFINITIVE the form of the verb with *to* in front of it and without any endings added, for example, *to walk*, *to have*, *to be*, *to go*. Compare with **base form**.

INTERROGATIVE ADJECTIVE a question word used with a noun to ask *who?*, *what?* or *which?* for example, *What* instruments do you play?; *Which* shoes do you like?

INTERROGATIVE PRONOUN one of the words *who*, *whose*, *whom*, *what* and *which* when they are used instead of a noun to ask questions, for example, *What's* happening?; *Who's* coming?

INVARIABLE used to describe a form which does not change.

IRREGULAR VERB a verb whose forms do not follow a general pattern or the normal rules. Compare with **regular verb**.

MASCULINE a form of noun, pronoun or adjective that is used to refer to a living being, thing or idea that is not classed as feminine.

NEGATIVE a question or statement which contains a word such as *not*, *never* or *nothing*, and is used to say that something is not happening, is not true or is absent, for example, *I never eat meat*; *Don't you love me?*

NOUN a 'naming' word for a living being, thing or idea, for example, *woman*, *desk*, *happiness*, *Andrew*.

NUMBER used to say how many things you are referring to or where something comes in a sequence. See also **ordinal number** and **cardinal number**.

OBJECT a noun or pronoun which refers to a person or thing that is affected by the action described by the verb. Compare with **direct object**, **indirect object** and **subject**.

OBJECT PRONOUN one of the set of pronouns including *me*, *him* and *them*, which are used instead of the noun as the object of a verb or preposition. Compare with **subject pronoun**.

ORDINAL NUMBER a number used to indicate where something comes in an order or sequence, for example, *first*, *fifth*, *sixteenth*. Compare with **cardinal number**.

PART OF SPEECH a word class, for example, *noun*, *verb*, *adjective*, *preposition*, *pronoun*.

PARTITIVE ARTICLE the words *some* or *any*, used to refer to part of a thing but not all of it, for example, *Have you got any money?*; *I'm going to buy some bread*.

PASSIVE a form of the verb that is used when the subject of the verb is the person or thing that is affected by the action, for example, *we were told*.

PAST PARTICIPLE a verb form which is used to form perfect and pluperfect tenses and passives, for example, *watched*, *swum*. Some past participles are also used as adjectives, for example, *a broken watch*.

PERFECT one of the verb tenses used to talk about the past, especially about actions that took place and were completed in the past. Compare with **imperfect**.

PERSON one of the three classes: the first person (*I*, *we*), the second person (*you* singular and *you* plural), and the third person (*he*, *she*, *it* and *they*).

PERSONAL PRONOUN one of the group of words including *I*, *you* and *they* which are used to refer to yourself, the people you are talking to, or the people or things you are talking about.

PLUPERFECT one of the verb tenses used to describe something that *had* happened or had been true at a point in the past, for example, *I had forgotten to finish my homework*.

PLURAL the form of a word which is used to refer to more than one person or thing. Compare with **singular**.

POSSESSIVE ADJECTIVE one of the words *my, your, his, her, its, our* or *their*, used with a noun to show that one person or thing belongs to another.

POSSESSIVE PRONOUN one of the words *mine, yours, hers, his, ours* or *theirs*, used instead of a noun to show that one person or thing belongs to another.

PREPOSITION is a word such as *at, for, with, into* or *from*, which is usually followed by a noun, pronoun or, in English, a word ending in *-ing*. Prepositions show how people and things relate to the rest of the sentence, for example, *She's <u>at</u> home; a tool <u>for</u> cutting grass; It's <u>from</u> David.*

PRESENT a verb form used to talk about what is true at the moment, what happens regularly, and what is happening now, for example, *I'm a student; I <u>travel</u> to college by train; I'm <u>studying</u> languages.*

PRESENT PARTICIPLE a verb form ending in *-ing* which is used in English to form verb tenses, and which may be used as an adjective or a noun, for example, *What are you <u>doing</u>?; the <u>setting</u> sun; <u>Swimming</u> is easy!*

PRONOUN a word which you use instead of a noun, when you do not need or want to name someone or something directly, for example, *it, you, none.*

PROPER NOUN the name of a person, place, organization or thing. Proper nouns are always written with a capital letter, for example, *Kevin, Glasgow, Europe, London Eye.*

QUESTION WORD a word such as *why, where, who, which* or *how* which is used to ask a question.

REFLEXIVE PRONOUN a word ending in *-self* or *-selves*, such as *myself* or *themselves*, which refers back to the subject, for example, *He hurt <u>himself</u>.; Take care of <u>yourself</u>.*

REFLEXIVE VERB a verb where the subject and object are the same, and where the action 'reflects back' on the subject. A reflexive verb is used with a reflexive pronoun such as *myself, yourself, herself*, for example, *I washed myself.; He cut himself.*

REGULAR VERB a verb whose forms follow a general pattern or the normal rules. Compare with **irregular verb**.

RELATIVE PRONOUN a word such as *that, who* or *which*, when it is used to link two parts of a sentence together.

SENTENCE a group of words which usually has a verb and a subject. In writing, a sentence has a capital letter at the beginning and a full stop, question mark or exclamation mark at the end.

SINGULAR the form of a word which is used to refer to one person or thing. Compare with **plural**.

STEM the main part of a verb to which endings are added.

STRESSED PRONOUN a word used instead of a noun when you want to emphasize something, for example, *Is this for <u>me</u>?; 'Who broke the window?' — '<u>He</u> did.'* Also called **emphatic pronoun**.

SUBJECT the noun in a sentence or phrase that refers to the person or thing that does the action described by the verb or is in the state described by the verb, for example, *<u>My cat</u> doesn't drink milk.* Compare with **object**.

SUBJECT PRONOUN a pronoun such as *I, he, she* and *they* which is used instead of a noun as the subject of a sentence. Pronouns stand in for nouns when it is clear who is being talked about, for example, *My brother isn't here at the moment. <u>He</u>'ll be back in an hour.* Compare with **object pronoun**.

SUBJUNCTIVE a verb form used in certain circumstances to express some sort of feeling, or to show doubt about whether something will happen or whether something is true. It is only used occasionally in modern English, for example, *If I were you, I wouldn't bother.*; *So be it*.

SUPERLATIVE an adjective or adverb with *-est* on the end of it or *most* or *least* in front of it, that is used to compare people, things or actions, for example, *thinnest, most quickly, least interesting*.

SYLLABLE a consonant+vowel unit that makes up all or part of a word, for example, *ca-the-dral (3 syllables), im-po-ssi-ble (4 syllables)*.

TENSE the form of a verb which shows whether you are referring to the past, present or future.

VERB a 'doing' word which describes what someone or something does, what someone or something is, or what happens to them, for example, *be, sing, live*.

VOWEL one of the letters *a, e, i, o* or *u*. Compare with **consonant**.

Nouns

> ### What is a noun?
> A **noun** is a 'naming' word for a living being, thing or idea, for example,
> *woman, happiness, Andrew*.

Using nouns

➤ In French, all nouns are either <u>masculine</u> or <u>feminine</u>. This is called their <u>gender</u>. Even words for things have a gender.

➤ Whenever you are using a noun, you need to know whether it is masculine or feminine as this affects the form of other words used with it, such as:
  • adjectives that describe it
  • articles (such as **le** or **une**) that go before it
  • pronouns (such as **il** or **elle**) that replace it

  ⇨ *For more information on **Adjectives**, **Articles** or **Pronouns**, see pages 32, 14 and 55.*

➤ You can find information about gender by looking the word up in a dictionary. When you come across a new noun, always learn the word for *the* or *a* that goes with it to help you remember its gender.
  • **le** or **un** before a noun tells you it is masculine
  • **la** or **une** before a noun tells you it is feminine

➤ We refer to something as <u>singular</u> when we are talking about just one of them, and as <u>plural</u> when we are talking about more than one. The singular is the form of the noun you will usually find when you look a noun up in the dictionary. As in English, nouns in French change their form in the plural.

➤ Adjectives, articles and pronouns are also affected by whether a noun is singular or plural.

> *Tip*
> Remember that you have to use the right word for *the* and *a* according to the gender of the French noun.

Gender

Nouns referring to people

➤ Most nouns referring to men and boys are <u>masculine</u>.
  un homme   a man   **un roi**   a king

➤ Most nouns referring to women and girls are <u>feminine</u>.
  une fille   a girl   **une reine**   a queen

➤ When the same word is used to refer to either men/boys or women/girls, its gender usually changes depending on the sex of the person it refers to.

un camarade	a (male) friend	**une camarade**	a (female) friend
un Belge	a Belgian (man)	**une Belge**	a Belgian (woman)

Grammar Extra!
Some words for people have only <u>one</u> possible gender, whether they refer to a male or a female.

un bébé	a (male or female) baby	**un guide**	a (male or female) guide
une personne	a (male or female) person	**une vedette**	a (male or female) star

---

➤ In English, we can sometimes make a word masculine or feminine by changing the ending, for example, *English<u>man</u>* and *English<u>woman</u>*, or *prince* and *prin<u>cess</u>*. In French, very often the ending of a noun changes depending on whether it refers to a man or a woman.

un Anglais	an Englishman	**une Anglaise**	an Englishwoman
un prince	a prince	**une princesse**	a princess
un employé	a (male) employee	**une employée**	a (female) employee

⇨ *For more information on **Masculine and feminine forms of words**, see page 7.*

Nouns referring to animals

➤ In English we can choose between words like *bull* or *cow*, depending on the sex of the animal we are referring to. In French too there are sometimes separate words for male and female animals.

un taureau	a bull	**une vache**	a cow

➤ Sometimes, the same word with different endings is used for male and female animals.

un chien	a (male) dog	**une chienne**	a (female) dog, a bitch

> *Tip*
> When you do not know or care what sex the animal is, you can usually use the masculine form as a general word.

➤ Words for other animals do not change according to the sex of the animal. Just learn the French word with its gender, which is always the same.

un poisson	a fish	**une souris**	a mouse

Nouns referring to things

➤ In English, we call all things – for example, *table, car, book, apple* – '*it*'. In French, however, things are either <u>masculine</u> or <u>feminine</u>. As things do not divide into sexes the way humans and animals do, there are no physical clues to help you with their gender in French. Try to learn the gender as you learn the word.

➤ There are lots of rules to help you:

- words ending in **-e** are generally <u>feminine</u>
  une boulangerie a baker's   **une banque** a bank

- words ending in a consonant (any letter except *a, e, i, o* or *u*) are generally <u>masculine</u>
  un aéroport an airport   **un film** a film

➤ There are some exceptions to these rules, so it is best to check in a dictionary if you are unsure.

➤ These endings are often found on <u>masculine nouns</u>.

Masculine ending	Examples	
-age	**un village** a village **un voyage** a journey **un étage** a floor **le fromage** cheese	but: **une image** a picture **une page** a page **la plage** the beach
-ment	**un appartement** a flat **un bâtiment** a building **le ciment** cement **un vêtement** a garment	
-oir	**un miroir** a mirror **un couloir** a corridor **le soir** the evening **un mouchoir** a handkerchief	
-sme	**le tourisme** tourism **le racisme** racism	
-eau	**un cadeau** a present **un chapeau** a hat **un gâteau** a cake **le rideau** the curtain	but: **la peau** skin **l'eau** water
-eu	**un jeu** a game	
-ou	**un chou** a cabbage **le genou** the knee	
-ier	**le cahier** the exercise book **un quartier** an area **un escalier** a staircase	
-in	**un magasin** a shop **un jardin** a garden **un dessin** a drawing **le vin** the wine	but: **la fin** the end **une main** a hand
-on	**un champignon** a mushroom **un ballon** a ball **le citron** the lemon	but: **une maison** a house **la saison** the season

➤ The following types of word are also masculine:

- names of the days of the week, and the months and seasons of the year

le lundi	Monday
septembre prochain	next September
le printemps	Spring

- the names of languages

le français	French
le portugais	Portuguese
Tu apprends le français depuis combien de temps?	How long have you been learning French?

- most metric weights and measures

un gramme	a gramme
un mètre	a metre
un kilomètre	a kilometre

- English nouns used in French

le football	football
un tee-shirt	a tee-shirt
un sandwich	a sandwich

➤ These endings are often found on <u>feminine nouns</u>.

Feminine ending	Examples	
-ance -anse -ence -ense	<u>la</u> **chance** luck, chance <u>une</u> **danse** a dance <u>la</u> **patience** patience <u>la</u> **défense** defence	but: <u>le</u> **silence** silence
-ion	<u>une</u> **région** a region <u>une</u> **addition** a bill <u>une</u> **réunion** a meeting <u>la</u> **circulation** traffic	but: <u>un</u> **avion** a plane
-té -tié	<u>une</u> **spécialité** a speciality <u>la</u> **moitié** half	but: <u>un</u> **été** a summer <u>le</u> **pâté** pâté

Grammar Extra!

A few words have different meanings depending on whether they are masculine or feminine. These are the most common:

Masculine	Meaning	Example	Feminine	Meaning	Example
un livre	a book	**un livre de poche** a paperback	**une livre**	a pound	**une livre sterling** a pound sterling
un mode	a method	**le mode d'emploi** the directions for use	**la mode**	fashion	**à la mode** in fashion
un poste	a set (*TV/radio*); a post (*job*); an extension (*phone*)	**un poste de professeur** a teaching job	**la poste**	post the post office	**mettre quelque chose à la poste** to post something
un tour	a turn; a walk	**faire un tour** to go for a walk	**une tour**	tower	**la tour Eiffel** the Eiffel Tower

---

KEY POINTS

✔ Most nouns referring to men, boys and male animals are <u>masculine</u>; most nouns referring to women, girls and female animals are <u>feminine</u>. The ending of a French noun often changes depending on whether it refers to a male or a female.

✔ Generally, words ending in **-e** are feminine and words ending in a consonant are masculine, though there are many exceptions to this rule.

✔ These endings are often found on masculine nouns:
-age, **-ment**, **-oir**, **-sme**, **-eau**, **-eu**, **-ou**, **-ier**, **-in** and **-on**.

✔ These endings are often found on feminine nouns:
-ance, **-anse**, **-ence**, **-ense**, **-ion**, **-té** and **-tié**.

✔ Days of the week, months and seasons of the year are masculine. So are languages, most metric weights and measures, and English nouns used in French.

Test yourself

1 **Complete the phrase by adding the feminine form of the noun.**

a un prince et une ....

b un Anglais et une ....

c un employé et une ....

d un roi et une ....

e un taureau et une ....

f un chien et une ....

g un Belge et ....

h un camarade et ....

i un serveur et ....

j un joueur et ....

2 **Translate the following phrases into French.**

a a mushroom, a cabbage, a lemon ....

b a flat, a house, a garden ....

c a tee-shirt, a hat, a handkerchief ....

d the hand, the knee, the skin ....

e the patience, the silence, the luck ....

f a page, a picture, a drawing ....

g a knife, a fork, a spoon ....

h a cat, a dog, a budgie ....

i a toothbrush, a towel, a shampoo ....

j a bakery, a café, a supermarket ....

3 **Match the noun in the left column to its description in the right column.**

a le lundi   an English noun used in French: masculine noun

b le français   a season: masculine noun

c un sandwich   a day of the week: masculine noun

d un gramme   a language: masculine noun

e le printemps   a metric weight: masculine noun

Masculine and feminine forms of words

➤ In French there are sometimes very different words for men and women, and for male and female animals, just as in English.

un homme	a man
une femme	a woman
un taureau	a bull
une vache	a cow
un neveu	a nephew
une nièce	a niece

➤ Many masculine French nouns can be made feminine simply by changing the ending. This is usually done by adding an **-e** to the masculine noun to form the feminine.

un ami	a (male) friend
une amie	a (female) friend
un employé	a (male) employee
une employée	a (female) employee
un Français	a Frenchman
une Française	a Frenchwoman

➤ If the masculine singular form already ends in **-e**, no further **e** is added.

un élève	a (male) pupil
une élève	a (female) pupil
un camarade	a (male) friend
une camarade	a (female) friend
un collègue	a (male) colleague
une collègue	a (female) colleague

Tip

If a masculine noun ends in a vowel, its pronunciation does not change when an **-e** is added to form the feminine. For example, **ami** and **amie** (meaning *friend*) are both pronounced the same.

If a masculine noun ends with a consonant that is not pronounced, for example, **-d, -s, -r** or **-t,** you DO pronounce that consonant when an **-e** is added in the feminine. For example, in **étudiant** (meaning *student*), you cannot hear the **t**; in **étudiante**, you can hear the **t**.

Tip

Some masculine nouns, such as **voisin** (meaning *neighbour*), end in what is called a nasal vowel and an **-n**. With these words, you pronounce the vowel 'through your nose' but DO NOT say the **n**. When an **-e** is added in the feminine – for example, **voisine** – the vowel becomes a normal one instead of a nasal vowel and you DO pronounce the **n**.

Some other patterns

➤ Some changes to endings from masculine to feminine are a little more complicated but still fall into a regular pattern.

Masculine ending	Feminine ending	Example	Meaning
-f	-ve	un veuf/une veuve	a widower/a widow
-x	-se	un époux/une épouse	a husband/a wife
-eur	-euse	un danseur/ une danseuse	a (male) dancer/ a (female) dancer
-teur	-teuse -trice	un chanteur/ une chanteuse un acteur/une actrice	a (male) singer/ a (female) singer an actor/an actress
-an	-anne	un paysan/ une paysanne	a (male) farmer/ a (female) farmer
-ien	-ienne	un Parisien/ une Parisienne	a (male) Parisian/ a (female) Parisian
-on	-onne	un lion/une lionne	a lion/a lioness
-er	-ère	un étranger/ une étrangère	a (male) foreigner/ a (female) foreigner
-et	-ette	le cadet/la cadette	the youngest (male) child/ the youngest (female) child
-el	-elle	un professionnel/ une professionnelle	a (male) professional/ a (female) professional

---

KEY POINTS

✔ Many masculine French nouns can be made to refer to females by adding an **-e**. If the masculine singular form already ends in **-e**, no further **e** is added.

✔ The pronunciation of feminine nouns is sometimes different from that of the corresponding masculine nouns.

✔ Other patterns include:

-f → -ve	-teur → -teuse or -trice	-er → -ère
-x → -se	-an, -ien and -on → -anne,	-et → -ette
-eur → -euse	-ienne and -onne	-el → -elle

For further explanation of grammatical terms, please see pages viii–xii.

Test yourself

4   **Complete the phrase with the correct article.**

a   .... ami, Paul

b   .... amie, Justine

c   .... employée, Madame Camus

d   .... Français, Michel Leduc

e   .... Française, Alice Sorel

f   .... Parisienne, Madame Durand

g   .... employé, Luc Zola

h   .... Parisien, Fabien Renoir

i   .... collègue, Emma Buchy

j   .... camarade, Pierre

5   **Match each noun to its translation.**

a   une veuve

b   un veuf

c   une lionne

d   une chanteuse

e   un étranger

a lioness

a foreign man

a female singer

a widow

a widower

6   **Replace the highlighted masculine nouns with the feminine form.**

a   Ils vendent leur maison à **un Anglais**. ....

b   Marie va à la piscine avec **un camarade**. ....

c   Le chef parle avec **un employé**. ....

d   C'est le palais d' **un roi**. ....

e   Tu as vraiment l'air d' **un prince**! ....

f   Elle vit avec **un Belge**. ....

g   Nous avons **un chien** et deux chats. ....

h   C'est la voiture d' **un Français**. ....

i   C'est un jouet pour **un garçon**. ....

j   Il y a **un homme** qui pleure. ....

7   **Translate the phrase with an article and a noun.**

a   a schoolboy ....

b   a schoolgirl................................

c   a female colleague ....

d   the youngest boy ....

e   the youngest girl ....

f   a female singer............................

g   an Englishwoman ....

h   the woman next door ....

i   the man next door ....

j   a Belgian woman ....

Forming plurals

Plurals ending in -s

➤ In English we usually make nouns plural by adding an -s to the end (*garden* → *gardens*; *house* → *houses*), although we do have some nouns which are <u>irregular</u> and do not follow this pattern (*mouse* → *mice*; *child* → *children*).

> *Tip*
> Remember that **les** is the plural form of **le**, **la** and **l'**. Any adjective that goes with a plural noun has to agree with it, as does any pronoun that replaces it.
>
> ⇨ *For more information on* **Adjectives**, **Articles** *and* **Pronouns**, *see pages 32, 14 and 55.*

➤ Most French nouns also form their plural by adding an **-s** to their singular form.

un jardin	a garden
des jardins	gardens
une voiture	a car
des voitures	cars
un hôtel	a hotel
des hôtels	hotels

➤ If the singular noun ends in **-s**, **-x** or **-z**, no further **-s** is added in the plural.

un fils	a son
des fils	sons
une voix	a voice
des voix	voices
un nez	a nose
des nez	noses

Plurals ending in -x

➤ The following nouns add an **-x** instead of an **-s** in the plural:

- nouns ending in **-eau**

un chapeau	a hat
des chapeaux	hats

- most nouns ending in **-eu**

un jeu	a game
des jeux	games

- a FEW nouns ending in **-ou** (MOST nouns ending in **-ou** add **-s** as usual)

un bijou	a jewel
des bijoux	jewels
un caillou	a pebble
des cailloux	pebbles
un chou	a cabbage
des choux	cabbages
un genou	a knee
des genoux	knees

For further explanation of grammatical terms, please see pages viii–xii.

un hibou	an owl
des hibou<u>x</u>	owls
un joujou	a toy
des joujou<u>x</u>	toys
un pou	a louse
des pou<u>x</u>	lice

> *Tip*
> Adding an **-s** or **-x** to the end of a noun does not usually change the way the word is pronounced. For example, **professeur** and **professeurs** and **chapeau** and **chapeaux** sound just the same when you say them out loud.

➤ If the singular noun ends in **-al** or **-ail**, the plural usually ends in **-aux**.

un journal	a newspaper
des journ<u>aux</u>	newspapers
un animal	an animal
des anim<u>aux</u>	animals
un travail	a job
des trav<u>aux</u>	jobs

> *Tip*
> The plural of **un œil** (*an eye*) is **des yeux** (*eyes*).

Plural versus singular

➤ A few words relating to clothing are plural in English but <u>NOT</u> in French.

<u>un</u> slip	pants
<u>un</u> short	shorts
<u>un</u> pantalon	trousers

➤ A few common words are plural in French but <u>NOT</u> in English.

<u>les</u> affaires	business
<u>les</u> cheveux	hair
<u>des</u> renseignements	information

Grammar Extra!
When nouns are made up of two separate words, they are called <u>compound nouns</u>, for example, **les grands-parents** (meaning *grandparents*), **des ouvre-boîtes** (meaning *tin-openers*). The rules for forming the plural of compound nouns are complicated and it is best to check in a dictionary to see what the plural is.

> ### KEY POINTS
>
> ✔ Most French nouns form their plural by adding an **-s** to their singular form. If the singular noun ends in **-s**, **-x** or **-z**, no further **-s** is added in the plural.
>
> ✔ Most nouns ending in **-eau** or **-eu** add an **-x** in the plural.
>
> ✔ Most nouns ending in **-ou** take an **-s** in the plural, with a few exceptions.
>
> ✔ If the singular noun ends in **-al** or **-ail**, the plural usually ends in **-aux**.
>
> ✔ Adding an **-s** or **-x** to the end of a noun does not generally affect the way the word is pronounced.
>
> ✔ A few common words are plural in English but not in French, and vice versa.

Test yourself

8 **Translate the noun, leaving the number as a figure.**

a 1 car ....

b 3 sons ....

c 2 voices ....

d 2 hotels ....

e 10 games ....

f 3 pebbles.......................................

g 1 cabbage ....

h 2 owls ....

i 3 newspapers ....

j 1000 jobs.......................................

9 **Write the plural form of the noun after the number.**

a 2 .... (jardin)

b 2 .... (ami)

c 2 .... (femme)

d 3 .... (animal)

e 2 .... (bijou)

f 2 .... (fils)

g 3 .... (chapeau)

h 2 .... (jeu)

i 2 .... (chou)

j 2 .... (genou)

10 **Write 1 in the gap if the noun is singular, and 2 if it is plural.**

a .... homme

b .... femmes

c .... camarades

d .... amies

e .... hibou

f .... jouets

g .... chapeaux

h .... voisin

i .... pantalon

j .... slip

11 **Translate the following phrases into French.**

a the hair and the skin ....

b business and tourism ....

c shorts and a tee-shirt ....

d trousers and a hat ....

e a job and a flat...

f the nose and the knees ....

g 8 mushrooms and 2 cabbages ....

h 2 sons and 1 nephew ....

i 1 spring and 2 summers ....

j a meeting and information ....

Articles

> **What is an article?**
> In English, an **article** is one of the words *the*, *a*, and *an* which is placed in front of a noun.

Different types of article

➤ There are three types of article:

- the <u>definite</u> article: *the* in English. This is used to identify a particular thing or person.
  I'm going to <u>the</u> supermarket.
  That's <u>the</u> woman I was talking to.

- the <u>indefinite</u> article: *a* or *an* in English, *some* or *any* (or no word at all) in the plural. This is used to refer to something unspecific, or that you do not really know about.
  Is there <u>a</u> supermarket near here?
  I need <u>a</u> day off.

- the <u>partitive</u> article: *some* or *any* (or no word at all) in English. This is used to talk about quantities or amounts.
  Can you lend me <u>some</u> sugar?
  They've got (<u>some</u>) problems.
  Did you buy <u>any</u> wine?

The definite article: le, la, l' and les

The basic rules

➤ In English we only have <u>one</u> definite article: *the*. In French, there is more than one definite article to choose from. All French nouns are either masculine or feminine and, just as in English, they can be either singular or plural. The word you choose for *the* depends on whether the noun it is used with is masculine or feminine, singular or plural. This may sound complicated, but it is not too difficult.

⇨ *For more information on **Nouns**, see page 1.*

	with masculine noun	with feminine noun
Singular	**le (l')**	**la (l')**
Plural	**les**	**les**

> *Tip*
> **le** and **la** change to **l'** when they are used in front of a word starting with a vowel and most words starting with **h**.

➤ **le** is used in front of <u>masculine singular nouns</u>.

le roi	the king
le chien	the dog
le jardin	the garden

➤ **la** is used in front of <u>feminine singular nouns</u>.

la reine	the queen
la souris	the mouse
la porte	the door

➤ **l'** is used in front of <u>singular nouns that start with a vowel</u> (*a*, *e*, *i*, *o*, or *u*), whether they are masculine or feminine.

l'ami (*masculine*)	the friend
l'eau (*feminine*)	the water
l'étage (*masculine*)	the floor

⒤ Note that **l'** is also used in front of most words starting with **h** but some others take **le** or **la** instead.

l'hôpital	the hospital
le hamster	the hamster
la hi-fi	the stereo

> *Tip*
> It is a good idea to learn the <u>article</u> or the <u>gender</u> with the noun when you come across a word for the first time, so that you know whether it is masculine or feminine. A good dictionary will also give you this information.

➤ **les** is used in front of <u>plural nouns</u>, whether they are masculine or feminine and whatever letter they start with.

les chiens	the dogs
les portes	the doors
les amis	the friends
les hôtels	the hotels

⒤ Note that you have to make the noun plural too, just as you would in English. In French, as in English, you usually add an **-s**.

⇨ *For more information on* **Forming plurals**, *see page 10.*
see page 10.

> *Tip*
> When **les** is used in front of a word that starts with a consonant, you DO NOT say the **s** on the end of **les**: **les chiens** *the dogs*. When **les** is used in front of a word that starts with a vowel, most words starting with **h**, and the French word **y**, you DO pronounce the **s** on the end of **les**. It sounds like the *z* in the English word *zip*: **les amis** *the friends*, **les hôtels** *the hotels*.

Using à with le, la, l' and les

➤ The French word **à** is translated into English in several different ways, including *at* or *to*. There are special rules when you use it together with **le** and **les**.

⇨ *For more information on the preposition à, see pages 227 and 228.*

➤ When **à** is followed by **le**, the two words become **au**.

au cinéma	to/at the cinema
au professeur	to the teacher

➤ When **à** is followed by **les**, the two words become **aux**.

aux maisons	to the houses
aux étudiants	to the students

➤ When **à** is followed by **la** or **l'**, the words do not change.

à la bibliothèque	to/at the library
à l'hôtel	to/at the hotel

> *Tip*
> **le** and **la** change to **l'** when they are used in front of a word starting with a vowel and most words starting with **h**.

Using de with le, la, l' and les

➤ The French word **de** is translated into English in several different ways, including *of* and *from*. There are special rules when you use it together with **le** and **les**.

⇨ *For more information on the preposition de, see pages 230 and 231.*

➤ When **de** is followed by **le**, the two words become **du**.

du cinéma	from/of the cinema
du professeur	from/of the teacher

➤ When **de** is followed by **les**, the two words become **des**.

des maisons	from/of the houses
des étudiants	from/of the students

➤ When **de** is followed by **la** or **l'**, the words do not change.

de la bibliothèque	from/of the library
de l'hôtel	from/of the hotel

> *Tip*
> **le** and **la** change to **l'** when they are used in front of a word starting with a vowel and most words starting with **h**.

KEY POINTS

✔ With masculine singular nouns → use **le**.
✔ With feminine singular nouns → use **la**.
✔ With nouns starting with a vowel, most nouns beginning with **h** and the French word **y** → use **l'**.
✔ With plural nouns → use **les**.
✔ **à + le = au**
  à + les = aux
  de + le = du
  de + les = des

Test yourself

1 **Complete the phrase with the correct form of the definite article.**

a ....fille

b ....bébé

c ....guide

d ....amies

e ....hôpital

f ....porte

g ....personne

h ....hamster

i ....printemps

j ....employée

2 **Translate the phrase into French.**

a the man and the woman...

b the house and the garden ....

c the Belgians and the French ....

d the Frenchman and the Englishwoman ....

e the youngest child, Marc ....

f the youngest child, Marie ....

g the star, Depardieu...

h the students and the teacher ....

i the mice and the cheese ....

j the spring and the summer ....

3 **Complete the phrase with the correct form of de or à + the definite article.**

a (à) .... cinéma

b (à) .... bibliothèque

c (de) .... appartement

d (à) .... plage

e (de) .... plages

f (de) .... étudiant

g (de) .... étudiante

h (de) .... étudiantes

i (à) .... hôpital

j (de) .... hôpitaux

Test yourself

4 **Cross out the phrase(s) that cannot complete the sentence.**

a La pollution vient   des fleurs/des voitures/des avions/des usines

b Je viens   du Royaume-Uni/des États-Unis/au Japon/de la région

c Je vais   à la bibliothèque/des professeurs/aux magasins/au cinéma

d Ce vin est   de la piscine/du village/de la région/du pays

e J'écris   aux étudiants/à l'Europe/au docteur/au professeur

f C'est le nom   au monsieur/du monsieur/du voisin/de l'hôtel

g La fête a lieu   au restaurant/à l'hôtel/au port/au piscine

h Les fleurs viennent   du marché/du court de tennis/du jardin/du sud

i Elle est   au bureau/au lycée/au marché/aux hôpitaux

Using the definite article

➤ The definite article in French (**le**, **la**, **l'** and **les**) is used in more or less the same way as we use *the* in English, but it is also used in French in a few places where you might not expect it.

➤ The definite article is used with words like *prices*, *flu* and *time* that describe qualities, ideas or experiences (called <u>abstract nouns</u>) rather than something that you can touch with your hand. Usually, *the* is missed out in English with this type of word.

<u>Les</u> prix montent.	Prices are rising.
J'ai <u>la</u> grippe.	I've got flu.
Je n'ai pas <u>le</u> temps.	I don't have time.

[i] Note that there are some set phrases using **avoir**, **avec** or **sans** followed by a noun, where the definite article is <u>NOT</u> used.

avoir faim	to be hungry (*literally: to have hunger*)
avec plaisir	with pleasure
sans doute	probably (*literally: without doubt*)

➤ You also use the definite article when you are talking about things like *coffee* or *computers* that you can touch with your hand (called <u>concrete nouns</u>) if you are talking generally about that thing. Usually, *the* is missed out in English with this type of word.

Je n'aime pas <u>le</u> café.	I don't like coffee.
<u>Les</u> ordinateurs coûtent très cher.	Computers are very expensive.
<u>Les</u> professeurs ne gagnent pas beaucoup.	Teachers don't earn very much.

➤ If you are talking about a part of your body, you usually use a word like *my* or *his* in English, but in French you usually use the definite article.

Tourne <u>la</u> tête à gauche.	Turn your head to the left.
Il s'est cassé <u>le</u> bras.	He's broken his arm.
J'ai mal à <u>la</u> gorge.	My throat hurts.

➤ In French you have to use the definite article in front of the names of countries, continents and regions.

<u>la</u> Bretagne	Brittany
<u>l'</u>Europe	Europe
<u>La</u> France est très belle.	France is very beautiful.
J'ai acheté ce poster <u>au</u> Japon.	I bought this poster in Japan.
Je viens <u>des</u> États-Unis.	I come from the United States.

[i] Note that if the name of the country comes after the French word **en**, meaning *to* or *in*, you do not use the definite article. **en** is used with the names of countries, continents and regions that are feminine in French.

Je vais <u>en Écosse</u> le mois prochain.	I'm going to Scotland next month.
Il travaille <u>en Allemagne</u>.	He works in Germany.

⇨ *For more information on the preposition **en**, see page 232.*

➤ You often use the definite article with the name of school subjects, languages and sports.

Tu aimes les maths?	Do you like maths?
J'apprends le français depuis trois ans.	I've been learning French for three years.
Mon sport préféré, c'est le foot.	My favourite sport is football.

🛈 Note that the definite article is not used after **en**.

Comment est-ce qu'on dit 'fils' en anglais?	How do you say 'fils' in English?
Sophie est nulle en chimie.	Sophie's no good at chemistry.

➤ When you use the verb **parler** (meaning *to speak*) in front of the name of the language, you do not always need to use the definite article in French.

Tu parles espagnol?	Do you speak Spanish?
Il parle bien l'anglais.	He speaks English well.

➤ You use **le** with dates, and also with the names of the days of the week and the seasons when you are talking about something that you do regularly or that is a habit.

Elle part le 7 mai.	She's leaving on the seventh of May.
Je vais chez ma grand-mère le dimanche.	I go to my grandmother's on Sundays.

🛈 Note that you do not use the definite article after **en**.

En hiver nous faisons du ski.	In winter we go skiing.

➤ You often find the definite article in phrases that tell you about prices and rates.

6 euros le kilo	6 euros a kilo
3 euros la pièce	3 euros each
On roulait à 100 kilomètres à l'heure.	We were doing 100 kilometres an hour.

KEY POINTS

✔ The definite article is used in French with:
- abstract nouns
- concrete nouns (*when you are saying something that is true about a thing in general*)
- parts of the body
- countries, continents and regions
- school subjects, languages and sports
- dates
- days of the week and the seasons (*when you are talking about something that you do regularly or that is a habit*)
- prices and rates

Test yourself

5 **Translate the sentence, remembering to use a definite article with the noun.**

a I don't like football. ....

b I don't like mice. ....

c Do you like cheese? ....

d I don't like dogs. ....

e Do you like cakes? ....

f Do you like Brittany? ....

g I don't like beaches. ....

h Do you like French? ....

i Do you like mushrooms?. ....

j I don't like wine. ....

6 **Complete the sentence with au, à la or aux.**

a J'ai mal...........genoux.

b J'ai mal...........tête.

c J'ai mal...........genou.

d J'ai mal...........main.

e J'ai mal ....ventre.

f J'ai mal ....gorge.

g Je vais............boulangerie.

h Je vais............Japon.

i Je vais............village.

j Je vais...........maison.

7 **Match the columns.**

a Mon sport préféré   c'est le brie

b Ma région préférée   c'est le ski

c Ma saison préférée   c'est le champagne

d Mon vin préféré   c'est le printemps

e Mon fromage préféré   c'est la Bretagne

8 **Complete the sentence with an article or with à/de and the article if necessary.**

a J'aime beaucoup..........Provence.

b Elle vient ....nord de la France.

c J'apprends..........italien.

d Ce fromage vient ....pays de Galles.

e Nous allons..........États-Unis.

f Je préfère la France..........Japon.

g Je préfère l'anglais..........maths.

h C'est une spécialité de.......... région.

i C'est un accent..........sud.

j Nous allons..........Portugal.

PRACTICE PRACTICE PRACTICE PRACTICE PRACTICE PRACTICE

The indefinite article: un, une and des

The basic rules

➤ In English we have the indefinite article *a*, which changes to *an* in front of a word that starts with a vowel. In the plural we say either *some*, *any* or nothing at all.

➤ In French, you choose from **un**, **une** and **des**, depending on whether the noun is masculine or feminine, and singular or plural.

	with masculine noun	with feminine noun
Singular	**un**	**une**
Plural	**des**	**des**

➤ **un** is used in front of <u>masculine singular nouns</u>.

un roi	a king
un chien	a dog
un jardin	a garden

➤ **une** is used in front of <u>feminine singular nouns</u>.

une reine	a queen
une souris	a mouse
une porte	a door

➤ **des** is used in front of <u>plural nouns</u>, whether they are masculine or feminine, and whatever letter they start with.

des chiens	(some/any) dogs
des souris	(some/any) mice
des amis	(some/any) friends

⚠ Note that **des** is also a combination of **de + les** and has other meanings, such as saying who something belongs to or where something is from.

⇨ *For more information on **des**, see page 230.*

> ### Tip
> When **des** is used in front of a word that starts with a consonant (any letter except *a, e, i, o* or *u*), you DO NOT say the **s** on the end of **des**: **des chiens** *(some/any) dogs*.
>
> When **des** is used in front of a word that starts with a vowel, and most words starting with **h**, you DO pronounce the **s** on the end. It sounds like the *z* in the English word *zip*: **des amis** *(some/any) friends*, **des hôtels** *(some/any) hotels*.

The indefinite article in negative sentences

➤ In English we use words like *not* and *never* to indicate that something is not happening or is not true. The sentences that these words are used in are called <u>negative</u> sentences.
    I <u>don't</u> know him.
    I <u>never</u> do my homework on time.

➤ In French, you use word pairs like **ne ... pas** (meaning *not*) and **ne ... jamais** (meaning *never*) to say that something is not happening or not true. When **un**, **une** or **des** is used after this type of expression, it has to be changed to **de**.

Je n'ai pas de vélo.	I don't have a bike.
Nous n'avons pas de cousins.	We don't have any cousins.

⇨ *For more information on* **Negatives**, *see page* 192.

Tip
de changes to **d'** in front of a word starting with a vowel and most words starting with **h**.

Je n'ai pas d'ordinateur.	I don't have a computer.
Il n'y a pas d'horloge dans la salle.	There isn't a clock in the room.

Grammar Extra!
There are some very common adjectives, like **beau**, **bon** and **petit**, that can come <u>BEFORE</u> the noun instead of after it. When an adjective comes before a plural noun, **des** changes to **de**.

J'ai reçu de beaux cadeaux.	I got some lovely presents.
Cette région a de très jolis villages.	This area has some very pretty villages.

⇨ *For more information on* **Word order with adjectives**, *see page* 39.

The meaning of des

➤ **des** can mean different things in English, depending on the sentence. *Some* is often the best word to use.

J'ai un chien, deux chats et <u>des</u> souris.	I've got a dog, two cats and <u>some</u> mice.
Tu veux <u>des</u> chips?	Would you like <u>some</u> crisps?

➤ In questions and negative sentences **des** means *any*, or is not translated at all.

Tu as <u>des</u> frères?	Have you got <u>any</u> brothers?
Il n'y a pas d'œufs.	There aren't <u>any</u> eggs.
Avez-vous <u>des</u> timbres?	Do you have stamps?

Using the indefinite article

➤ The indefinite article is used in French in much the same way as we use *a*, *some* and *any* in English, but there are two places where the indefinite article is <u>NOT</u> used:

- with the adjective **quel** (meaning *what a*), in sentences like

Quel dommage!	What <u>a</u> shame!
Quelle surprise!	What <u>a</u> surprise!
Quelle bonne idée!	What <u>a</u> good idea!

  ⇨ For more information on *quel*, see page 204.

- when you say what jobs people do

Il est professeur.	He's <u>a</u> teacher.
Ma mère est infirmière.	My mother's <u>a</u> nurse.

> *Tip*
> When you use **c'est** (to mean *he/she is*), you <u>DO</u> use **un** or **une**. When you use **ce sont** (to mean *they are*), you <u>DO</u> use **des**.
>
> | | |
> |---|---|
> | **C'est <u>un</u> médecin.** | He's/She's a doctor. |
> | **Ce sont <u>des</u> acteurs.** | They're actors. |
>
> ⇨ For more information on *c'est* and *ce sont*, see page 91.

KEY POINTS
- ✔ With masculine singular nouns → use **un**.
- ✔ With feminine singular nouns → use **une**.
- ✔ With plural nouns → use **des**.
- ✔ **un**, **une** and **des** → change to **de** or **d'** in negative sentences.
- ✔ The indefinite article is not usually used when you say what jobs people do, or in exclamations with **quel**.

Test yourself

9 **Complete the phrase with the correct indefinite article.**

a un homme, ... femme et des enfants

b une maison et .... jardin

c un chou et .... champignons

d des collègues et .... amis

e un appartement et .... travail

f .... journaux et un livre

g .... short et un tee-shirt

h un danseur et .... danseuse

i une actrice et .... chanteurs

j un professeur et .... étudiants

10 **Translate the sentences.**

a I haven't got a computer. ....

b I haven't got a job. ....

c I haven't got a car. ....

d I haven't got problems. ....

e There isn't a swimming pool. ....

f There isn't any wine. ....

g There isn't a mirror. ....

h I haven't got a hat. ....

i There's no bakery. ....

j There isn't a hospital. ....

11 **Match the answer to the question.**

a **Tu as des frères?**   Oui, il y a une boulangerie.

b **Tu as des animaux?**   Oui, j'ai un ballon.

c **Avez-vous des enfants?**   Non, j'ai une sœur.

d **Il y a des magasins?**   Oui, j'ai un chien.

e **Tu as des jouets?**   Oui, j'ai un fils.

12 **Complete the translation, starting with the word provided.**

a She's a dancer. **Elle** ....

b He's a singer. **C'** ....

c He's an actor. **Il**...........................

d She's a waitress. **Elle**...................

e She's a singer. **C'** ....

f She's a doctor. **Elle** ....

g He's a singer. **Il**...........................

h She's a teacher. **C'** ....

i She's a hairdresser. **Elle** ....

The partitive article: du, de la, de l' and des

The basic rules

➤ **du**, **de la**, **de l'** and **des** can all be used to give information about the amount or quantity of a particular thing. They are often translated into English as *some* or *any*.

➤ In French, you choose between **du**, **de la**, **de l'** and **des**, depending on whether the noun is masculine or feminine, singular or plural.

	with masculine noun	with feminine noun
Singular	du (de l')	de la (de l')
Plural	des	des

> *Tip*
> **de + le** and **de la** change to **de l'** when they are used in front of a word starting with a vowel, most words starting with **h**, and the French word **y**.

➤ **du** is used in front of <u>masculine singular nouns</u>.

| <u>du</u> **beurre** | (some/any) butter |
| <u>du</u> **jus d'orange** | (some/any) orange juice |

> ⓘ Note that **du** is also a combination of **de + le** and has other meanings, such as saying who something belongs to or where something is from.

> ⇨ *For more information on **du**, see page 230.*

➤ **de la** is used in front of <u>feminine singular nouns</u>.

| <u>de la</u> **viande** | (some/any) meat |
| <u>de la</u> **margarine** | (some/any) margarine |

➤ **de l'** is used in front of <u>singular nouns that start with a vowel</u> and most nouns starting with **h**, whether they are masculine or feminine.

<u>de l'</u>**argent** (*masculine*)	(some/any) money
<u>de l'</u>**eau** (*feminine*)	(some/any) water
<u>de l'</u>**herbe** (*feminine*)	(some/any) grass

➤ **des** is used in front of <u>plural nouns</u>, whether they are masculine or feminine and whatever letter they start with.

<u>des</u> **gâteaux**	(some/any) cakes
<u>des</u> **lettres**	(some/any) letters
<u>des</u> **hôtels**	(some/any) hotels

> ⓘ Note that **des** is also a combination of **de + les** and has other meanings, such as saying who something belongs to or where something is from.

> ⇨ *For more information on **des**, see page 230.*

The partitive article in negative sentences

➤ In French, you use word pairs like **ne ... pas** (meaning *not*) and **ne ... jamais** (meaning *never*) to say that something is not happening or not true. In this type of expression, **du**, **de la**, **de l'** and **des** all change to **de**.

Nous <u>n'</u>avons <u>pas de</u> beurre.	We don't have any butter.
Je <u>ne</u> mange <u>jamais de</u> viande.	I never eat meat.
Il <u>n'</u>y a <u>pas de</u> timbres.	There aren't any stamps.

⇨ *For more information on **Negatives**, see page 192.*

> *Tip*
> **de** changes to **d'** in front of a word starting with a vowel and most nouns starting with **h**.
>
> | | |
> |---|---|
> | **Il n'a pas <u>d'</u>argent.** | He doesn't have any money. |
> | **Il n'y a pas <u>d'</u>horloge dans la salle.** | There isn't a clock in the room. |

Grammar Extra!

There are some very common adjectives, like **beau**, **bon** and **petit**, that can come <u>BEFORE</u> the noun instead of after it. When an adjective comes before a plural noun, **des** changes to **de**.

J'ai reçu de beaux cadeaux.	I got some lovely presents.
Cette région a de très jolis villages.	This area has some very pretty villages.

⇨ *For more information on **Word order with adjectives**, see page 39.*

The meaning of du, de la, de l' and des

➤ **du**, **de la**, **de l'** and **des** are often translated into English as *some* or *any*, but there are times when no word is used in English to translate the French.

Il me doit <u>de l'</u>argent.	He owes me (some) money.
Je vais acheter <u>de la</u> farine et <u>du</u> beurre pour faire un gâteau.	I'm going to buy (some) flour and butter to make a cake.
Est-ce qu'il y a <u>des</u> lettres pour moi?	Are there any letters for me?
Elle ne veut pas <u>de</u> beurre.	She doesn't want any butter.
Je ne prends pas <u>de</u> lait.	I don't take milk.

> *Tip*
> Remember that **du, de la, de l'** and **des** can <u>NEVER</u> be missed out in French, even if there is no word in English.

> **KEY POINTS**
> ✔ With masculine singular nouns → use **du**.
> ✔ With feminine singular nouns → use **de la**.
> ✔ With singular nouns starting with a vowel and some nouns beginning with **h** → use **de l'**.
> ✔ With plural nouns → use **des**.
> ✔ **du**, **de la**, **de l'** and **des** → change to **de** or **d'** in negative sentences.

Test yourself

13 **Complete the sentence with du, de la, de l' or des.**

a   Je vais acheter..........vin.

b   Je vais acheter ....champignons.

c   J'ai reçu..........lettres.

d   Tu as..........patience!

e   Tu veux .... gâteau?

f   Je veux..........eau.

g   Je vais acheter..........journaux.

h   Tu as .... chance!

i   Tu as .... argent?

j   Je vais acheter .... beurre.

14 **Cross out the ingredients that don't fit.**

a   un gâteau   du beurre/du vin/du sucre/du ciment

b   un sandwich   du tourisme/du fromage/de l'eau/du pain

c   une soupe   de l'eau/des tomates/du café/du sel

d   une pizza   du lait/des olives/du fromage/de la farine

e   le petit déjeuner   du café/du pain/du vin/du jus d'orange

f   un pique-nique   des sandwichs/du riz au lait/de l'eau/du chocolat

g   une salade   du beurre/des tomates/du vinaigre/des olives

h   un curry   de la viande/du lait/du sucre/du riz

i   une quiche   des œufs/des oranges/des chips/du fromage

j   un petit déjeuner   de la glace/du café/des céréales/des croissants

15 **Translate the sentence.**

a   I'm going to buy some yoghurt. ....

b   I'm going to buy butter and milk. ....

c   Would you like some honey?...

d   Milk and sugar? ....

e   Is there any orange juice? ....

f   Is there any coffee for me? ....

g   Is there any lemonade? ....

h   Would you like some jam? ....

i   She doesn't want margarine. ....

j   I don't eat cheese. ....

Test yourself

16 Put d', de or des in the gap.

a   Du café? — Non merci, je ne veux pas ....café.

b   Des hôtels? — Oui, il y a..........hôtels.

c   Des jardins? — Oui, il y a..........beaux jardins.

d   Des journaux? — Non, il n'y a pas..........journaux.

e   De l'argent? — Non, il n'y a pas..........argent.

f   Des enfants? — Non, il n'y a pas..........enfants.

g   Des images? — Oui, il y a..........très jolies images.

h   Des réponses? — Non, il n'y a pas .... réponses.

i   De l'huile? — Non, il n'y a pas..........huile.

j   Des oiseaux? — Oui, il y a .... oiseaux intéressants.

Adjectives

What is an adjective?
An **adjective** is a 'describing' word that tells you more about a person or thing, such as their appearance, colour, size or other qualities, for example, *pretty*, *blue*, *big*.

Using adjectives

➤ Adjectives are words like *clever*, *expensive* and *silly* that tell you more about a noun (a living being, thing or idea). They can also tell you more about a pronoun, such as *he* or *they*. Adjectives are sometimes called 'describing words'. They can be used right next to a noun they are describing, or can be separated from the noun by a verb like *be*, *look*, *feel* and so on.

  a <u>clever</u> girl
  an <u>expensive</u> coat
  a <u>silly</u> idea
  He's just being <u>silly</u>.

  ➪ *For more information on* **Nouns** *and* **Pronouns**, *see pages 1 and 55.*

➤ In English, the only time an adjective changes its form is when you are making a comparison.
  She's <u>cleverer</u> than her brother.
  That's the <u>silliest</u> idea I ever heard!

➤ In French, however, most adjectives <u>agree</u> with what they are describing. This means that their endings change depending on whether the person or thing you are referring to is masculine or feminine, and singular or plural.

un mot français	a French word
une chanson française	a French song
des traditions françaises	French traditions

➤ In English we put adjectives <u>BEFORE</u> the noun they describe, but in French you usually put them <u>AFTER</u> it.

  un chat <u>noir</u>   a <u>black</u> cat

  ➪ *For further information, see* **Word order with adjectives** *on page 39.*

KEY POINTS
✔ Most French adjectives change their form, according to whether the person or thing they are describing is masculine or feminine, singular or plural.
✔ In French adjectives usually go after the noun they describe.

Test yourself

1 **Match the names and descriptions.**

a   David Beckham   des actrices françaises

b   Serena et Venus Williams   une chanteuse anglaise

c   Gérard Depardieu   des joueurs de golf espagnols

d   Thierry Henri et Zinedine Zidane   un joueur de tennis espagnol

e   Isabelle Huppert et Catherine Deneuve   un footballeur anglais

f   Amy Winehouse   un acteur français

g   Michael Schumacher   un chanteur gallois

h   Seve Ballesteros et Raquel Carriedo   des footballeurs français

i   Tom Jones   des joueuses de tennis américaines

j   Rafael Nadal   un pilote de course allemand

2 **Fill the gap with** américain **(masculine singular),** américaine **(feminine singular),** américains **(masculine plural), or** américaines **(feminine plural).**

a   une voiture ....

b   un film ....

c   des personnes ....

d   mes amies ....

e   des journaux ....

f   des villes ....

g   des hôtels ....

h   l'histoire ....

i   l'avion ....

j   les traditions ....

Making adjectives agree

The basic rules

➤ In dictionaries, regular French adjectives are usually shown in the masculine singular form. You need to know how to change them to make them agree with the noun or pronoun that they are describing.

➤ To make an adjective agree with the noun or pronoun it describes, you simply add the following endings in most cases:

	with masculine noun	with feminine noun
Singular	-	-e
Plural	-s	-es

un chat <u>noir</u>	a black cat
une chemise <u>noire</u>	a black shirt
des chats <u>noirs</u>	black cats
des chemises <u>noires</u>	black shirts

Making adjectives feminine

➤ With most adjectives you add an **-e** to the masculine singular form to make it feminine.
un chat noir a black cat → **une chemise noir<u>e</u>** a black shirt
un sac lourd a heavy bag → **une valise lourd<u>e</u>** a heavy suitcase

➤ If the adjective already ends in an **-e** in the masculine, you do not add another -**e**.
un sac jaune a yellow bag → **une chemise jaune** a yellow shirt
un garçon sage a good boy → **une fille sage** a good girl

➤ Some changes to endings are a little more complicated but still follow a regular pattern. Sometimes you have to double the consonant as well as adding an **-e**. On the next page there is a table showing these changes.

Masculine ending	Feminine ending	Example	Meaning
-f	-ve	**neuf/neuve**	new
-x	-se	**heureux/heureuse**	happy
-er	-ère	**cher/chère**	dear, expensive
-an	-anne	**paysan/paysanne**	farming, country
-en	-enne	**européen/européenne**	European
-on	-onne	**bon/bonne**	good, right
-el	-elle	**cruel/cruelle**	cruel
-eil	-eille	**pareil/pareille**	similar
-et	-ette	**net/nette**	clear
	-ète	**complet/complète**	complete, full

un <u>bon</u> repas a good meal → **de <u>bonne</u> humeur** in a good mood
un homme <u>cruel</u> a cruel man → **une remarque <u>cruelle</u>** a cruel remark

For further explanation of grammatical terms, please see pages viii–xii.

➤ Some very common adjectives have irregular feminine forms.

Masculine form	Feminine form	Meaning
blanc	blanche	white, blank
doux	douce	soft, sweet, mild, gentle
faux	fausse	untrue
favori	favorite	favourite
frais	fraîche	fresh, chilly, cool
gentil	gentille	nice, kind
grec	grecque	Greek
gros	grosse	big, fat
long	longue	long
nul	nulle	useless
roux	rousse	red, red-haired
sec	sèche	dry, dried
turc	turque	Turkish

mon sport <u>favori</u> my favourite sport → **ma chanson <u>favorite</u>** my favourite song
un ami <u>grec</u> a Greek (male) friend → **une amie <u>grecque</u>** a Greek (female) friend

➤ A very small group of French adjectives have an <u>extra</u> masculine singular form that is used in front of words that begin with a vowel (*a*, *e*, *i*, *o* or *u*) and most words beginning with **h**. These adjectives also have an irregular feminine form.

Masculine form in front of a word beginning with a consonant	Masculine form in front of a word beginning with a vowel or most words beginning with h	Feminine form	Meaning
beau	bel	belle	lovely, beautiful, good-looking, handsome
fou	fol	folle	mad
nouveau	nouvel	nouvelle	new
vieux	vieil	vieille	old

un <u>bel</u> appartement	a beautiful flat
le <u>Nouvel</u> An	New Year
un <u>vieil</u> arbre	an old tree

Making adjectives plural

➤ With most adjectives you add an **-s** to the masculine singular or feminine singular form to make it plural.

> **un chat noir** a black cat → **des chats noirs** black cats
> **une valise lourde** a heavy suitcase → **des valises lourdes** heavy suitcases

> *Tip*
> When an adjective describes a masculine <u>and</u> a feminine noun or pronoun, use the masculine plural form of the adjective.
>
> **La maison et le jardin sont <u>beaux</u>.** The house and garden are beautiful.
> **Sophie et son petit ami sont très <u>gentils</u>.** Sophie and her boyfriend are very nice.

➤ If the masculine singular form already ends in an **-s** or an **-x**, you do not add an **-s**.

> **un fromage français** a French cheese → **des fromages français** French cheeses
> **un homme dangereux** a dangerous man → **des hommes dangereux** dangerous men

➤ If the masculine singular form ends in **-eau** or **-al**, the masculine plural is usually **-eaux** or **-aux**.

> **le nouveau professeur** the new teacher → **les nouv<u>eaux</u> professeurs** the new teachers
> **le rôle principal** the main role → **les rôles princip<u>aux</u>** the main roles

> **Tip**
>
> Adding an **-s** or an **-x** does not change the pronunciation of a word. For example, **noir** and **noirs** sound just the same, as do **nouveau** and **nouveaux**.
>
> When the **-s** or **-x** ending comes before a word starting with a vowel or most words starting with **h**, you have to pronounce the **s** or **x** on the end of the adjective. It sounds like the *z* in the English word *zip*.
>
> **les anciens élèves** the former pupils
> **de grands hôtels** big hotels

Invariable adjectives

➤ A small number of adjectives (mostly relating to colours) do not change in the feminine or plural. They are called <u>invariable</u> because their form <u>NEVER</u> changes, no matter what they are describing. These adjectives are often made up of more than one word – for example, **bleu marine** (meaning *navy blue*), or else come from the names of fruit or nuts – for example, **orange** (meaning *orange*), **marron** (meaning *brown*).

   des chaussures <u>marron</u> brown shoes
   une veste <u>bleu marine</u> a navy blue jacket

KEY POINTS

✔ To make an adjective agree with a feminine singular noun or pronoun, you usually add **-e** to the masculine singular. If the adjective already ends in an **-e**, no further **-e** is added.

✔ Several adjectives ending in a consonant double their consonant as well as adding **-e** in the feminine.

✔ **beau**, **fou**, **nouveau** and **vieux** have an irregular feminine form and an extra masculine singular form that is used in front of words that begin with a vowel and most words beginning with **h**: **bel**, **fol**, **nouvel**, **vieil**.

✔ To make an adjective agree with a masculine plural noun or pronoun, you usually add **-s** to the masculine singular. If the adjective already ends in an **-s** or an **-x**, no further **-s** is added.

✔ If the adjective ends in **-eau** or **-al**, the masculine plural is usually **-eaux** or **-aux**.

✔ To make an adjective agree with a feminine plural noun or pronoun, you usually add **-es** to the masculine singular.

✔ Some adjectives relating to colours never change their form.

Test yourself

3 Translate the phrase into French.

a a black hat ....

b black tee-shirts ....

c black trousers ....

d a black car ....

e black shorts ....

f a black door ....

g Black students ....

h a Black female colleague ....

i Black friends ....

j female Black singers ....

4 Complete the phrase with the correct form of the adjective.

a des mots .... (allemand)   **f** de l'eau .... (minéral)

b une étudiante .... (français)   **g** des sacs .... (lourd)

c des danses .... (espagnol)   **h** une image .... (net)

d une tradition .... (allemand)   **i** une femme....................... (cruel)

e des chansons .... (anglais)   **j** une maison .... (pareil)

5 Match the noun to an appropriate adjective.

a une chemise   extrêmement gentille

b ma cousine   très longue

c une phrase   favorite

d une histoire   blanche

e une personne   complètement fausse

Word order with adjectives

The basic rules

➤ When adjectives are used right beside the noun they are describing, they go <u>BEFORE</u> it in English. French adjectives usually go <u>AFTER</u> the noun.

l'heure <u>exacte</u>	the <u>right</u> time
la page <u>suivante</u>	the <u>following</u> page

➤ Adjectives describing colours, shapes or nationalities always go <u>AFTER</u> the noun.

des cravates <u>rouges</u>	red ties
une table <u>ronde</u>	a round table
un mot <u>français</u>	a French word

➤ Some very common adjectives usually come <u>BEFORE</u> the noun.

beau	lovely, beautiful, good-looking, handsome
bon	good, right
court	short
grand	tall, big, long, great
gros	big, fat
haut	high
jeune	young
joli	pretty
long	long
mauvais	bad, poor
meilleur	better
nouveau	new
petit	small, little
premier	first
vieux	old
une belle journée	a lovely day
Bonne chance!	Good luck!

➤ There is a small group of common adjectives whose meaning changes depending on whether they come before the noun or go after it.

Adjective	Example before noun	Meaning	Example after noun	Meaning
ancien	**un ancien collègue**	a <u>former</u> colleague	**un fauteuil ancien**	an <u>antique</u> chair
cher	**Chère Julie**	<u>Dear</u> Julie	**une robe chère**	an <u>expensive</u> dress
propre	**ma propre chambre**	my <u>own</u> bedroom	**un mouchoir propre**	a <u>clean</u> handkerchief

Tip

dernier (meaning *last*) and **prochain** (meaning *next*) go UNDERLINE nouns relating to time, for example, **semaine** (meaning *week*) and **mois** (meaning *month*). Otherwise they go BEFORE the noun.

la semaine <u>dernière</u>	last week
la <u>dernière</u> fois que je t'ai vu	the last time I saw you
la semaine <u>prochaine</u>	next week
la <u>prochaine</u> fois que j'y vais	the next time I go there

---

Grammar Extra!

When certain adjectives are used with certain nouns, they may take on a meaning you wouldn't have guessed. You may need to check these in your dictionary and learn them. Here are a few:

mon petit ami	my boyfriend
les petits pois	peas
les grandes vacances	the summer holidays
une grande personne	an adult, a grown-up

Using more than one adjective

➤ In French you can use more than one adjective at a time to describe someone or something. If one of the adjectives usually comes <u>BEFORE</u> the noun and the other usually goes <u>AFTER</u> the noun, the word order follows the usual pattern.

une <u>jeune</u> femme <u>blonde</u>	a young blonde woman
un <u>nouveau</u> film <u>intéressant</u>	an interesting new film

➤ If both adjectives usually come <u>AFTER</u> the noun, they are joined together with **et** (meaning *and*).

un homme mince <u>et</u> laid	a thin, ugly man
une personne intelligente <u>et</u> drôle	an intelligent, funny person

---

KEY POINTS

✔ Most French adjectives go after the noun they describe.
✔ Some very common adjectives usually come before the noun: **bon/mauvais**, **court/long**, **grand/petit**, **jeune/nouveau/vieux**, **gros**, **haut**, **beau**, **joli**, **premier**, **meilleur**.
✔ The meaning of some adjectives such as **ancien**, **cher** and **propre** varies according to the position in the sentence.

Test yourself

6 **Translate the phrase into French.**

a   a hot day ....

b   a white shirt and a black tie ....

c   French wines and English cheeses ....

d   a pretty girl and a good-looking boy ....

e   the right answer ....

f   a short meeting ....

g   a high building ....

h   an old man and a little boy ....

i   a bad choice ....

j   a better idea ....

7 **Cross out the names or items the phrase cannot refer to.**

a   **un ancien collègue**   Jacques Leduc/Marie Vargas/Luc Vincent/ma cousine

b   **une ancienne élève**   Max/Lucie/Thomas/Paul

c   **un bâtiment ancien**   une ferme/une caravane/un skateboard/une église

d   **un ami cher**   Alice/André/Maurice/Marc

e   **une voiture chère**   un cyclomoteur/un tracteur/une BMW/un camion

f   **un vêtement propre**   un pantalon/un jeu/une chemise/un short

g   **mon petit ami**   Julien/Delphine/Nicolas/ Susanne

h   **une grande personne**   un bébé/Madame Gautier/Monsieur Amiot/
                               notre professeur

i   **une jeune femme blonde**   Marie/Tina/Nicolas/Jeanne

j   **un homme riche**   Pierre/Isabelle/Thierry/Thérèse

Test yourself

8 **Formulate a phrase, putting the words in the correct order.**

a une/vieille/française/femme ....

b un/nouveau/américain/film ....

c une /intéressante/nouvelle/idée...

d une/chère/et/élégante/robe ....

e une/mince/jeune/femme ....

f un/bon/indien/repas...

g un/bon/chaud/chocolat ....

h une/ronde/belle/table...

i un/sage/et/intelligent/enfant...

j une/rouge/et/noire/cravate..

9 **Complete the following sentences with the correct form of the adjective.**

a Elle arrive la semaine .... **(prochain)**

b Quelqu'un veut les ....fraises? **(dernier)**

c Il arrive toujours au .... moment. **(dernier)**

d Le premier mai, c'est la .... fois que je t'ai vu. **(dernier)**

e Lundi, c'est la .... fois que j'y vais. **(prochain)**

f Les .... examens commencent mardi. **(prochain)**

g Les .... questions sont les plus difficiles. **(prochain)**

h Les mois .... il a fait très chaud. **(dernier)**

i Le mois .... on part en vacances. **(prochain)**

j Ses .... mots étaient inaudibles. **(dernier)**

Comparatives and superlatives of adjectives

Making comparisons using comparative adjectives

> **What is a comparative adjective?**
> A **comparative adjective** in English is one with -er on the end of it or *more*
> or *less* in front of it, that is used to compare people or things, for example,
> *slower, less important, more beautiful*.

➤ In French, to say that something is *easier, more expensive* and so on, you use **plus** (meaning *more*) before the adjective.

Cette question est <u>plus</u> facile.	This question is easier.
Cette veste est <u>plus</u> chère.	This jacket is more expensive.

➤ To say something is *less expensive, less complicated* and so on, you use **moins** (meaning *less*) before the adjective.

Cette veste est <u>moins</u> chère.	This jacket is less expensive.
un projet <u>moins</u> compliqué	a less complicated plan

➤ To introduce the person or thing you are making the comparison with, use **que** (meaning *than*).

Elle est plus petite <u>que</u> moi.	She's smaller than me.
Cette question est plus facile <u>que</u> la première.	This question is easier than the first one.

➤ To say that something or someone is *as ... as* something or someone else, use **aussi ... que**.

Il est <u>aussi</u> inquiet <u>que</u> moi.	He's as worried as me.
Cette ville n'est pas <u>aussi</u> grande <u>que</u> Bordeaux.	This town isn't as big as Bordeaux.

Making comparisons using superlative adjectives

> **What is a superlative adjective?**
> A **superlative adjective** in English is one with -est on the end of it or *most*
> or *least* in front of it, that is used to compare people or things, for example,
> *thinnest, most beautiful, least interesting*.

➤ In French, to say that something or someone is *easiest, prettiest, most expensive* and so on, you use:

- **le plus** with <u>masculine singular</u> adjectives
- **la plus** with <u>feminine singular</u> adjectives
- **les plus** with <u>plural</u> adjectives (for both masculine and feminine)

le guide <u>le plus</u> utile	the <u>most</u> useful guidebook
la question <u>la plus</u> facile	the easi<u>est</u> question
<u>les plus</u> grands hôtels	the big<u>gest</u> hotels
<u>les plus</u> petites voitures	the small<u>est</u> cars

➤ To say that something or someone is *the least easy, the least pretty, the least expensive* and so on, you use:

- **le moins** with <u>masculine singular</u> adjectives
- **la moins** with <u>feminine singular</u> adjectives
- **les moins** with <u>plural</u> adjectives (for both masculine and feminine).

le guide <u>le moins</u> utile	the <u>least</u> useful guidebook
Cette question est <u>la moins</u> facile.	This question is the <u>least</u> easy (*or* the hard<u>est</u>).
les mois <u>les moins</u> agréables	the <u>least</u> pleasant months
<u>les moins</u> belles photos	the <u>least</u> attractive photos

> *Tip*
>
> When the adjective comes <u>AFTER</u> the noun, you repeat the definite article (**le**, **la** or **les**).
>
> **les mois <u>les</u> moins agréables**   the least pleasant months
>
> When the adjective comes <u>BEFORE</u> the noun, you do not repeat the definite article.
>
> **les moins belles photos**   the least attractive photos
>
> ⇨ *For more information on **Word order with adjectives**, see page 39.*

➤ In phrases like *the biggest hotel in London* and *the oldest person in the village*, you use **de** to translate *in*.

le plus grand hôtel <u>de</u> Londres	the biggest hotel in London
la personne la plus âgée <u>du</u> village	the oldest person in the village

⇨ *For more information on **de** and **du**, see page 230 and 231.*

Irregular comparative and superlative adjectives

➤ Just as English has some irregular comparative and superlative forms – *better* instead of '*more good*', and *worst* instead of '*most bad*' – French also has a few irregular forms.

Adjective	Meaning	Comparative	Meaning	Superlative	Meaning
bon	good	**meilleur**	better	**le meilleur**	the best
mauvais	bad	**pire** **plus mauvais**	worse	**le pire** **le plus mauvais**	the worst
petit	small	**moindre** **plus petit**	smaller, lesser	**le moindre** **le plus petit**	the smallest, the least, the slightest

J'ai une <u>meilleure</u> idée.	I've got a <u>better</u> idea.
Il ne fait pas <u>le moindre</u> effort.	He doesn't make the <u>slightest</u> effort.

> Tip
> Choose the right form of the adjective to match the noun or pronoun, depending on whether it is masculine or feminine, singular or plural. Don't forget to change **le** to **la** or **les** in superlatives.

Grammar Extra!

bien and its comparative and superlative forms **mieux** and **le mieux** can be both adjectives and adverbs.

Il est <u>bien</u>, ce restaurant. (=*adjective*)	This restaurant is good.
Elle va <u>mieux</u> aujourd'hui. (=*adverb*)	She's better today.

⇨ *For more information on **Adverbs**, see page 209.*

KEY POINTS

✔ To compare people or things in French you use **plus** + adjective, **moins** + adjective or **aussi ... que**.

✔ *than* in comparatives is translated by **que**.

✔ French superlatives are formed with **le/la/les plus** + adjective and **le/la/les moins** + adjective.

✔ *in* after superlatives is translated by **de**.

✔ **bon, mauvais** and **petit** have irregular comparatives and superlatives: **bon/meilleur/le meilleur**, **mauvais/pire/le pire**, **petit/moindre/ le moindre**.

Test yourself

10 **Look at the two things being compared, and choose moins or plus to fill the gap.**

a   30° comparé à 25°, c'est .... chaud.

b   £200 comparé à £2000, c'est .... cher.

c   500 km comparé à 430 km, c'est .... loin.

d   2 heures comparé à 3 heures, c'est ....court.

e   3 heures comparé à 2 heures, c'est .... long.

f   10 kg comparé à 8 kg, c'est .... lourd.

g   8 kg comparé à 10 kg, c'est.............léger.

h   8 kg comparé à 10 kg, c'est.............lourd.

i   1999 comparé à 2010, c'est .... récent.

j   120 km/h comparé à 100 km/h, c'est .... rapide.

11 **Make comparisons, using est (= is) and plus ... que, moins... que or aussi... que, according to whether you see +, -, or =.**

a   Lucien/Serge/intelligent/+ ....

b   Serge/Lucien/intelligent/- ....

c   Lucien/son frère/grand/+ ....

d   Élodie/moi/petite/+..

e   Marie/Chantal/sympathique/- ....

f   Lucien/Chantal/sympathique/= ....

g   Charles/Xavier/optimiste/+ ....

h   Véronique/Sébastien/impatiente/- ....

i   Luc/moi/inquiet/= ....

j   Florent/son frère/sportif/+ ....

Test yourself

12 Translate the phrase into French.

a   the most interesting newspaper ....

b   the most expensive car ....

c   the most expensive hotels ....

d   the most popular female singers ....

e   the smallest gardens ....

f   the biggest hospitals ....

g   the least optimistic person..

h   the least attractive drawings ....

i   the least attractive dresses ....

j   the biggest shop in London ....

13 Complete the sentence with the correct article and form of the superlative adjective.

a   Elle est .... chanteuse de la chorale. **(meilleur)**

b   Le rouge, c'est .... choix. **(meilleur)**

c   Il dormait pendant .... moments du voyage. **(pire)**

d   Il fait .... travail possible. **(plus mauvais)**

e   Thierry et Thomas, c'est .... joueurs de l'équipe. **(meilleur)**

f   Il ne nous apporte jamais .... aide. **(moindre)**

g   C'est une émission sans .... intérêt. **(moindre)**

h   Je n'ai pas .... appétit. **(moindre)**

i   Anne et Marlène, c'est .... étudiantes de la classe. **(plus mauvais)**

j   André, c'est .... garçon de la classe. **(plus petit)**

Demonstrative adjectives: ce, cette, cet and ces

> **What is a demonstrative adjective?**
> A **demonstrative adjective** is one of the words *this*, *that*, *these* and *those* used with a noun in English to point out a particular thing or person, for example, *this* woman, *that* dog.

➤ In French you use **ce** to point out a particular thing or person. Like all adjectives in French, **ce** changes its form depending on whether you are referring to a noun that is masculine or feminine, singular or plural.

	Masculine	**Feminine**	**Meaning**
Singular	ce (cet)	cette	this that
Plural	ces	ces	these those

Tip
cet is used in front of masculine singular nouns which begin with a vowel and most words beginning with **h**.
cet oiseau   this/that bird
cet hôpital   this/that hospital

➤ **ce** comes <u>BEFORE</u> the noun it refers to.

Combien coûte <u>ce</u> manteau?	How much is this/that coat?
Comment s'appelle <u>cette</u> entreprise?	What's this/that company called?
<u>Ces</u> livres sont très intéressants.	These/Those books are very interesting.
<u>Ces</u> couleurs sont jolies.	These/Those colours are pretty.

➤ If you want to emphasize the difference between something that is close to you and something that is further away, you can add:

- **-ci** on the end of the noun for things that are closer
  Prends cette valise-<u>ci</u>.   Take this case.

- **-là** on the end of the noun for things that are further away
  Est-ce que tu reconnais cette personne-<u>là</u>?   Do you recognize that person?

> **KEY POINTS**
> ✔ The adjective **ce** corresponds to *this* and *that* in the singular, and *these* and *those* in the plural.
> ✔ The forms are **ce** and **cette** in the singular, and **ces** in the plural. **cet** is used with masculine singular nouns beginning with a vowel and most words beginning with **h**.
> ✔ You can add **-ci** on the end of the noun for things that are closer, or **-là** for things that are further away, to emphasize their nearness or distance.

For further explanation of grammatical terms, please see pages viii–xii.

Test yourself

14 **Fill the gap with the correct form of the demonstrative adjective.**

a .... veste est plus chère.

b .... projet est moins compliqué.

c .... questions sont plus faciles.

d .... ville n'est pas aussi grande que Lille.

e .... hôtel est moins cher.

f Combien coûte .... robe?

g Combien coûtent .... tomates?

h Comment s'appelle .... enfant?

i Combien coûte .... pantalon?

j Comment s'appelle .... chien?

15 **Translate the sentence into French, using ce, cet, cette or ces.**

a This car is beautiful. ....

b That colour is lovely. ....

c This hospital is big. ....

d That garden is nice. ....

e These trousers are better. ....

f These mushrooms are good. ....

g I'm going to buy that mirror. ....

h Do you want these roses? ....

i I like this tee-shirt and those shorts. ....

j I'm going to buy this jacket and those shirts. ....

k I've got these bags and that case. ....

16 **Translate the phrase using a demonstrative adjective with –ci for _here_ and –là for _over there_.**

a that person over there ....

b this jacket here ....

c these children here ....

d those women over there ....

e this button here ....

f that hotel over there ....

g this word here ....

h that guide over there ....

i these apples here ....

j those cakes over there ....

Possessive adjectives

> **What is a possessive adjective?**
> In English a **possessive adjective** is one of the words *my, your, his, her, its, our* or *their* used with a noun to show that one person or thing belongs to another.

➤ Here are the French possessive adjectives. Like all French adjectives, these agree with the noun they refer to.

with masculine singular noun	with feminine singular noun	with plural noun (masculine or feminine)	Meaning
mon	ma (mon)	mes	my
ton	ta (ton)	tes	your
son	sa (son)	ses	his her its one's
notre	notre	nos	our
votre	votre	vos	your
leur	leur	leurs	their

Tip

You use **mon, ton** and **son** with feminine singular nouns in front of words that begin with a vowel and most words beginning with **h**. This makes them easier to say.

mon assiette	my plate
ton histoire	your story
son erreur	his/her mistake
mon autre sœur	my other sister

➤ Possessive adjectives come <u>BEFORE</u> the noun they describe.

Voilà <u>mon</u> mari.	There's my husband.
<u>Mon</u> frère et <u>ma</u> sœur habitent à Glasgow.	My brother and sister live in Glasgow.
Est-ce que <u>tes</u> voisins vendent <u>leur</u> maison?	Are your neighbours selling their house?
Rangez <u>vos</u> affaires.	Put your things away.

Tip

Possessive adjectives agree with what they describe, <u>NOT</u> with the person who owns that thing. For example, **sa** can mean *his*, *her*, *its* and *one's*, but can only ever be used with a feminine singular noun.

Paul cherche <u>sa</u> montre.	Paul's looking for <u>his</u> watch.
Paul cherche <u>ses</u> lunettes.	Paul's looking for <u>his</u> glasses.
Catherine a appelé <u>son</u> frère.	Catherine called <u>her</u> brother.
Catherine a appelé <u>sa</u> sœur.	Catherine called <u>her</u> sister.

➤ The equivalent of *your* in French is **ton/ta/tes** for someone you call **tu**, or **votre/vos** for someone you call **vous**.

⇨ *For more information on the difference between **tu** and **vous**, see page 56.*

ℹ Note that possessive adjectives are <u>not</u> normally used with parts of the body. Use **le, la, l'** or **les** instead.

J'ai mal <u>à la main</u>.   My hand hurts.

⇨ *For more information on **Articles**, see page 14.*

KEY POINTS

✔ The French possessive adjectives are:
  • **mon/ton/son/notre/votre/leur** in the masculine singular
  • **ma/ta/sa/notre/votre/leur** in the feminine singular
  • **mes/tes/ses/nos/vos/leurs** in the plural
✔ Possessive adjectives come before the noun they refer to. They agree with what they describe, rather than with the person who owns that thing.
✔ You use **mon**, **ton** and **son** with feminine singular nouns when the following word begins with a vowel. You also use them with most words beginning with **h**.
✔ Possessive adjectives are not normally used with parts of the body. Use **le, la, l'** or **les** instead.

Test yourself

17 Fill the gap with the correct possessive adjective.

a mon mari et .... enfants

b .... frère et mes sœurs

c ton père et .... mère

d ta veste et .... chemise

e ses chaussures et .... pantalon

f son jardin et .... maison

g son nom et .... adresse

h .... noms et vos adresses

i nos collègues et .... chef

j leur famille et .... amis

18 Translate the following into French. Note that voilà can be used for _here is_, _here are_, _there is_, or _there are_.

a There's her husband. ....

b There's my car. ....

c Here's your paper, sir. ....

d There are your bags, madam. ....

e There's his mother. ....

f Here are your toys, Pierre. ....

g There's his house. ....

h There are my things. ....

i There's our train. ....

j There's his other sister. ....

19 Cross out the names the noun could not refer to.

a sa femme   Julie/Marc/Matthieu/Sarah

b mon fromage préféré   le beurre/le camembert/le roquefort/le rosbif

c son petit ami   Catherine/Hugo/Jean-Claude/Martin

d ma ville préférée   l'Australie/Paris/Lyon/la Seine

e leur vin préféré   le café/le champagne/le bordeaux/le bourgogne

f sa langue préférée   l'anglais/les maths/le français/la biologie

g mes fleurs préférées   les petits pois/les roses/les fraises/les marguerites

h leurs amies anglaises   Paul et Martin/Heinrich et Horst/Sarah et Tina/
                                   Christine et Jane

i mes affaires   mon sac/mon adresse/ma montre/mes lunettes

j son sport préféré   le foot /la philosophie/le cyclisme/le golf

Indefinite adjectives

What is an indefinite adjective?

An **indefinite adjective** is one of a small group of adjectives that are used to talk about people or things in a general way without saying exactly who or what they are, for example, *several*, *all*, *every*.

➤ In French, this type of adjective comes <u>BEFORE</u> the noun it refers to. Here are the most common French indefinite adjectives:

Masculine singular	Feminine singular	Masculine plural	Feminine plural	Meaning
autre	autre	autres	autres	other
chaque	chaque	-	-	every, each
même	même	mêmes	mêmes	same
-	-	quelques	quelques	some, a few
tout	toute	tous	toutes	all, every

J'ai d'<u>autres</u> projets.	I've got other plans.
J'y vais <u>chaque</u> année.	I go every year.
J'ai le <u>même</u> manteau.	I have the same coat.
Il a <u>quelques</u> amis à Paris.	He has some friends in Paris.
Il reste <u>quelques</u> bouteilles.	There are a few bottles left.
Il travaille <u>tout</u> le temps.	He works all the time.

Tip

You can also use **tout** to talk about how often something happens.

tous les jours	every day
tous les deux jours	every other day

ⓘ Note that these words can also be used as <u>pronouns</u>, standing in place of a noun instead of being used with one. **chaque** and **quelques** have a slightly different form when they are used in this way.

⇨ *For more information on **Pronouns**, see page 55.*

KEY POINTS

✔ The most common French indefinite adjectives are **autre**, **chaque**, **même**, **quelques** and **tout**.
✔ They come before the noun when they are used in this way.

Test yourself

20 Translate the sentence into French.

a I've got other friends. ....

b I've got some problems. ....

c I go every month. ....

d I've got the same shoes. ....

e There are a few potatoes left. ....

f I've got other trousers. ....

g He's got the same problem. ....

h There are a few tickets left. ....

i I've got all the work. ....

j Here are all the girls. ....

Pronouns

What is a pronoun?
A **pronoun** is a word you use instead of a noun, when you do not need or want to name someone or something directly, for example, *it*, *you*, *none*.

➤ There are several different types of pronoun:

- Personal pronouns such as *I, you, he, her* and *they*, which are used to refer to yourself, the person you are talking to, or other people and things. They can be either subject pronouns (*I, you, he* and so on) or object pronouns (*him, her, them* and so on).

- Possessive pronouns like *mine* and *yours*, which show who someone or something belongs to.

- Indefinite pronouns like *someone* or *nothing*, which refer to people or things in a general way without saying exactly who or what they are.

- Relative pronouns like *who, which* or *that*, which link two parts of a sentence together.

- Demonstrative pronouns like *this* or *those*, which point things or people out.

- Reflexive pronouns, a type of object pronoun that forms part of French reflexive verbs like **se laver** (meaning *to wash*) or **s'appeler** (meaning *to be called*).

  ➪ *For more information on **Reflexive verbs**, see page 123.*

- The two French pronouns, **en** and **y**, which are used in certain constructions.

- The pronouns **qui?** (meaning *who?, whom?*), **que?** (meaning *what?*), **quoi?** (meaning *what?*) and **lequel?** (meaning *which one?*), which are used in asking questions.

  ➪ *For more information on **Questions**, see page 197.*

➤ Pronouns often stand in for a noun to save repeating it.
  I finished my homework and gave <u>it</u> to my teacher.
  Do you remember Jack? I saw <u>him</u> at the weekend.

➤ Word order with personal pronouns is usually different in French and English.

Personal pronouns: subject

What is a subject pronoun?
A **subject pronoun** is a word such as *I, he, she* and *they*, which performs the action expressed by the verb. Pronouns stand in for nouns when it is clear who is being talked about, for example, *My brother isn't here at the moment. <u>He</u>'ll be back in an hour.*

Using subject pronouns

➤ Here are the French subject pronouns:

Singular	Meaning	Plural	Meaning
je (j')	I	nous	we
tu *or* vous	you	vous	you
il	he it	ils	they (*masculine*)
elle	she it	elles	they (*feminine*)
on	one (we/you/they)		

Je pars en vacances demain.
Nous habitons à Nice.

I'm going on holiday tomorrow.
We live in Nice.

> *Tip*
> je changes to j' in front of words beginning with a vowel, most words beginning with h, and the French word y.
>
> **J'arrive!**   I'm just coming!
> **Bon, j'y vais.**   Right, I'm off.

tu or vous?

➤ In English we have only <u>one</u> way of saying *you*. In French, there are <u>two</u> words: **tu** and **vous**. The word you use depends on:

- whether you are talking to one person or more than one person

- whether you are talking to a friend or family member, or someone else

➤ If you are talking to one person <u>you know well</u>, such as a friend, a young person or a relative, use **tu**.
    Tu me prêtes ce CD?   Will you lend me this CD?

➤ If you are talking to one person <u>you do not know so well</u>, such as your teacher, your boss or a stranger, use **vous**.
    Vous pouvez entrer.   You may come in.

> *Tip*
> If you are in doubt as to which form of *you* to use, it is safest to use **vous** so you will not offend anybody.

For further explanation of grammatical terms, please see pages viii–xii.

➤ If you are talking to <u>more than one person</u>, you have to use **vous**, no matter how well you know them.

Vous comprenez, les enfants?	Do you understand, children?

🗓 Note that the adjectives you use with **tu** and **vous** have to agree in the feminine and plural forms.

Vous êtes <u>certain</u>, Monsieur Leclerc? (*masculine singular*)	Are you sure, Mr Leclerc?
Vous êtes <u>certains</u>, les enfants? (*masculine plural*)	Are you sure, children?

Grammar Extra!
Any past participles (the form of the verb ending in **-é**, **-i** or **-u** in French) used with **être** in tenses such as the perfect also have to agree in the feminine and plural forms.

Vous êtes <u>partie</u> quand, Estelle? (*feminine singular*)	When did you leave, Estelle?
Estelle et Sophie — vous êtes <u>parties</u> quand? (*feminine plural*)	Estelle and Sophie — when did you leave?

⇨ For more information on the **Past participle**, see page 151–152.

---

il/elle and ils/elles

➤ In English we generally refer to things (such as *table*, *book*, *car*) only as *it*. In French, **il** (meaning *he, it*) and **elle** (meaning *she, it*) are used to talk about a thing, as well as about a person or an animal. You use **il** for <u>masculine nouns</u> and **elle** for <u>feminine nouns</u>.

<u>Il</u> est déjà parti.	He's already left.
<u>Elle</u> est actrice.	She's an actress.
<u>Il</u> mord, ton chien?	Does your dog bite?
Prends cette chaise. <u>Elle</u> est plus confortable.	Take this chair. It's more comfortable.

➤ **il** is also used to talk about the weather, the time and in certain other set phrases.

<u>Il</u> pleut.	It's raining.
<u>Il</u> est deux heures.	It's two o'clock.
<u>Il</u> faut partir.	We/You have to go.

➤ **ils** (meaning *they*) and **elles** (meaning *they*) are used in the plural to talk about things, as well as about people or animals. Use **ils** for <u>masculine nouns</u> and **elles** for <u>feminine nouns</u>.

<u>Ils</u> vont appeler ce soir.	They're going to phone tonight.
'Où sont Anne et Rachel?' — '<u>Elles</u> sont à la piscine.'	'Where are Anne and Rachel?' — 'They're at the swimming pool.'
'Est-ce qu'il reste des billets?' — 'Non, <u>ils</u> sont tous vendus.'	'Are there are any tickets left?' — 'No, they're all sold.'
'Tu aimes ces chaussures?' — 'Non, <u>elles</u> sont affreuses!'	'Do you like those shoes?' — 'No, they're horrible!'

➤ If you are talking about a masculine and a feminine noun, use **ils**.

Que font <u>ton père et ta mère</u> **quand <u>ils</u> partent en vacances?**	What do your father and mother do when they go on holiday?
'Où sont <u>le poivre et la moutarde</u>?'	'Where are the pepper and the mustard?'
— '<u>Ils</u> sont déjà sur la table.'	— 'They're already on the table.'

on

➤ **on** is frequently used in informal, everyday French to mean *we*.

<u>On</u> va à la plage demain.	We're going to the beach tomorrow.
<u>On</u> y va?	Shall we go?

➤ **on** can also have the sense of *someone* or *they*.

<u>On</u> m'a volé mon porte-monnaie.	Someone has stolen my purse.
<u>On</u> m'a dit que tu étais malade.	They told me you were ill.

> *Tip*
>
> **on** is often used to avoid a passive construction in French.
>
> **On vous demande au téléphone.**   You're wanted on the phone.
>
> ⇨ *For more information on the **Passive**, see page 165.*

➤ You can also use **on** as we use *you* in English when we mean people in general.

<u>On</u> peut visiter le château en été.	You can visit the castle in the summer.
D'ici <u>on</u> peut voir les côtes françaises.	From here you can see the French coast.

> *Tip*
>
> The form of the verb you use with **on** is the same as the **il/elle** form.
>
> ⇨ *For more information on **Verbs**, see pages 96–190.*

> ### KEY POINTS
> ✔ The French subject pronouns are: **je (j')**, **tu**, **il**, **elle**, **on** in the singular, and **nous**, **vous**, **ils**, **elles** in the plural.
> ✔ To say *you* in French, use **tu** if you are talking to one person you know well or to a young person. Use **vous** if you are talking to one person you do not know so well or to more than one person.
> ✔ **il/ils** (masculine singular/plural) and **elle/elles** (feminine singular/plural) are used to refer to things, as well as to people or animals. **il** is also used in certain set phrases.
> ✔ If there is a mixture of masculine and feminine nouns, use **ils**.
> ✔ **on** can mean *we*, *someone*, *you*, *they*, or people in general. It is often used instead of a passive construction.

Test yourself

1　**Cross out the names and things the pronoun could not refer to.**

a　**il**　　Robert/mon amie/le sel/mon chien

b　**elle**　mon pantalon/ma chemise/ma voiture/mon ami

c　**nous**　toi et moi/vous et moi/les autres/mes amis et moi

d　**vous**　mon mari et moi/toi et ton mari/Madame Renoir/Monsieur Buchy

e　**ils**　　les oiseaux/les souris/les Français/ les personnes âgées

f　**elles**　mes camarades/mes affaires/tes questions/tes examens

g　**tu**　　sa Majesté la reine/ tous les enfants de la classe /mon amie/un bébé

h　**on**　　une chaise/les affaires/tout le monde/mon mari et moi

i　**il**　　le temps/l'heure/le poivre et la moutarde/la circulation

j　**ils**　　les filles et les garçons/la viande et le vin/Sophie et Laurent/ Sylvie et Christine

2　**Fill the gap with il, elle, ils or elles.**

a　Où est ta sœur? — .... est à la piscine.

b　Où sont Yves et Charlotte? — .... sont à Paris.

c　Où sont les Anglais? — .... sont à l'hôtel.

d　Anne et Rachel sont déjà là? — Non, ... arrivent à deux heures.

e　Prends ces chaussures, ... sont plus confortables.

f　Prends cette assiette, ... est plus grande.

g　Prends ce pantalon, ... est moins cher.

h　Prends ces fraises, ... sont plus mûres.

i　Je n'ai pas de journaux, ... sont tous vendus.

j　Je n'ai pas de timbres, ... sont à la maison.

3　**Match the noun to the pronoun that would replace it.**

a　l'addition　　　　　　　　ils

b　les personnes　　　　　　il

c　les trains　　　　　　　　elles

d　mon frère et mes sœurs　elle

e　l'appartement　　　　　　ils

Test yourself

4 Translate the sentence into French.

a Where's Paul? — He's in Paris. ....

b Take some cheese, it's good. ....

c I like this wine, it's excellent. ....

d It's raining. ....

e Where are Pierre and Sonia? — They're in Calais.

....

f Where's your car? — It's at home. ....

g Take some strawberries, they're good.

....

h We're going to the cinema tomorrow.

....

i Do you like my jacket? — Yes, it's lovely.

....

j Where are the forks? — They're on the table.

....

Personal pronouns: direct object

> ### What is a direct object pronoun?
> A **direct object pronoun** is a word such as *me*, *him*, *us* and *them*, which is used instead of the noun to stand in for the person or thing most directly affected by the action expressed by the verb.

Using direct object pronouns

➤ Direct object pronouns stand in for nouns when it is clear who or what is being talked about, and save having to repeat the noun.

I've lost my glasses. Have you seen <u>them</u>?
'Have you met Jo?' — 'Yes, I really like <u>her</u>!'

➤ Here are the French direct object pronouns:

Singular	Meaning	Plural	Meaning
me (m')	me	**nous**	us
te (t')	you	**vous**	you
le (l')	him it	**les**	them (*masculine and feminine*)
la (l')	her it		

Ils vont <u>nous</u> aider.   They're going to help us.
Je <u>la</u> vois.   I can see her/it.
'Tu aimes les carottes?' —   'Do you like carrots?' —
  'Non, je <u>les</u> déteste!'   'No, I hate them!'

ⓘ Note that you cannot use direct object pronouns after a preposition like **à** or **de**, or when you want to emphasize something.

⇨ *For more information on* **Emphatic pronouns**, *see page 69.*

> *Tip*
> **me** changes to **m'**, **te** to **t'**, and **le/la** to **l'** in front of words beginning with a vowel, most words beginning with **h**, and the French word **y**.
>
> **Je <u>t'</u>aime.**   I love you.
> **Tu <u>m'</u>entends?**   Can you hear me?

➤ In orders and instructions **moi** is used instead of **me**, and **toi** is used instead of **te**.
  Aidez-<u>moi</u>!   Help me!
  Assieds-<u>toi</u>.   Sit down.

➤ **le** is sometimes used to refer back to an idea or information that has already been given. The word *it* is often missed out in English.
  'Ta chemise est très sale.' — **'Je <u>le</u> sais.'**   'Your shirt's very dirty.' — 'I know.'

Word order with direct object pronouns

➤ The direct object pronoun usually comes <u>BEFORE</u> the verb.

Je t'aime.	I love you.
Les voyez-vous?	Can you see them?
Elle ne nous connaît pas.	She doesn't know us.

    i Note that in orders and instructions the direct object pronoun comes <u>AFTER</u> the verb.

    Asseyez-vous.   Sit down.

➤ In tenses like the perfect that are formed with **avoir** or **être** and the past participle (the part of the verb that ends in **-é**, **-i** or **-u** in French), the direct object pronoun comes <u>BEFORE</u> the part of the verb that comes from **avoir** or **être**.

    Il m'a vu.   He saw me.

➤ When a verb like **vouloir** (meaning *to want*) or **pouvoir** (meaning *to be able to, can*) is followed by another verb in the infinitive (the '*to*' form of the verb), the direct object pronoun comes <u>BEFORE</u> the infinitive.

Il voudrait la revoir.	He'd like to see her again.
Puis-je vous aider?	Can I help you?

KEY POINTS

✔ The French direct object pronouns are: **me (m')**, **te (t')**, **le/la (l')** in the singular, and **nous**, **vous**, **les** in the plural.

✔ Except in orders and instructions the direct object pronoun comes before the verb.

Test yourself

5 **Fill the gap with the correct direct object pronoun.**

a   Tu vois cette fille? — Oui, je .... vois.

b   Regarde ces danseurs! — Oui, je .... regarde.

c   Tu m'entends? Oui, je .... entends bien.

d   Tu .... aimes? — Oui, je t'aime.

e   Écoute-moi! — Je .... écoute.

f   Tu aimes les chats? — Oui, je .... adore.

g   Ils vous invitent à la fête? — Oui, ils .... invitent.

h   Tu aimes cette chanson? — Non, je .... déteste!

i   Tu vois Pierre? — Non, je ne .... vois pas.

j   Janine? Je ne .... connais pas.

6 **Replace the highlighted words with a hyphen and an object pronoun.**

a   Aidez **la petite fille!** ....

b   Prenez **vos clés**! ....

c   Prends **ton billet et ton passeport**! ....

d   Invite **ton amie**! ....

e   Essayez **ce vin**! ....

f   Écoutez **ton père et moi**! ....

g   Refais **ce travail**! ....

h   Range **ta chambre**! ....

i   Appelez **Joseph et moi**! ....

7 **Match the two columns.**

a   **Susanne est gentille.**   Je vais l'acheter.

b   **Tu es gentille.**   Je vais les acheter.

c   **J'aime ce pantalon.**   Il voudrait la revoir.

d   **Marie est jolie.**   Elle va nous aider.

e   **J'aime ces chaussures.**   Tu vas m'aider.

Test yourself

8 **Translate the sentence into French.**

a Do you like Sarah? — No, I hate her!

....

b Can you hear him? ....

c You see that bird? — Yes, I see it. ....

d Do you know the answer? — No, I don't know it. ....

e Henri and Sophie are in the garden. — Yes, I can see them.

....

f Do you like this wine? — Yes, I like it very much.

....

g The castle's lovely, you can visit it in summer.

....

h Help me! ....

i I like that photo. — Take it! ....

j Jonathon, where are my keys, can you see them?

....

Personal pronouns: indirect object

> **What is an indirect object pronoun?**
> When a verb has two objects (a <u>direct</u> one and an <u>indirect</u> one), the **indirect object pronoun** is used instead of a noun to show the person or thing the action is intended to benefit or harm, for example, *me* in *He gave <u>me</u> a book; Can you get <u>me</u> a towel?*

Using indirect object pronouns

➤ It is important to understand the difference between direct and indirect object pronouns in English, as they can have different forms in French:

- an <u>indirect object</u> answers the question *who to/for?* or *to/for what?*
  He gave me a book. → *Who did he give the book to?* → me (=*indirect object pronoun*)
  Can you get me a towel? → *Who can you get a towel for?* → me (=*indirect object pronoun*)

- if something answers the question *what* or *who*, then it is the <u>direct object</u> and <u>NOT</u> the indirect object
  He gave me a book. → *What did he give me?* → a book (=*direct object*)
  Can you get me a towel? → *What can you get me?* → a towel (=*direct object*)

➤ Here are the French indirect object pronouns:

Singular	Meaning	Plural	Meaning
me (m')	me, to me, for me	**nous**	us, to us, for us
te (t')	you, to you, for you	**vous**	you, to you, for you
lui	him, to him, for him her, to her, for her it, to it, for it	**leur**	them, to them, for them (*masculine and feminine*)

Il <u>nous</u> écrit tous les jours.   He writes to us every day.
Qu'est-ce que tu <u>lui</u> as acheté?   What did you buy him?

> *Tip*
> **me** changes to **m'** and **te** to **t'** in front of words beginning with a vowel, most words beginning with **h**, and the French word **y**.
>
> **Il <u>m'</u>a donné un livre.**   He gave me a book.
> **Tu <u>m'</u>apportes une serviette?**   Can you get me a towel?

➤ The pronouns shown in the table are used instead of the preposition **à** with a noun.
J'écris <u>à Suzanne</u>. I'm writing to Suzanne. → **Je <u>lui</u> écris.** I'm writing to her.
Donne du lait <u>au chat</u>. Give the cat some milk. → **Donne-<u>lui</u> du lait.** Give it some milk.

➤ Some French verbs like **demander à** (meaning *to ask*) and **téléphoner à** (meaning *to phone*) take an <u>indirect object</u> while English uses a direct object.

Il <u>leur</u> téléphone tous les soirs.   He phones <u>them</u> every evening.

➤ On the other hand, some French verbs like **attendre** (meaning *to wait for*), **chercher** (meaning *to look for*) and **regarder** (meaning *to look at*) take a <u>direct object</u> to translate an English preposition + pronoun.

Je <u>les</u> attends devant la gare.   I'll wait <u>for them</u> outside the station.

Word order with indirect object pronouns

➤ The indirect object pronoun usually comes <u>BEFORE</u> the verb.

Dominique <u>vous</u> écrit une lettre.   Dominique's writing you a letter.
Il ne <u>nous</u> parle pas.   He doesn't speak to us.
Il ne veut pas <u>me</u> répondre.   He won't answer me.

i Note that in orders and instructions telling someone to do something, the indirect object pronoun comes <u>AFTER</u> the verb.

Donne-<u>lui</u> ça!   Give her that!

> **KEY POINTS**
> ✔ The French indirect object pronouns are: **me (m')**, **te (t')**, **lui** in the singular, and **nous**, **vous**, **leur** in the plural.
> ✔ Except in orders and instructions telling someone to do something, the direct object pronoun comes <u>before</u> the verb.

9 **Match a sentence starting with a name to one starting with a pronoun.**

a Bernard téléphone à ses parents tous les jours.

Il nous écrit à Noël.

b Laurent téléphone à son frère tous les jours.

Il lui téléphone tous les jours.

c Nathalie parle souvent à sa sœur.

Il leur téléphone tous les jours.

d Paul écrit à mon mari et moi à Noël.

Il lui écrit à Noël.

e Pierre écrit à sa sœur à Noël.

Elle lui parle souvent.

10 **Apporte-moi une serviette! is an order which sounds more polite phrased as a question: Tu m'apportes une serviette? Change the orders into questions, adding s to the verb.**

a Apporte-moi un verre! ....

b Apporte-lui du lait! ....

c Apporte-nous ton cahier! ....

d Apporte-leur des chaises! ....

e Donne-moi la main! ....

f Donne-lui le ballon! ....

g Donne-leur les cadeaux! ....

h Donne-nous ce bâton! ....

i Téléphone-leur ce soir! ....

j Téléphone-moi demain! ....

11 **Fill the gap with the correct indirect object pronoun.**

a Tu vas parler à ta mère ce soir? — Oui, je vais .... parler ce soir.

b Vous allez parler aux employés demain? — Oui, je vais .... parler demain.

c Vous parlez souvent au professeur? — Oui, je .... parle souvent.

d Il donne des cadeaux aux enfants? — Oui, il .... donne des cadeaux.

e Tu écris à Pauline? — Oui, je .... écris.

f Il te parle? — Non, il ne .... parle pas.

g Tu vas demander à tes parents? — Oui, je vais .... demander.

h Il salue son voisin? — Non, il ne .... parle jamais.

i Elle peut voir ton jardin? — Oui, je vais le .... montrer.

j Nous pouvons voir vos photos? — Oui, je vais .... les montrer.

12 Translate the sentence into French.

a She gave me a glass of wine. ....

b Give her some milk. ....

c Madame Reyer, Lise is writing you a card.

....

d She doesn't speak to us. ....

e Give me the keys! ....

f Give her the money! ....

g Will you give me the money? ....

h I'm going to phone them this evening.

....

i He's going to tell them the truth. ....

j She won't answer me. ....

Emphatic pronouns

> **What is an emphatic pronoun?**
> An **emphatic pronoun** is used instead of a noun when you want to emphasize something, for example *Is this for me?*

Using emphatic pronouns

➤ In French, there is another set of pronouns which you use after prepositions, when you want to emphasize something and in certain other cases. These are called <u>emphatic pronouns</u> or <u>stressed pronouns</u>.

Singular	Meaning	Plural	Meaning
moi	I me	nous	we us
toi	you	vous	you
lui	he him	eux	they (*masculine*) them
elle	she her	elles	they (*feminine*) them
soi	oneself (yourself, ourselves)		

Je pense souvent à <u>toi</u>.	I often think about you.
C'est pour <u>moi</u>?	Is this for me?
Venez avec <u>moi</u>.	Come with me.
Il a besoin de <u>nous</u>.	He needs us.

➤ **soi** (meaning *oneself*) is used with the subject pronoun **on** and with words like **tout le monde** (meaning *everyone*) or **chacun** (meaning *each one*).

Il faut avoir confiance en <u>soi</u>.	You have to have confidence in yourself.
Tout le monde est rentré chez <u>soi</u>.	Everyone went home.

When to use emphatic pronouns

➤ Emphatic pronouns are used in the following circumstances:

- after a preposition

C'est <u>pour moi</u>?	Is this for me?

- for emphasis, especially where a contrast is involved

<u>Toi</u>, tu ressembles à ton père, mais <u>elle</u> non.	You look like your father, she doesn't.
Il m'énerve, <u>lui</u>!	He's getting on my nerves!

- on their own without a verb

'Qui a cassé la fenêtre?' — '<u>Lui</u>.'	'Who broke the window?' — 'He did.'
'Je suis fatiguée.' — '<u>Moi aussi</u>.'	'I'm tired.' — 'Me too.'

- after **c'est** and **ce sont** (meaning *it is*)
  C'est <u>toi</u>, Simon?   Is that you, Simon?
  Ce sont <u>eux</u>.   It's them.

⇨ *For more information on* ***c'est*** *and* ***ce sont***, *see page 91.*

- in comparisons
  Tu es plus jeune que <u>moi</u>.   You're younger than me.
  Il est moins grand que <u>toi</u>.   He's smaller than you (are).

- when the subject of the sentence is made up of two pronouns, or of a pronoun and a noun
  Mon père et elle ne s'entendent pas.   My father and she don't get on.

Grammar Extra!
You can add **-même** or **-mêmes** to the emphatic pronouns when you particularly want to emphasize something. These forms correspond to English *myself*, *ourselves* and so on.

Form with -même	Meaning
moi-même	myself
toi-même	yourself
lui-même	himself, itself
elle-même	herself, itself
soi-même	oneself (yourself, ourselves)
nous-mêmes	ourselves
vous-même vous-mêmes	yourself yourselves
eux-mêmes	themselves (*masculine*)
elles-mêmes	themselves (*feminine*)

Je l'ai fait <u>moi-même</u>.   I did it myself.
Elle l'a choisi <u>elle-même</u>.   She chose it herself.

> ### KEY POINTS
> ✔ The French emphatic pronouns are: **moi**, **toi**, **lui**, **elle**, **soi** in the singular, and **nous**, **vous**, **eux**, **elles** in the plural.
> ✔ They are used:
>   - after a preposition
>   - for emphasis
>   - on their own without a verb
>   - after **c'est** and **ce sont**
>   - in comparisons
>   - when the subject of the sentence is made up of two pronouns, or of a pronoun and a noun
> ✔ You can add **-même** or **-mêmes** to the emphatic pronouns when you particularly want to emphasize something.

Test yourself

13 **Replace the highlighted words with an emphatic pronoun.**

a Je pense souvent à **Michelle**. ....

b Il pense souvent à **sa petite amie**. ....

c C'est pour **Matthieu et Catherine**? ....

d Il a besoin **de ses sœurs**. ....

e Je pense souvent à **mes amies**. ....

f Venez avec **votre mari**. ....

g Je viens sans **mes enfants**. ....

h Il a besoin de **toi et de ton mari**. ....

i Tu viens avec **mon frère et moi**? ....

j Elle vit avec **Michel**. ....

14 **Match the alternative versions.**

a **Tu es là, chérie?**   C'est vous, Madame?

b **Luc a cassé le joujou.**   C'est lui qui les a cassés.

c **Lucie a cassé le vase.**   C'est toi, chérie?

d **Vous êtes là, Madame Ducasse?** C'est elle qui l'a cassé.

e **Laurent a cassé les verres.**   C'est lui qui l'a cassé.

15 **Translate the sentence.**

a He's tired. — So am I. ....

b She's optimistic. — We are too. ....

c I'm at the hotel, are you too? ....

d She is as worried as him. ....

e You are as pretty as her, Emma. ....

f She's smaller than me. ....

g She's nice, he's not. ....

h You're rich, I'm not. ....

i They're richer than us. ....

j I often think about him. — So do I. ....

Test yourself

16 **Add an emphatic pronoun joined with a hyphen to même or mêmes.**

a   Ils l'ont fait ....

b   Ma cousine nettoie la maison ....

c   Nous avons repeint la maison ....

d   J'ai fait ma robe ....

e   Les petites filles l'ont choisi ....

f   Tu l'as fait .... ?

g   On peut le peindre ....

h   Je me coupe les cheveux ....

i   Marc et Chantal ont construit leur maison ....

j   Vous l'avez dessiné .... ?

Possessive pronouns

What is a possessive pronoun?

A **possessive pronoun** is one of the words *mine, yours, hers, his, ours* or *theirs*, which are used instead of a noun to show that one person or thing belongs to another, for example, *Ask Carole if this pen is hers*.

➤ Here are the French possessive pronouns:

Masculine singular	Feminine singular	Masculine plural	Feminine plural	Meaning
le mien	la mienne	les miens	les miennes	mine
le tien	la tienne	les tiens	les tiennes	yours
le sien	la sienne	les siens	les siennes	his hers
le nôtre	la nôtre	les nôtres	les nôtres	ours
le vôtre	la vôtre	les vôtres	les vôtres	yours
le leur	la leur	les leurs	les leurs	theirs

Ces CD-là, ce sont les miens.   Those CDs are mine.
Heureusement que tu as tes clés.   It's lucky you've got your keys.
 J'ai oublié les miennes.   I forgot mine.

Tip

In French, possessive pronouns agree with what they describe, NOT with the person who owns that thing. For example, **le sien** can mean *his* or *hers*, but can only be used to replace a masculine singular noun.

'C'est le vélo de Paul?' —   'Is that Paul's bike?' —
  'Oui, c'est le sien.'   'Yes, it's his.'

'C'est le vélo d'Isabelle?' —   'Is that Isabelle's bike?' —
  'Oui, c'est le sien.'   'Yes, it's hers.'

Grammar Extra!

Remember that **à** with the definite article **le** becomes **au**, and **à** with **les** becomes **aux,** so:

à + le mien → **au mien**
à + les miens → **aux miens**
à + les miennes → **aux miennes**
Tu préfères ce manteau <u>au mien</u>?   Do you prefer this coat to mine?

Remember that **de** with the definite article **le** becomes **du**, and **de** with **les** becomes **des**, so:

de + le mien → **du mien**
de + les miens → **des miens**
de + les miennes → **des miennes**
J'ai oublié mes clés. J'ai besoin   I've forgotten my keys. I need yours.
  <u>des tiennes</u>.

⇨ *For more information on **Articles**, see page 14.*

KEY POINTS

✔ The French possessive pronouns are **le mien**, **le tien**, **le sien** for singular subject pronouns, and **le nôtre**, **le vôtre** and **le leur** for plural subject pronouns. Their forms change in the feminine and the plural.
✔ In French, the pronoun you choose has to agree with the noun it replaces, and <u>not</u> with the person who owns that thing.

Test yourself

17 Match the sentences.

a	Tes chaussures sont plus belles.	Je préfère la sienne.
b	Ton frère est plus gentil.	J'ai besoin du vôtre.
c	J'ai oublié mon guide.	J'ai besoin de la tienne.
d	Je n'aime pas ma chambre.	Je le préfère au mien.
e	Je n'ai pas de crème solaire.	Je les préfère aux miennes.

18 Complete the sentence with the correct form of the possessive pronoun.

a   C'est ton sac? — Non, ce n'est pas ....

b   C'est votre place? — Oui, c'est ....

c   C'est l'adresse de ton camarade? — Oui, c'est ....

d   C'est la voiture de tes parents? — Oui, c'est ....

e   C'est l'appartement de son petit ami? — Oui, c'est ....

f   C'est la maison de ta petite amie? — Oui, c'est ....

g   Ce sont les meubles de ta grand-mère? — Oui, ce sont ....

h   Ce sont les affaires de ton mari? — Non, ce ne sont pas ....

i   C'était l'idée de tes camarades? — Non, ce n'était pas ....

j   C'est le chien des voisins? — Oui, c'est ....

19 Cross out the phrases that cannot refer to the noun.

a	l'argent sur la table	c'est la nôtre/c'est le sien/c'est le mien/c'est la leur
b	ces journaux	ce sont les miens/ce sont les nôtres/ce sont les leurs/ ce sont les siennes
c	ce jardin	c'est le leur/c'est le sien/c'est la mienne/ce n'est pas le nôtre
d	cette tasse de thé	c'est le tien/ ce n'est pas le tien/c'est la mienne/ ce sont les leurs
e	ces chaussures	c'est le mien/ce sont les siennes/ce sont les leurs/ ce sont les miennes
f	ce short	c'est le sien/ce sont les siens/c'est le vôtre/c'est le leur
g	ce portable	c'est la mienne/c'est le sien/ce n'est pas le mien/ c'est la vôtre

Test yourself

h   **ces clés**   ce sont les siens/ce sont les leurs/ce sont les nôtres/
ce ne sont pas les vôtres

i   **ces sandwichs**   ce sont les miens/ ce sont les miennes/ce sont les leurs/
ce sont les tiennes

j   **la faute**   c'est la tienne/ce n'est pas la mienne/ce n'est pas la nôtre/
c'est le leur

20 Translate the sentence into French.

a   It's not his car, it's mine. ....

b   His house is lovely, I prefer it to mine.

....

c   Their teacher is good, I prefer him to ours.

....

d   That room is his. ....

e   This team is good. It's better than ours.

....

f   Their flat is bigger than ours. ....

g   My bag is heavier than hers. ....

h   Those things are theirs. ....

i   I haven't got any shampoo, I need yours.

....

j   Her life is more difficult than mine.

....

en and y

➤ **en** and **y** do not usually refer to people. How we translate them into English depends on where **en** and **y** are found in French.

en

➤ **en** is used with verbs and phrases normally followed by **de** to avoid repeating the same word.

Si tu as un problème, tu peux m'en parler.	If you've got a problem, you can talk to me about it.
	(**en** replaces **de** in **parler de quelque chose**)
Est-ce que tu peux me prêter ce livre? J'en ai besoin.	Can you lend me that book? I need it.
	(**en** replaces **de** in **avoir besoin de quelque chose**)
Il a un beau jardin et il en est très fier.	He's got a beautiful garden and is very proud of it.
	(**en** replaces **de** in **être fier de quelque chose**)

➤ **en** can also replace the <u>partitive article</u> (**du**, **de la**, **de l'**, **des**).

Je n'ai pas d'argent. Tu en as?	I haven't got any money. Have you got any?
'Tu peux me prêter des timbres?'	'Can you lend me some stamps?' —
— 'Non, je dois en acheter.'	'No, I need to buy some.'

⇨ *For more information on the **Partitive article**, see page 27.*

➤ **en** is also used:
- as a preposition
- with the present participle of verbs

⇨ *For more information on **Prepositions** and the **Present participle**, see pages 227 and 170.*

➤ When **en** is used with **avoir,** with **il y a** or with numbers, it is often not translated in English but can <u>NEVER</u> be missed out in French.

'Est-ce que tu as un dictionnaire?'	'Have you got a dictionary?' —
— 'Oui, j'en ai un.'	'Yes, I've got one.'
'Combien d'élèves y a-t-il dans ta classe?' — 'Il y en a trente.'	'How many pupils are there in your class?' — 'There are thirty.'
J'en veux deux.	I want two (of them).

y

➤ **y** is used with verbs and phrases normally followed by **à** to avoid repeating the same word.

'Je pensais à l'examen.' —	'I was thinking about the exam.' —
'Mais arrête d'y penser!'	'Well, stop thinking about it!'
	(**y** replaces **à** in **penser à quelque chose**)
'Je ne m'attendais pas à ça.' —	'I wasn't expecting that.' —
'Moi, je m'y attendais.'	'Well, I was expecting it.'
	(**y** replaces **à** in **s'attendre à quelque chose**)

➤ **y** can also mean *there*. It can be used to replace phrases that would use prepositions such as **dans** (meaning *in*) and **sur** (meaning *on*).

Elle y passe tout l'été.	She spends the whole summer there.
Regarde dans le tiroir. Je pense que les clés y sont.	Look in the drawer. I think the keys are in there.

Word order with en and y

➤ en and y usually come <u>BEFORE</u> the verb.

J'en veux.	I want some.
Elle en a parlé avec lui.	She talked to him about it.
En êtes-vous content?	Are you pleased with it/them?
Comment fait-on pour y aller?	How do you get there?
N'y pense plus.	Don't think about it any more.

➤ In orders and instructions telling someone to do something, **en** or **y** come <u>AFTER</u> the verb and are attached to it with a hyphen (-).

Prenez-en.	Take some.
Restez-y.	Stay there.

Tip

The final **-s** of **-er** verbs is usually dropped in the **tu** form used for orders and instructions. When an **-er** verb in the **tu** form is used before **en** or **y**, however, the **-s** is not dropped, to make it easier to say.

Donne des bonbons à ton frère.	Give some sweets to your brother.
Donnes-en à ton frère.	Give some to your brother.
Va dans ta chambre!	Go to your room!
Vas-y!	Go on!

⇨ *For more information on the* **Imperative***, see page* 119.

➤ en and y come <u>AFTER</u> other direct or indirect object pronouns.

Donnez-leur-en.	Give them some.
Il m'en a parlé.	He spoke to me about it.

⇨ *For more information on* **Direct object pronouns** *and* **Indirect object pronouns***, see pages* 61 *and* 65.

KEY POINTS

✔ **en** is used with verbs and expressions normally followed by **de** to avoid repeating the same word.
✔ **en** can also replace the partitive article.
✔ When **en** is used with **avoir** and **il y a** or with numbers, it is often not translated in English but can never be missed out in French.
✔ **y** is used with verbs and expressions normally followed by **à** to avoid repeating the same word.
✔ **y** can also mean *there* and may replace expressions that would be used with **dans** and **sur** or some other preposition indicating a place.
✔ **en** and **y** usually come before the verb, except in orders and instructions telling someone to do something, when **en** or **y** follows the verb and is attached to it with a hyphen.
✔ **en** and **y** come after other direct or indirect object pronouns.

Test yourself

21 **Replace the highlighted words with a phrase consisting of en followed by the verb. When followed by en, me, te, se and ne become m', t', s' and n'.**

a Tu **as de l'argent**? ....

b Tu **veux du sucre**? ....

c Tu peux me **parler de ce problème**. ....

d Il peut se **servir de son vélo**. ....

e Je peux me **servir de ton ordinateur**? ....

f Il ne **veut pas de lait**. ....

g Vous **avez de l'eau**? ....

h Vous **voulez du vin**? ....

i Tu veux **goûter du fromage**? ....

j Je dois **acheter de la viande**. ....

22 **Match the sentences that are related.**

a Elle aime beaucoup la France.   Je ne m'y attendais pas.

b Tu peux me prêter de l'argent?   J'en ai besoin.

c Je n'ai pas de beurre.   Tu peux m'en parler.

d Il y a un problème?   Elle y passe tout l'été.

e Quelle surprise!   Je dois en acheter.

23 **Cross out the unlikely items.**

a Je n'en veux pas.   Je ne bois jamais d'alcool./C'est très bon./
                             Je suis fatiguée./Ce n'est pas bon.

b Je vais en acheter.   Je ne l'aime pas./J'en ai besoin./Je n'en ai pas./
                             C'est un ingrédient important.

c Elle en est très fière. Son jardin est beau./Sa maison est belle./
                             Sa maison est petite./Sa maison est bien rangée.

d J'en suis ravi.   C'est nul./C'est magnifique./C'est très bon./
                             C'est beau.

e J'en suis sûre.   C'est certain./Je suis dans le doute./
                             Je le sais bien./Tout le monde le sait.

f Elle en est contente.   Il est très petit./C'est une bonne nouvelle./
                             Il est beau./Il est lourd.

g Je ne m'y attendais pas.

C'est bizarre./C'est naturel./C'est une surprise./
C'était prévisible.

h N'y pense plus.

C'est important./Ce n'est pas grave./
C'est drôle./C'est de ta faute.

i Elles m'en ont parlé.

C'est un problème./C'est un secret./
C'est une idée intéressante./
Elles en parlent seulement aux amis.

j J'y vais souvent.

J'aime bien cette ville./
Mes parents habitent cette ville./
C'est une ville agréable./
Comment fait-on pour y aller?

24 Translate the sentence into French, using y or en.

a One dictionary? I've got three. ....

b I want a dog. No, I want two. ....

c How many plates are there on the table? — There are four.

....

d Look on the table, I think your mobile is there.

....

e There's ice cream? I want some! ....

f I don't think about it any more. ....

g You've got money – give your sister some!

....

h We need money – give us some! ....

i I need money – give me some! ....

j How do you get there? ....

Using different types of pronoun together

➤ Sometimes you find a direct object pronoun and an indirect object pronoun in the same sentence.

He gave <u>me</u> (*indirect object*) <u>them</u> (*direct object*).
He gave <u>them</u> (*direct object*) to <u>me</u> (*indirect object*).

➤ When this happens in French, you have to put the indirect and direct object pronouns in a certain order.

Indirect	Direct	Indirect	
me	le	lui	en
te	la	leur	y
nous	les		
vous			

Dominique <u>vous l'</u>envoie demain.	Dominique's sending it to you tomorrow.
Il <u>te les</u> a montrés?	Has he shown them to you?
Je <u>les lui</u> ai lus.	I read them to him/her.
Ne <u>la leur</u> donne pas.	Don't give it to them.
Elle ne <u>m'en</u> a pas parlé.	She didn't speak to me about it.

KEY POINTS

✔ If a direct and an indirect object pronoun are used in the same sentence, you usually put the indirect object pronoun before the direct object pronoun.

✔ With **lui** and **leur**, this order is reversed and you put the direct object pronoun before the indirect object pronoun.

Test yourself

25 Fill the gap with two pronouns. veux, veut etc mean _want_.

   a   Matthieu demande cet argent? Ne .... donne pas!

   b   Lucie veut la voiture? Ne .... donne pas!

   c   Les filles demandent les clés? Je vais .... donner.

   d   Tu veux ce CD? Je .... donne.

   e   Elle veut prendre mon tee-shirt favori. Je ne .... donne pas.

   f   Vous voulez de l'eau? Je .... donne.

   g   Ils veulent ton mot de passe? Ne .... donne pas!

   h   Je veux du sucre, maman. — Je .... donne, chérie.

   i   Ce monsieur veut du pain. Je .... donne.

   j   Je veux voir votre jardin. Je .... montre.

26 Match the related items.

   a   Ils veulent voir vos photos.   Je vais t'en envoyer.

   b   Marie adore cette histoire.   Je vais vous l'envoyer.

   c   J' adore les roses rouges.   Je vais la lui lire.

   d   Il demande du cognac.   Je vais les leur montrer.

   e   Nous avons besoin de l'adresse.   Ne lui en donne pas!

Indefinite pronouns

What is an indefinite pronoun?
An **indefinite pronoun** is one of a small group of pronouns such as *everything*, *nobody* and *something* which are used to refer to people or things in a general way without saying exactly who or what they are.

➤ Here are the most common French indefinite pronouns:

- **chacun** (*masculine singular*)/**chacune** (*feminine singular*) each, everyone

Nous avons <u>chacun</u> donné dix euros.	We each gave ten euros.
<u>Chacun</u> fait ce qu'il veut.	Everyone does what they like.
Toutes les villas ont <u>chacune</u> leur piscine.	Each villa has its own swimming pool.

- **personne** nobody/no one, anybody/anyone

Il <u>n'</u>y a <u>personne</u> à la maison.	There's no one at home.
Elle <u>ne</u> veut voir <u>personne</u>.	She doesn't want to see anybody.

⇨ *For more information on **Negatives**, see page 192.*

Tip
You can use **personne** on its own to answer a question.

Qui connaît la réponse? <u>Personne</u>.	Who knows the answer? No one.

If the sentence contains a verb you have to use **ne** with it.

Personne <u>n'</u>est venu.	Nobody came.

- **quelque chose** something, anything

J'ai <u>quelque chose</u> pour toi.	I've got something for you.
Avez-vous <u>quelque chose</u> à déclarer?	Do you have anything to declare?

- **quelqu'un** somebody/someone, anybody/anyone

Il y a <u>quelqu'un</u> à la porte.	There's someone at the door.
<u>Quelqu'un</u> a vu mon parapluie?	Has anybody seen my umbrella?

- **rien** nothing, anything

Elle n'a <u>rien</u> dit.	She didn't say anything.
<u>Rien</u> n'a changé.	Nothing's changed.

⇨ *For more information on **Negatives**, see page 192.*

> *Tip*
> You can use **rien** on its own to answer a question.
>
> **'Qu'est-ce tu as acheté?' — 'Rien.'**   'What did you buy?' — 'Nothing.'
>
> If the sentence contains a verb you have to use **ne** with it.
>
> **Il n'a rien mangé.**   He's eaten nothing.

- **tout** everything
  Il organise tout.   He's organizing everything.
  Tout va bien?   Is everything OK?

- **tous** (*masculine plural*)/**toutes** (*feminine plural*) all
  Je les connais tous.   I know them all.
  Elles sont toutes arrivées?   Are they all here?

➤ You can use **quelque chose de/rien de** and **quelqu'un de/personne de** with adjectives
  if you want to say *nothing interesting*, *something new* and so on.
  rien d'intéressant   nothing interesting

> **KEY POINTS**
> ✔ **rien** and **personne** can be used on their own to answer questions,
>   but need to be used with **ne** when there is a verb in the sentence.
> ✔ **quelque chose/rien** and **quelqu'un/personne** can be followed by
>   **de** + adjective.

Test yourself

27 Replace the highlighted noun with an indefinite pronoun.

a J'ai **un cadeau** pour toi. ....

b Il y a **une petite fille** au jardin. ....

c Il m'a dit **un secret**. ....

d **Une jeune femme** répond aux questions. ....

e J'ai **une camarade** qui m'accompagne. ....

f Ils ont **des fleurs** pour Christine. ....

g Tu veux **un café**? ....

h C'est **une personne** qui parle beaucoup. ....

i Vous avez besoin de **ces serviettes**? ....

j J'ai **un renseignement** à vous demander. ....

28 Match the related items.

a Ici on est libre.   Rien n'a changé.

b Elle est malade.   Nous avons donné 20 euros chacun.

c La crise continue.   Les maisons ont chacune leur grand jardin.

d On a fait une collecte.   Chacun fait ce qu'il veut.

e C'est un beau quartier.   Elle ne veut voir personne.

29 Fill the gap with rien or personne.

a Je n'en parle avec ....

b Le musée est nul: il n'y a .... d'intéressant.

c La réunion était nulle: il n'y avait .... d'intéressant.

d Qui s'occupe de la maison? — ....

e Tout est différent? — Non, ... n'a changé.

f Qu'est-ce que tu vas faire? — .... du tout.

g C'est cher? — Non, ça ne coûte ....

h Qui t'accompagne en Afrique? ....

i Qu'est-ce qu'il te donne? — Il ne me donne ....

j Qui vous aide à la maison? — .... ne m'aide.

Test yourself

30 Cross out the items that do not make sense.

a   Quelqu'un a vu mon parapluie?

Je vais en ville./Je reste à la maison./
Oui, il est là./Il pleut.

b   Je les connais tous.

C'est un collègue./Ce sont des amis./
Ce sont des voisins./Ce sont mes cousins.

c   Tout va bien.

Il n'y a de problème./Je suis inquiet./
Je suis content./C'est le désastre.

d   J'ai quelque chose pour eux.

des joujoux/des bonbons/
une nouvelle amie/un ballon

e   Elle n'a rien dit.

Elle est timide./Elle est silencieuse./
Elle est jolie./Elle est pleine de tact.

f   Il n'a rien mangé.

Le repas était très bon./Il n'avait pas faim./
Il était malade./La soupe était trop salée.

g   Elle organise tout.

Elle est énergique./Elle est sportive./
Elle n'a rien à faire./Elle ne dit rien.

h   Il n'y a personne au restaurant.

Il est tard./Il est cinq heures du matin./
Ce n'est pas un bon restaurant./Il pleut.

i   Elles sont toutes arrivées.

tes amies/tes cousines/tes cadeaux/
les lettres

j   Qui connaît la réponse?

toi/quelques/personne/lui

Relative pronouns: qui, que, lequel, auquel, duquel

> ## What is a relative pronoun?
> In English a **relative pronoun** is one of the words *who*, *which* and *that* (and the more formal *whom*) which can be used to introduce information that makes it clear which person or thing is being talked about, for example, *The man who has just come in is Ann's boyfriend*; *The vase that you broke was quite valuable*.
>
> Relative pronouns can also introduce further information about someone or something, for example, *Peter, who is a brilliant painter, wants to study art*; *Jane's house, which was built in 1890, needs a lot of repairs*.

➤ In French, the relative pronouns are **qui**, **que**, **lequel**, **auquel**, and **duquel**.

qui and que

➤ **qui** and **que** can both refer to people or things.

	Relative pronoun	Meaning
Subject	qui	who which that
Direct object	que	who, whom which that

Mon frère, <u>qui</u> a vingt ans, est à l'université.	My brother, who's twenty, is at university.
Est-ce qu'il y a un bus <u>qui</u> va au centre-ville?	Is there a bus that goes to the town centre?
Les amis <u>que</u> je vois le plus sont Léa et Mehdi.	The friends (that) I see most are Léa and Mehdi.
Voilà la maison <u>que</u> nous voulons acheter.	That's the house (which) we want to buy.

> *Tip*
> **que** changes to **qu'** in front of a word beginning with a vowel and most words beginning with **h**.

➤ **qui** is also used after a preposition such as **à**, **de** or **pour** to talk about <u>people</u>.

la personne <u>à qui</u> il parle	the person he is speaking to
les enfants <u>pour qui</u> j'ai acheté des bonbons	the children I bought sweets for

> *Tip*
> In English we often miss out the object pronouns *who*, *which* and *that*. For example, we can say both *the friends <u>that</u> I see most*, or *the friends I see most*, and *the house <u>which</u> we want to buy*, or *the house we want to buy*. In French you can <u>NEVER</u> miss out **que** or **qui** in this way.

lequel, laquelle, lesquels, lesquelles

➤ **lequel** (meaning *which*) is used after a preposition such as **à**, **de** or **pour** to talk about <u>things</u>. It has to agree with the noun it replaces.

	Masculine	Feminine	Meaning
Singular	lequel	laquelle	which
Plural	lesquels	lesquelles	which

le livre <u>pour lequel</u> elle est connue	the book she is famous for
la table <u>sur laquelle</u> j'ai mis mon sac	the table I put my bag on

➤ Remember that **à** and **de** combine with the definite article **le** to become **au** and **du**, and with **les** to become **aux** and **des**. **lequel/lesquels/lesquelles** combine with **à** and **de** as shown in the table. **laquelle** doesn't change.

	+ lequel	+ laquelle	+ lesquels	+ lesquelles	Meaning
à	auquel	à laquelle	auxquels	auxquelles	to which
de	duquel	de laquelle	desquels	desquelles	of which

⇨ *For more information on **à** and **de**, see pages 227, 228 and 230.*

Grammar Extra!
dont means *whose, of whom, of which, about which* and so on. It can refer to people or things, but its form <u>NEVER</u> changes.

la femme <u>dont</u> la voiture est en panne	the woman whose car has broken down
les films <u>dont</u> tu parles	the films you're talking about

---

> ### KEY POINTS
> ✔ **qui** and **que** can both refer to people or things: **qui** is the subject of the part of the sentence it is found in; **que** is the object.
> ✔ In English we often miss out the object pronouns *who, which* and *that*, but in French you can <u>never</u> miss out **que** or **qui**.
> ✔ After a preposition you use **qui** if you are referring to people, and **lequel** if you are referring to things – **lequel** agrees with the noun it replaces.
> | | |
> |---|---|
> | **à** + **lequel** → **auquel** | **de** + **lequel** → **duquel** |
> | **à** + **lesquels** → **auxquels** | **de** + **lesquels** → **desquels** |
> | **à** + **lesquelles** → **auxquelles** | **de** + **lesquelles** → **desquelles** |

Test yourself

31 **Fill the gap with qui or que.**

a C'est la dame .... a le petit chien blanc.

b C'est l'amie .... je vois le plus.

c Je parle souvent au monsieur .... habite à côté.

d Ma sœur, ... est plus jeune que moi, habite chez nos parents.

e C'est une personne .... j'admire beaucoup.

f Voilà les chaussures .... je veux acheter.

g Il y a un train .... arrive vers 18 heures?

h C'est le bus .... je prends chaque matin.

i C'est le modèle .... coûte le plus cher.

j C'est le modèle .... j'ai choisi.

32 **Translate the sentence into French, remembering to use a relative pronoun even when there is no pronoun in English.**

a It's the bus that goes to the town centre.

....

b My sister, who is very intelligent, is at university.

....

c That's the car I'm going to buy. ....

d It's the sport I like the most. ....

e Élodie is the friend I'm writing to. ....

f Who's the person he's speaking to? ....

g Who's the girl he's dancing with? ....

h They are the children I'm buying this ball for.

....

i That's the man I adore! ....

j That's the model that costs most. ....

Test yourself

33 Cross out the words that cannot refer to the noun.

a	la chaise	sur lequel/sur laquelle/sur que/sur qui
b	les films	pour lesquels/pour lesquelles/pour qui/que
c	l'argent	que/sans lequel/qui/sans qui
d	l'eau	avec qui/avec lequel/avec laquelle/que
e	les problèmes	auxquelles/auquels/qui/que
f	l'histoire	que/duquel/de laquelle/à laquelle
g	ses erreurs	desquels/auxquels/auxquelles/desquelles
h	la table	sur laquelle/sous laquelle/à laquelle/duquel
i	les lycées	auxquelles/desquels/que/pour lesquels
j	l'hôpital	sans laquelle/sans lequel/auquel/qui

34 Match the noun with the description.

a	les problèmes	dont le vélo a disparu
b	l'argent	dont j'ai besoin
c	le beau jardin	dont elle souffre
d	l'enfant	dont tu parles
e	la maladie	dont elle est très fière

Demonstrative pronouns: ce, cela/ça, ceci, celui

> **What is a demonstrative pronoun?**
> In English a **demonstrative pronoun** is one of the words *this*, *that*, *these*, and *those*
> used instead of a noun to point people or things out, for example, _That_ *looks fun*.

ce

➤ **ce** is usually used with the verb **être** (meaning *to be*) in the expressions **c'est** (meaning *it's*, *that's*), **c'était** (meaning *it was*, *that was*), **ce sont** (meaning *it's*, *that's*) and so on.

C'est moi.	It's me.
C'était mon frère.	That was my brother.
Ce sont eux.	It's them.

> *Tip*
> **ce** becomes **c'** when it is followed by a part of the verb that starts with **e** or **é**.
> **ce** becomes **ç'** when it is followed by a part of the verb that starts with **a**.
>
> **Ç'a été difficile.** It was difficult.
>
> Note that after **c'est** and **ce sont** and so on you have to use the emphatic form of the pronoun, for example, **moi** instead of **je**, **eux** instead of **ils** and so on.
>
> **C'est <u>moi</u>.** It's me.
>
> ⇨ *For more information on* **Emphatic pronouns**, *see page 69.*

➤ **ce** is used:

- with a noun or a question word to identify a person or thing

Qui est-<u>ce</u>?	Who is it?, Who's this/that?
Ce sont des professeurs.	They're teachers.
Qu'est-ce que <u>c</u>'est?	What's this/that?
C'est un ouvre-boîte.	It's a tin-opener.

- with an adjective to refer to a statement, idea and so on that cannot be classed as either masculine or feminine

C'est très intéressant.	That's/It's very interesting.
C'est dangereux.	That's/It's dangerous.
Ce n'est pas grave.	It doesn't matter.

- for emphasis

C'est moi qui ai téléphoné.	It was me who phoned.
Ce sont les enfants qui ont fait le gâteau.	It was the children who made the cake.

cela, ça and ceci

➤ **cela** and **ça** mean *it, this* or *that*. Both refer to a statement, an idea or an object. **ça** is used instead of **cela** in everyday, informal French.

Ça ne fait rien.	It doesn't matter.
Écoute-moi <u>ça</u>!	Listen to this!
<u>Cela</u> dépend.	That/It depends.
Je n'aime pas <u>cela</u>.	I don't like that.
Donne-moi <u>ça</u>!	Give me that!

> *Tip*
> **ça** and **cela** are used in a more general way than **il** and **elle**, which are usually linked to a noun that has already been mentioned.
>
> **Alors, <u>ma nouvelle voiture, elle</u> te plaît?** So, do you like my new car?
> **<u>Ça</u> te plaît d'aller à l'étranger?** Do you like going abroad?

➤ **ceci** means *this* and is not as common as **cela** and **ça**. It is used to talk about something that has not yet been mentioned.

Lisez <u>ceci</u>.	Read this.

➤ **ceci** is also used to hand or show someone something.

Prends <u>ceci</u>. Tu en auras besoin.	Take this. You'll need it.

celui, celle, ceux, celles

➤ **celui** and **celle** mean *the one*; **ceux** and **celles** mean *the ones*. The form you choose depends on whether the noun it is replacing is masculine or feminine, and singular or plural.

	Masculine	Feminine	Meaning
Singular	celui	celle	the one
Plural	ceux	celles	the ones

➤ **celui** and its other forms are used before:

- **qui, que** or **dont**

'Quelle robe préférez-vous?'	'Which dress do you like best?'
— **'<u>Celle qui</u> est en vitrine.'**	— 'The one in the window.'
Prends <u>ceux que</u> tu préfères.	Take the ones you like best.
<u>celui dont</u> je t'ai parlé	the one I told you about
<u>celui qui</u> est proche de la fontaine	the one near the fountain

➤ **celui** and its other forms can be used with **de** to show who something belongs to. In English, we would use *'s*.

Je n'ai pas d'appareil photo mais je peux emprunter <u>celui de</u> ma sœur.	I haven't got a camera but I can borrow my sister<u>'s</u>.
Comparez vos réponses à <u>celles de</u> votre voisin.	Compare your answers with your neighbour<u>'s</u>.

➤ You can add the endings **-ci** and **-là** to **celui** and its other forms to emphasize the difference between something that is close to you and something that is further away.

- use **-ci** for something that is closer to you

- use **-là** for something that is further away

	Masculine	Feminine	Meaning
Singular	celui-ci celui-là	celle-ci celle-là	this, this one that, that one
Plural	ceux-ci ceux-là	celles-ci celles-là	these, these ones those, those ones

On prend quel fromage? <u>Celui-ci</u> ou <u>celui-là</u>?

Which cheese shall we get? This one or that one?

Ces chemises ont deux poches mais <u>celles-là</u> n'en ont pas.

These shirts have two pockets but those have none.

KEY POINTS

✔ **ce** is often found in the expressions **c'est**, **ce sont** and so on.

✔ **ce** is also used:
- to identify a person or thing
- to refer to a statement, idea and so on that cannot be classed as either masculine or feminine
- for emphasis

✔ **cela** and **ça** mean *it*, *this* or *that*; **ceci** means *this*, but is not as common.

✔ **celui** and **celle** mean *the one*; **ceux** and **celles** mean *the ones*. They are often found with the endings -**ci** and -**là** and are used to distinguish between things which are close and things which are further away.

Test yourself

35 **C'est moi qui le veux is a more emphatic way of saying Je le veux. Make the sentences more emphatic by replacing the highlighted pronoun with c'est or ce sont + emphatic pronoun + qui.**

a **Je** paye toujours. ....

b **Il** joue le mieux. ....

c **Elles** veulent du vin blanc. ....

d **Ils** causent beaucoup d'accidents. ....

e **Tu** as besoin d'argent. ....

f **Je** fais la plupart du travail. ....

g **Ils** nous aident le plus. ....

h **Vous** prenez la décision, Madame. ....

i Michel et Luc,**vous** devez choisir. ....

j Gaëlle,**tu** dois répondre à cette question. ....

36 Match the items.

a **Donne-moi ça!**   Oui, c'est très triste.

b **Ça te plaît de faire de longues**   C'est vraiment ridicule.
    promenades?

c **Ma robe n'est pas très élégante.**   Ça ne fait rien.

d **Écoute-moi ça!**   J'en ai besoin.

e **Ce sont les enfants qui souffrent**   Non, je préfère regarder la télé.
    le plus.

37 Fill the gap with the correct demonstrative pronoun.

a Quel menu prends-tu? — .... qui est le moins cher.

b Quelles chaussures vas-tu acheter? — .... qui sont les plus confortables.

c Vas-tu venir avec nous? — .... dépend du temps.

d Je n'ai pas d'ordinateur. J'utilise .... de ma sœur.

e Quelle est sa voiture? — C'est .... qui est toute sale.

f J'aime ces photos-ci, mais .... sont affreuses.

g Ce sont vos enfants? — Non, les miens sont .... qui jouent sur le trampoline.

h Voilà les brochures. Prenez .... dont vous avez besoin.

i Prenez ...., peut-être que vous allez en avoir besoin.

j Quels restaurants sont les meilleurs? — .... qui ont des chefs français.

Test yourself

38 **Cross out the answers that do not fit the question.**

a Quelles baskets préfères-tu?

Celles de Jean./Ceux de Pierre./
Celles qui sont les plus chères./
Ceux qui sont les plus confortables.

b Quel est ton café préféré?

Celle à côté de la banque./
Celui qui est proche de la poste./
Celui-là./Celui-ci.

c C'est un problème?

Non, ça ne fait rien./
Non, celui qui ne fait rien./
Non, ce n'est pas grave./Cela dépend.

d Je peux prendre celui-ci?

Celui-là est à Max./Ne touche pas à ça!/
Oui, prends-le./Celui-là est mon frère.

e Ça te plaît d'aller en France?

Oui, mais c'est petit./Oui, mais c'est cher./
Non, cela ne m'intéresse pas./Ça me plaît.

f Ce sont les photos de Lucille?

Non, celles de Nadège./
Je ne reconnais pas celles-là./
Non, celle-là est à mon frère./
Regardez-moi ça!

g Je n'ai pas de portable.

Écoute-moi ça!/Prenez celle-ci./
Vous voulez utiliser celui-ci?/
Prenez celui de Paul.

h Quel gâteau prenez-vous?

Celle au milieu./Celui-là/Celui-ci./
Celui qui est devant vous.

i Qui est cette fille?

Celle-là?/Ça dépend./
Celle dont je t'ai parlé./
Celle de la poste.

j Quel hôtel est le plus cher?

Ceci./Celui d'en face./Celui qui est là-haut./
Celui-là.

Verbs

> **What is a verb?**
> A **verb** is a 'doing' word which describes what someone or something does, what someone or something is, or what happens to them, for example, *be*, *sing*, *live*.

The three conjugations

➤ Verbs are usually used with a noun, with a pronoun such as *I*, *you* or *she*, or with somebody's name. They can relate to the present, the past and the future; this is called their <u>tense</u>.

   ⇨ *For more information on **Nouns** and **Pronouns**, see pages 1 and 55.*

➤ Verbs are either:

- <u>regular</u>; their forms follow the normal rules

- <u>irregular</u>; their forms do not follow the normal rules

➤ Regular English verbs have a <u>base form</u> (the form of the verb without any endings added to it, for example, *walk*). The base form can have *to* in front of it, for example, *to walk*. This is called the <u>infinitive</u>. You will find one of these forms when you look a verb up in your dictionary.

➤ French verbs also have an infinitive, which ends in **-er**, **-ir** or **-re**, for example, **donner** (meaning *to give*), **finir** (meaning *to finish*), **attendre** (meaning *to wait*). <u>Regular</u> French verbs belong to one of these three verb groups, which are called <u>conjugations</u>. We will look at each of these three conjugations in turn on the next few pages.

➤ English verbs have other forms apart from the base form and infinitive: a form ending in *-s* (*walks*), a form ending in *-ing* (*walking*), and a form ending in *-ed* (*walked*).

➤ French verbs have many more forms than this, which are made up of endings added to a <u>stem</u>. The stem of a verb can usually be worked out from the infinitive.

➤ French verb endings change, depending on who you are talking about: **je** (*I*), **tu** (*you*), **il/elle/on** (*he/she/it/one*) in the singular, or **nous** (*we*), **vous** (*you*) and **ils/elles** (*they*) in the plural. French verbs also have different forms depending on whether you are referring to the present, future or past.

➤ Some verbs in French do not follow the normal rules, and are called <u>irregular verbs</u>. These include some very common and important verbs like **avoir** (meaning to *have*), **être** (meaning *to be*), **faire** (meaning *to do*, *to make*) and **aller** (meaning *to go*). There is information on many of these irregular verbs in the following sections.

   ⇨ *For **Verb tables**, see supplement.*

KEY POINTS

✔ French verbs have different forms depending on what noun or pronoun they are used with, and on their tense.

✔ They are made up of a stem and an ending. The stem is usually based on the infinitive.

✔ Regular verbs fit into one of three patterns or conjugations: **-er**, **-ir**, or **-re** verbs.

✔ Irregular verbs do not follow the normal rules.

The present tense

> **What is the present tense?**
> The **present tense** is used to talk about what is true at the moment,
> what happens regularly and what is happening now, for example, I'_m a student_,
> I _travel_ to college by train, I'_m studying_ languages.

➤ You use a verb in the present tense to talk about:

- things that are happening now
  It'_s raining_.
  The phone'_s ringing_.

- things that happen all the time or at certain intervals, or things that you do as a habit
  It always _snows_ in January.
  I _play_ football on Saturdays.

- things that are true at the present time:
  She'_s_ not very well.
  It'_s_ a beautiful house.

➤ There is more than one way to express the present tense in English. For example, you can say either I _give_, I _am giving_, or occasionally I _do give_. In French you use the same form (**je donne**) for all of these.

➤ In English you can also use the present tense to talk about something that is going to happen in the near future. You can do the same in French.

Je <u>vais</u> en France le mois prochain.	I'_m going_ to France next month.
Nous <u>prenons</u> le train de dix heures.	We'_re getting_ the ten o'clock train.

> _Tip_
> Although English sometimes uses parts of the verb _to be_ to form the present tense of other verbs (for example, I _am_ listening, she'_s_ talking), French <u>NEVER</u> uses the verb **être** in this way.

The present tense: regular -er (first conjugation) verbs

➤ If an infinitive in French ends in **-er**, it means the verb belongs to the <u>first conjugation</u>, for example, **donner**, **aimer**, **parler**.

➤ To know which form of the verb to use in French, you need to work out what the stem of the verb is and then add the correct ending. The stem of **-er** verbs in the present tense is formed by taking the <u>infinitive</u> and chopping off **-er**.

Infinitive	Stem (without -er)
donner (_to give_)	donn-
aimer (_to like, to love_)	aim-
parler (_to speak, to talk_)	parl-

For further explanation of grammatical terms, please see pages viii–xii.

➤ Now you know how to find the stem of a verb, you can add the correct ending. Which one you choose will depend on whether you are referring to **je**, **tu**, **il**, **elle**, **on**, **nous**, **vous**, **ils** or **elles**.

⇨ *For more information on **Pronouns**, see page 55.*

➤ Here are the present tense endings for **-er** verbs:

Pronoun	Ending	Add to stem, e.g. donn-	Meanings
je (j')	-e	je donn<u>e</u>	I give I am giving
tu	-es	tu donn<u>es</u>	you give you are giving
il elle on	-e	il donn<u>e</u> elle donn<u>e</u> on donn<u>e</u>	he/she/it/one gives he/she/it/one is giving
nous	-ons	nous donn<u>ons</u>	we give we are giving
vous	-ez	vous donn<u>ez</u>	you give you are giving
ils elles	-ent	ils donn<u>ent</u> elles donn<u>ent</u>	they give they are giving

Marie <u>regarde</u> la télé.	Marie is watching TV.
Le train <u>arrive</u> à deux heures.	The train arrives at 2 o'clock.

Tip
je changes to **j'** in front of a word starting with a vowel (*a*, *e*, *i*, *o* or *u*), most words starting with **h**, and the French word **y**.

ⓘ Note that there are a few regular **-er** verbs that are spelled slightly differently from the way you might expect.

⇨ *For more information on **Spelling changes in -er verbs**, see page 109.*

KEY POINTS
✔ Verbs ending in **-er** belong to the first conjugation and form their present tense stem by losing the **-er** from the infinitive.
✔ The present tense endings for **-er** verbs are:
-e, **-es**, **-e**, **-ons**, **-ez**, **-ent**.

Test yourself

1 Fill the gap with the correct form of the present tense.

a Nos tantes nous .... de beaux cadeaux. **(donner)**

b Vous .... bien le français, Madame. **(parler)**

c Tu .... trop. **(parler)**

d J' .... jouer au foot. **(aimer)**

e Mes cousins .... à Paris. **(habiter)**

f Claire .... parce qu'elle est heureuse. **(chanter)**

g Tu .... très vite. **(marcher)**

h Jean .... le match à la télé. **(regarder)**

i Demain on .... le travail. **(commencer)**

j Nous l' .... beaucoup. **(admirer)**

2 Match the person to the description.

a C'est un médecin.   Ils ne mangent pas de viande.

b Ils sont végétariens.   Nous habitons près de la Seine.

c Elle est factrice.   Il travaille à l'hôpital.

d Nous sommes parisiens.   J'aime beaucoup les plantes.

e Je suis jardinière.   Elle marche beaucoup.

3 Make a sentence using the elements given with the verb in the present tense. Remember that when the object of the verb is a pronoun it usually comes before the verb.

a nous/utiliser/le/souvent ....

b vous/donner/lui/beaucoup d'argent ....

c Marie/adorer/la ....

d en ce moment/il/parler/lui/au téléphone ....

e maintenant/ils/jouer/mieux ....

f je/demander/lui/demain ....

g sa petite amie/regarder/le ....

h nous/arriver/y/à deux heures ....

i vous/rester/y/longtemps? ....

j mes amies/passer/un mois/à Lille ....

Test yourself

4 **Translate the sentence into French. You can make questions in French simply by adding a question mark.**

a Do you love him? (*Use* **tu**.) ....

b He's playing outside at the moment. ....

c The children adore our dog. ....

d We like Paris very much. ....

e Are you giving it to him? (*Use* **tu**.) ....

f We're spending a month in France with them. ....

g She's staying at home today. ....

h Are you eating that? (*Use* **tu**.) ....

i Are you looking for your keys? (*Use* **vous**.) ....

j Why are you crying? (*Use* **tu**.) ....

The present tense: regular -ir (second conjugation) verbs

➤ If an infinitive ends in **-ir**, it means the verb belongs to the <u>second conjugation</u>, for example, **finir**, **choisir**, **remplir**.

➤ The stem of **-ir** verbs in the present tense is formed by taking the <u>infinitive</u> and chopping off **-ir**.

Infinitive	Stem (without **-ir**)
finir (to finish)	**fin-**
choisir (to choose)	**chois-**
remplir (to fill, to fill in)	**rempl-**

➤ Now add the correct ending, depending on whether you are referring to **je**, **tu**, **il**, **elle**, **on**, **nous**, **vous**, **ils** or **elles**.

⇨ For more information on **Pronouns**, see page 55.

➤ Here are the present tense endings for **-ir** verbs:

Pronoun	Ending	Add to stem, e.g. fin-	Meanings
je (j')	-is	je fin<u>is</u>	I finish I am finishing
tu	-is	tu fin<u>is</u>	you finish you are finishing
il **elle** **on**	-it	il fin<u>it</u> elle fin<u>it</u> on fin<u>it</u>	he/she/it/one finishes he/she/it/one is finishing
nous	-issons	nous fin<u>issons</u>	we finish we are finishing
vous	-issez	vous fin<u>issez</u>	you finish you are finishing
ils **elles**	-issent	ils fin<u>issent</u> elles fin<u>issent</u>	they finish they are finishing

Le cours <u>finit</u> à onze heures.   The lesson finishes at eleven o'clock.
Je <u>finis</u> mes devoirs.   I'm finishing my homework.

> *Tip*
> **je** changes to **j'** in front of a word starting with a vowel, most words starting with **h**, and the French word **y**.

➤ The **nous** and **vous** forms of **-ir** verbs have an extra syllable.
    tu fi|nis   (*two syllables*)
    vous fi|ni|ssez   (*three syllables*)

KEY POINTS

✔ Verbs ending in **-ir** belong to the second conjugation and form their present tense stem by losing the **-ir** from the infinitive.

✔ The present tense endings for **-ir** verbs are:
-is, -is, -it, -issons, -issez, -issent.

✔ Remember the extra syllable in the **nous** and **vous** forms.

Test yourself

5 **Fill the gap with the correct form of the present tense.**

a Aujourd'hui mes parents .... une voiture neuve. **(choisir)**

b Nous .... le travail demain. **(finir)**

c Tu .... ce formulaire? **(remplir)**

d En ce moment il .... un nouveau record. **(établir)**

e À quelle heure .... le concert? **(finir)**

f Comme dessert je .... toujours la tarte Tatin. **(choisir)**

g Ils .... leur réputation sur la qualité de leurs produits. **(bâtir)**

h Il est tard, vous .... bientôt? **(finir)**

i Susanne est fatiguée, elle .... le pas. **(ralentir)**

j Nous .... la piscine. **(remplir)**

6 **Match the related sentences.**

a	**Le concert dure deux heures.**	Je ralentis tout de suite.
b	**Ils sont végétariens.**	Je remplis son verre d'eau.
c	**Il y a une voiture de police.**	Nous choisissons un dessert.
d	**Elle ne boit pas de vin.**	Il finit à vingt heures quinze.
e	**Le fromage n'est pas bon.**	Ils choisissent toujours les salades.

7 **Make a sentence using the elements given with the verb in the present tense. Remember that when the object of the verb is a pronoun it usually comes before the verb.**

a elles/finir/leurs devoirs ....

b nous/investir/dans/l'immobilier ....

c en ce moment/il/finir/l'introduction/en ....

d ton verre est vide/je/remplir/le? ....

e aujourd'hui/nous/finir/la plupart/en ....

f celles-ci sont jolies/vous/choisir/les? ....

g je/choisir/les meilleures/en ....

h on voit la police/on/ralentir ....

i Laure a de l'argent/elle/investir/
le/dans la boutique ....

j Ils ont leurs formulaires/ils/remplir/les ....

Test yourself

8 **Translate the sentence into French. You can make questions in French simply by adding a question mark.**

    a They're finishing their game. ....

    b Does she always choose fish? ....

    c Does the class finish at noon? ....

    d We're finishing the job tomorrow. ....

    e They're choosing the team today. ....

    f You're investing in her future. (*Use* ***vous***.) ....

    g Do you finish at six this evening? (*Use* ***tu***.) ....

    h I'm filling the swimming pool. ....

    i Why are you slowing down? (*Use* ***vous***.) ....

    j I pay for them, I choose them. ....

The present tense: regular -re (third conjugation) verbs

➤ If an infinitive ends in **-re**, it means the verb belongs to the <u>third conjugation</u>, for example, **attendre**, **vendre**, **entendre**.

➤ The stem of **-re** verbs in the present tense is formed by taking the <u>infinitive</u> and chopping off **-re**.

Infinitive	Stem (without -re)
attendre (*to wait*)	**attend-**
vendre (*to sell*)	**vend-**
entendre (*to hear*)	**entend-**

➤ Now add the correct ending, depending on whether you are referring to **je**, **tu**, **il**, **elle**, **on**, **nous**, **vous**, **ils** or **elles**.

⤳ *For more information on* **Pronouns**, *see page* 55.

➤ Here are the present tense endings for **-re** verbs:

Pronoun	Ending	Add to stem, e.g. attend-	Meanings
je (j')	-s	j'attend<u>s</u>	I wait I am waiting
tu	-s	tu attend<u>s</u>	you wait you are waiting
il elle on	-	il attend elle attend on attend	he/she/it/one waits he/she/it/ one is waiting
nous	-ons	nous attend<u>ons</u>	we wait we are waiting
vous	-ez	vous attend<u>ez</u>	you wait you are waiting
ils elles	-ent	ils attend<u>ent</u> elles attend<u>ent</u>	they wait they are waiting

J'<u>attends</u> ma sœur.   I'm waiting for my sister.
Chaque matin nous <u>attendons</u>   Every morning we wait for the train
  le train ensemble.   together.

> *Tip*
> **je** changes to **j'** in front of a word starting with a vowel, most words starting with **h**, and the French word **y**.

KEY POINTS
✔ Verbs ending in **-re** belong to the third conjugation and form their present tense stem by losing the **-re** from the infinitive.
✔ The present tense endings for **-re** verbs are: **-s, -s, -, -ons, -ez, -ent**.

For further explanation of grammatical terms, please see pages viii–xii.

Test yourself

9 **Fill the gap with the correct form of the present tense.**

    a   J'.................... mon amie. **(attendre)**

    b   Richard et Delphine .... leur maison. **(vendre)**

    c   Vous .... votre appartement? **(vendre)**

    d   Tu .... ce bruit? **(entendre)**

    e   Elle est sourde, elle n'.................... rien. **(entendre)**

    f   Elles .... toutes les deux un bébé. **(attendre)**

    g   Cet animal .... son territoire. **(défendre)**

    h   Jeanne n'est pas là, nous l'.................... . **(attendre)**

    i   Ils .... la sirène, ils quittent tout de suite le bureau. **(entendre)**

    j   Je .... mes tomates au marché. **(vendre)**

10 **Match the related sentences.**

    a   Le service n'est pas bon.   Tu la répètes.

    b   Mes amis ont besoin d'argent.   Je te défends.

    c   Ma cousine attend un enfant.   Elle ne fume pas.

    d   Je n'entends pas ta question.   Ils vendent leur voiture.

    e   Tu es mon amie.   On attend longtemps.

11 **Make a sentence using the elements given with the verb in the present tense. Remember that when the object of the verb is a pronoun it usually comes before the verb.**

    a   je/entendre/te/bien ....

    b   Tu/attendre/la/longtemps?...

    c   voilà sa voiture/il/vendre/la ....

    d   vous/défendre/les? ....

    e   elle/tendre/lui/la main ....

    f   les lionnes/défendre/leurs petits ....

    g   Anne est en retard/nous/attendre/la..

    h   ces meubles/vous/vendre/les?...

    i   ça/dépendre/du temps ....

    j   on/entendre/beaucoup/en..

Test yourself

12 Translate the sentence into French. You can make questions in French simply by adding a question mark.

a   Are you waiting for her? (*Use* **vous**.) ....

b   My car's too small, I'm selling it. ....

c   We hear their TV. ....

d   That depends on the price. ....

e   He defends his friends. ....

f   Do you hear me? (*Use* **tu**.) ....

g   The girls are waiting for the bus. ....

h   The computer's useless, they're selling it. ....

i   They hear the bells every morning. ....

j   She's expecting a baby. ....

The present tense: spelling changes in -er verbs

➤ Learning the patterns shown on pages 98–99 means you can now work out the forms of most -er verbs. A few verbs, though, involve a small spelling change. This is usually to do with how a word is pronounced. In the tables below the form(s) with the irregular spelling is/are <u>underlined</u>.

Verbs ending in -cer

➤ With verbs such as **lancer** (meaning *to throw*), which end in **-cer**, **c** becomes **ç** before an **a** or an **o**. This is so the letter **c** is still pronounced as in the English word *ice*.

Pronoun	Example verb: lancer
je	lance
tu	lances
il, elle, on	lance
nous	<u>lançons</u>
vous	lancez
ils, elles	lancent

Verbs ending in -ger

➤ With verbs such as **manger** (meaning *to eat*), which end in **-ger**, **g** becomes **ge** before an **a** or an **o**. This is so the letter **g** is still pronounced like the **s** in the English word *leisure*.

Pronoun	Example verb: manger
je	mange
tu	manges
il, elle, on	mange
nous	<u>mangeons</u>
vous	mangez
ils, elles	mangent

Verbs ending in -eler

➤ With verbs such as **appeler** (meaning *to call*), which end in **-eler**, the **l** doubles before **-e**, **-es** and **-ent**. The double consonant (**ll**) affects the pronunciation of the word. In **appeler**, the first **e** sounds like the vowel sound at the end of the English word *teacher*, but in **appelle** the first **e** sounds like the one in the English word *pet*.

Pronoun	Example verb: appeler
j'	<u>appelle</u>
tu	<u>appelles</u>
il, elle, on	<u>appelle</u>
nous	appelons
vous	appelez
ils, elles	<u>appellent</u>

➤ The exceptions to this rule are **geler** (meaning *to freeze*) and **peler** (meaning *to peel*), which change in the same way as **lever** (*see page 111*).

➤ Verbs like this are sometimes called '1, 2, 3, 6 verbs' because they change in the first person singular (**je**), second person singular (**tu**), and third person singular and plural (**il/elle/on** and **ils/elles**).

Verbs ending in -eter

➤ With verbs such as **jeter** (meaning *to throw*), which end in **-eter**, the **t** doubles before **-e**, **-es** and **-ent**. The double consonant (**tt**) affects the pronunciation of the word. In **jeter**, the first **e** sounds like the vowel sound at the end of the English word *teacher*, but in **jette** the first **e** sounds like the one in the English word *pet*.

Pronoun	Example verb: jeter
je	jette
tu	jettes
il, elle, on	jette
nous	jetons
vous	jetez
ils, elles	jettent

➤ The exceptions to this rule include **acheter** (meaning *to buy*), which changes in the same way as **lever** (*see page 111*).

➤ Verbs like this are sometimes called '1, 2, 3, 6 verbs'.

Verbs ending in -yer

➤ With verbs such as **nettoyer** (meaning *to clean*), which end in **-yer**, the **y** changes to **i** before **-e**, **-es** and **-ent**.

Pronoun	Example verb: nettoyer
je	nettoie
tu	nettoies
il, elle, on	nettoie
nous	nettoyons
vous	nettoyez
ils, elles	nettoient

➤ Verbs ending in **-ayer**, such as **payer** (meaning *to pay*) and **essayer** (meaning *to try*), can be spelled with either a **y** or an **i**. So **je paie** and **je paye**, for example, are both correct.

➤ Verbs like this are sometimes called '1, 2, 3, 6 verbs'.

Changes involving accents

➤ With verbs such as **lever** (meaning *to raise*), **peser** (meaning *to weigh*) and **acheter** (meaning *to buy*), **e** changes to **è** before the consonant + **-e**, **-es** and **-ent**. The accent changes the pronunciation too. In **lever** the first **e** sounds like the vowel sound at the end of the English word *teacher*, but in **lève** and so on the first **e** sounds like the one in the English word *pet*.

Pronoun	Example verb: lever
je	<u>lève</u>
tu	<u>lèves</u>
il, elle, on	<u>lève</u>
nous	levons
vous	levez
ils, elles	<u>lèvent</u>

➤ With verbs such as **espérer** (meaning *to hope*), **régler** (meaning *to adjust*) and **préférer** (meaning *to prefer*), **é** changes to **è** before the consonant + **-e**, **-es** and **-ent**.

Pronoun	Example verb: espérer
j'	<u>espère</u>
tu	<u>espères</u>
il, elle, on	<u>espère</u>
nous	espérons
vous	espérez
ils, elles	<u>espèrent</u>

➤ Verbs like this are sometimes called '<u>1, 2, 3, 6 verbs</u>'.

KEY POINTS

✔ In verbs ending in **-cer** and **-ger**:
  c → ç and g → ge in the **nous** form.
✔ In verbs ending in **-eler** and **-eter**:
  l → ll and t → tt in all but the **nous** and **vous** forms.
✔ In verbs ending in **-yer**:
  y → i in all but the **nous** and **vous** forms (optional in **-ayer** verbs).

13 **Fill the gap with the correct form of the present tense.**

a Je te .... le ballon! **(lancer)**

b Nous .... un nouveau modèle. **(lancer)**

c Tu .... à la cantine? **(manger)**

d Nous .... du porc ce soir. **(manger)**

d Vous nous .... demain? **(appeler)**

f Ils nous .... souvent. **(appeler)**

g Je ne le veux pas, je le .... **(jeter)**

h La cuisine est sale, tu la .... demain? **(nettoyer)**

i En hiver il .... souvent. **(geler)**

j J' .... vous voir bientôt. **(espérer)**

14 **Cross out the unlikely items.**

a Nous en mangeons au petit déjeuner.   du pain/de la glace/de la confiture/ du beurre

b Tu le jettes à la poubelle.   de l'argent/du papier/de l'eau/le trognon de pomme

c On les pèle.   les pommes de terre/les carottes/les cerises/ les oranges

d Je le préfère.   le mauvais temps/le chocolat au lait/le pain complet/ le thé

e Elle s'appelle   Madame Aubery/Marc/Nathalie/Docteur LeDuc

f Nous l'appelons   souvent/tous les samedis/ce soir/quand il gèle

g Il espère   la revoir/y aller/se casser le bras/trouver un travail

h Il pèse 100 kg.   Il mange peu./Il mange trop./Il n'aime pas manger./ Il fait un régime.

i La maison est toute propre.   Je la nettoie souvent./Je n'aime pas le fouillis./ Je n'aime pas le ménage./Tu m'aides à la nettoyer?

j La question est facile.   Nous nous levons./Ils lèvent la main./Je lève la main./ Nous levons la main.

Test yourself

15 **Translate the sentence into French. You can make questions simply by adding a question mark to a statement.**

a Are we eating with them? ....

b She's called Alice ....

c My neighbours throw a lot away ....

d I'm throwing these old trainers away. ....

e I'm peeling the onions, you two are peeling the potatoes.

....

f Are you sending them a card? (*Use* **tu**.) ....

g He eats too much. ....

h I prefer hot countries. ....

i We hope to see them again. ....

j In winter they adjust the thermostat. ....

16 **Match the sentences that have a connection.**

a Les examens commencent jeudi.   Je les considère comme mes meilleurs amis.

b Ils m'envoient toujours un beau cadeau pour mon anniversaire.   Tu l'essaies?

c Ce restaurant est très cher.   Ils en achètent beaucoup.

d Cette jupe est jolie.   J'espère avoir de bons résultats.

e Mes parents adorent le fromage.   Nous mangeons ailleurs.

The present tense: irregular verbs

➤ Some verbs in French do not follow the normal rules. These verbs include some very common and important verbs like **avoir** (meaning *to have*), **être** (meaning *to be*), **faire** (meaning *to do, to make*) and **aller** (meaning *to go*). The present tense of these four verbs is given in full below.

⇨ For **Verb tables**, *see supplement.*

The present tense of avoir

Pronoun	avoir	Meaning: *to have*
j'	ai	I have
tu	as	you have
il elle on	a	he/she/it/one has
nous	avons	we have
vous	avez	you have
ils elles	ont	they have

J'ai deux sœurs.   I have two sisters.
Il a les yeux bleus.   He has blue eyes.
Elle a trois ans.   She's three.
Qu'est-ce qu'il y a?   What's the matter?

The present tense of être

Pronoun	être	Meaning: *to be*
je	suis	I am
tu	es	you are
il elle on	est	he/she/it/one is
nous	sommes	we are
vous	êtes	you are
ils elles	sont	they are

Je suis heureux.   I'm happy.
Mon père est instituteur.   My father's a primary school teacher.
Il est deux heures.   It's two o'clock.

The present tense of faire

Pronoun	faire	Meaning: *to do, to make*
je	fais	I do/make I am doing/making
tu	fais	you do/make you are doing/making
il elle on	fait	he/she/it/one does/makes he/she/it/one is doing/ making
nous	faisons	we do/make we are doing/making
vous	faites	you do/make you are doing/making
ils elles	font	they do/make they are doing/making

Je <u>fais</u> un gâteau.	I'm making a cake.
Qu'est-ce que tu <u>fais</u>?	What are you doing?
Il <u>fait</u> chaud.	It's hot.
Ça ne <u>fait</u> rien.	It doesn't matter.

The present tense of aller

Pronoun	aller	Meaning: *to go*
je	vais	I go I am going
tu	vas	you go you are going
il elle on	va	he/she/it/one goes he/she/it/one is going
nous	allons	we go we are going
vous	allez	you go you are going
ils elles	vont	they go they are going

Je <u>vais</u> à Londres.	I'm going to London.
'Comment <u>allez</u>-vous?' — 'Je <u>vais</u> bien.'	'How are you?' — 'I'm fine.'
'Comment ça <u>va</u>?' — 'Ça <u>va</u> bien.'	'How are you?' — 'I'm fine.'

Irregular -ir verbs

➤ Many irregular verbs that end in **-ir**, such as **partir** (meaning *to go*) and **tenir** (meaning *to hold*), have a common pattern in the singular. The **je** and **tu** forms often end in **-s**, and the **il/elle/on** form often ends in **-t**.

Pronoun	partir	tenir
je	par<u>s</u>	tien<u>s</u>
tu	par<u>s</u>	tien<u>s</u>
il/elle/on	par<u>t</u>	tien<u>t</u>

Je <u>pars</u> demain.	I'm leaving tomorrow.
Elle <u>tient</u> le bébé.	She is holding the baby.

⇨ For **Verb tables**, see supplement.

KEY POINTS

✔ Some very important French verbs are irregular, including **avoir**, **être**, **faire** and **aller**. They are worth learning in full.
✔ The **-s**, **-s**, **-t** pattern occurs frequently in irregular **-ir** verbs.

Test yourself

17 Complete the sentence with the correct form of the present tense.

a Ils .... deux fils et une fille. **(avoir)**

b Nous n' .... pas d'enfants. **(avoir)**

c .... -vous à Marseille? **(aller)**

d Tu .... besoin d'aide? **(avoir)**

e Qu'est-ce que vous .... ce soir? **(faire)**

f Il .... midi, nous mangeons bientôt. **(être)**

g Qu'est-ce qu'ils .... quand il pleut? **(faire)**

h Je .... en vacances demain. **(partir)**

i Nous .... tous les deux professeurs de français. **(être)**

j Et Marie, elle .... bien? **(aller)**

18 Match the question to the statement.

a Tu pleures.   Est-ce qu'ils se battent?

b J'ai deux frères.   On lui fait un gâteau?

c Il fait très chaud aujourd'hui.   Qu'est-ce qu'il y a?

d Demain c'est son anniversaire.   On va à la piscine?

e Les enfants font beaucoup de bruit.   Comment s'appellent-ils?

19 J'ai les yeux bleus is another way of saying Mes yeux sont bleus. Replace the highlighted words in this way, using avoir + the definite article.

a **Tes yeux sont** très grands. ....

b **Leurs cheveux sont** bouclés. (*Use* **ils**.) ....

c **Ses hanches sont** plutôt larges. (*Use* **elle**.) ....

d **Vos cheveux sont** très secs. ....

e **Nos mains sont** gelées. ....

f **Mes mains sont** propres. ....

g **Son bras est** cassé. (*Use* **elle**.) ....

h **Mon cœur est** brisé. ....

i **Ses pieds sont** trop grands. (*Use* **il**.) ....

j **Leurs jambes sont** bien musclées. (*Use* **elles**.) ....

20 Translate the sentence into French.

a What are they doing at the weekend? (*Use ils*.)

....

b My parents are fine, thanks. ....

c Jeanne is very young: she's five. ....

d We always go to France: this year we're going with friends.

....

e What's wrong? — Nothing. ....

f Lisa's a dentist: she makes a lot of money.

....

g It's cold: I'm going to switch on the heating.

....

h It's late: I'm going to bed. ....

i We haven't got tickets. — It doesn't matter.

....

j The train leaves from platform five.

....

The imperative

> **What is the imperative?**
> An **imperative** is a form of the verb used when giving orders and instructions, for example, *Shut the door!; Sit down!; Don't go!*

Using the imperative

➤ In French, there are two forms of the imperative that are used to give instructions or orders to someone. These correspond to **tu** and **vous**.

⇨ *For more information on the difference between **tu** and **vous**, see page 56.*

➤ There is also a form of the imperative that corresponds to **nous**. This means the same as *let's* in English. It is not used as often as the **tu** and **vous** forms.

Forming the present tense imperative

➤ For regular verbs, the imperative is the same as the **tu**, **nous** and **vous** forms of the present tense, except that you do not say the pronouns **tu, nous** and **vous**. Also, in the **tu** form of **-er** verbs like **donner**, the final **-s** is dropped.

Pronoun	-er verbs: donner	Meaning	-ir verbs: finir	Meaning	-re verbs: attendre	Meaning
tu	donne	give	finis	finish	attends	wait
nous	donnons	let's give	finissons	let's finish	attendons	let's wait
vous	donnez	give	finissez	finish	attendez	wait

Donne-moi ça!	Give me that!
Finissez vos devoirs et allez vous coucher.	Finish your homework and go to bed.
Attendons le bus.	Let's wait for the bus.

Tip
When a **tu** imperative comes before **en** or **y**, the final **-s** is kept to make the words easier to pronounce. The **s** is pronounced like the *z* in the English word *zip*:
Vas-y! Go on!
Donnes-en à ton frère. Give some to your brother.

Where to put the object pronoun

➤ An object pronoun is a word like **la** (meaning *her/it*), **me/moi** (meaning *me*) or **leur** (meaning *to them*) that is used instead of a noun as the object of a sentence. In orders and instructions, the position of these object pronouns in the sentence changes depending on whether you are telling someone <u>TO DO</u> something or <u>NOT TO DO</u> something.

⇨ *For more information on **Object pronouns**, see page 61.*

➤ If you are telling someone <u>NOT TO DO</u> something, you put the object pronouns <u>BEFORE</u> the verb.

Ne <u>me</u> dérange pas.	Don't disturb me.
Ne <u>leur</u> parlons pas.	Let's not speak to them.
Ne <u>le</u> regardez pas.	Don't look at him/it.

➤ If you are telling someone <u>TO DO</u> something, you put the object pronouns <u>AFTER</u> the verb and join the two words with a hyphen. The word order is the same as in English.

Excusez-<u>moi</u>.	Excuse me.
Aide-<u>nous</u>.	Help us.
Attendons-<u>la</u>.	Let's wait for her/it.

➤ Orders and instructions telling someone to do something may contain <u>direct object</u> and <u>indirect object pronouns</u>. When this happens, the pronouns go in this order:

DIRECT	BEFORE	INDIRECT	
le		moi	nous
la		toi	vous
les		lui	leur

Prête-<u>les-moi</u>!	Lend them to me! *or* Lend me them!
Donnez-<u>la-nous</u>!	Give it to us! *or* Give us it!

⇨ *For imperatives using **Reflexive verbs**, see page 123.*

Imperative forms of irregular verbs

➤ **avoir** (meaning *to have*), **être** (meaning *to be*), **savoir** (meaning *to know*) and **vouloir** (meaning *to want*) have irregular imperative forms.

Pronoun	avoir	être	savoir	vouloir
tu	aie	sois	sache	veuille
nous	ayons	soyons	sachons	veuillons
vous	ayez	soyez	sachez	veuillez

<u>Sois</u> **sage.**	Be good.
<u>Veuillez</u> **fermer la porte.**	Please shut the door.

> **KEY POINTS**
> ✔ The imperative has three forms: **tu**, **nous** and **vous**.
> ✔ The forms are the same as the **tu**, **nous** and **vous** forms of the present tense, except that the final **-s** is dropped in the **tu** form of **-er** verbs.
> ✔ Object pronouns go before the verb when you are telling someone not to do something, but after the verb with a hyphen when you are telling someone to do something.
> ✔ **avoir**, **être**, **savoir** and **vouloir** have irregular imperative forms.

Test yourself

21 **Tu m'apportes un verre? is more polite than using the imperative: Apporte-moi un verre! Change the question into an order, remembering that the pronoun may change.**

a Tu me regardes, Martin? ....

b Vous m'écoutez, les enfants? ....

c Tu en donnes à ta sœur, Pierre? ....

d Si tu en as besoin, tu lui demandes?..

e Vous nous attendez, Monsieur?...

f Vous me suivez, Madame? ....

g Tu en goûtes un peu? ....

h Vous finissez vos devoirs avant le dîner? ....

i Vous nous aidez? ....

j Tu m'excuses? ....

22 **Replace the highlighted negative command with a positive one.**

a **Ne pars pas** sans eux!...

b **Ne restez pas** à la maison! ....

c **Ne prends pas** le dernier morceau! ....

d **Ne le fais pas**, je t'en prie!..

e **Ne me réveillez pas** tôt! ....

f **Ne leur prêtez pas** votre voiture! ....

g **N'en parle pas** à tes amis! ....

h Elle est très occupée, **ne l'appelle pas** avant midi!

....

i C'est compliqué: **n'y pensez pas**! ....

j Elle est toujours en retard, **ne l'attendons pas**!

....

Test yourself

23 Cross out the items the speaker is not likely to be referring to.

a	Finissez-les!	vos glaces/vos places/vos devoirs/vos dessins
b	Refais-le!	le travail/le rapport/le test/l'omelette
c	Fêtez-le!	l'échec/votre anniversaire/ce grand succès/ cette bonne nouvelle
d	Donne-les-moi!	les billets/les clés/les réunions/les journaux
e	Écoute-les	ces peintures/tes parents/ces chansons/mes idées
f	Regarde-la!	ma sœur/la télé/l'appartement/mon amie
g	Parlez-nous-en	du problème/du travail/du projet/de la chaise
h	Profitons-en!	de la pluie/du beau temps/du congé/de l'examen
i	Envoie-les-moi!	tes photos/ton fils/les détails/les cent euros
j	Demande-le-lui!	la question/l'argent/le nom/le billet

24 Match the sentences that have a connection.

a	Soyez sages, les enfants!	Ça va prendre du temps.
b	Sois tranquille!	Ils arrivent bientôt.
c	Ayez de la patience!	Ne faites pas de bêtises.
d	Veuillez les attendre ici.	Ce n'est pas une idée pratique.
e	Soyons réalistes.	Il ne va rien lui arriver.

Reflexive verbs

> ### What is a reflexive verb?
> A **reflexive verb** is one where the subject and object are the same, and where the action 'reflects back' on the subject. It is used with a reflexive pronoun such as *myself*, *yourself* and *herself* in English, for example, *I washed myself; He cut himself.*

Using reflexive verbs

➤ In French, reflexive verbs are much more common than in English, and many are used in everyday French. They are shown in dictionaries as **se** plus the infinitive (**se** means *himself, herself, itself, themselves* or *oneself*). **se** is called a reflexive pronoun.

> *Tip*
> **se** changes to **s'** in front of a word starting with a vowel, most words starting with **h**, and the French word **y**.

➤ Reflexive verbs are often used to describe things you do (to yourself) every day or that involve a change of some sort (going to bed, sitting down, getting angry, going to sleep). Some of the most common French reflexive verbs are listed here:

s'amuser	to play, to enjoy oneself
s'appeler	to be called
s'arrêter	to stop
s'asseoir	to sit down
se baigner	to go swimming
se coucher	to go to bed
se dépêcher	to hurry
s'habiller	to get dressed
s'intéresser à (quelque chose)	to be interested in (something)
se laver	to wash, to have a wash
se lever	to get up, to rise, to stand up
se passer	to take place, to happen
se promener	to go for a walk
se rappeler	to remember
se réveiller	to wake up
se trouver	to be (situated)

Qu'est-ce qui se passe?	What's happening?
Le soleil se lève à cinq heures.	The sun rises at five o'clock.
Asseyez-vous!	Sit down!

ⓘ Note that **se**, **s'** and other reflexive pronouns are very rarely translated as *himself* and so on in English.

➤ Some French verbs can be used with a reflexive pronoun or without a reflexive pronoun, for example, the verbs **appeler** and **s'appeler**, and **arrêter** and **s'arrêter**. Sometimes, however, their meaning may change.

Appelle le chien.	<u>Call</u> the dog.
Je <u>m'appelle</u> Jacques.	<u>I'm called</u> Jacques.
Il <u>arrête</u> le moteur.	He <u>switches off</u> the engine.
Elle <u>s'arrête</u> devant une vitrine.	She <u>stops</u> in front of a shop window.

Forming the present tense of reflexive verbs

➤ To use a reflexive verb in French, you need to decide which reflexive pronoun to use. The forms shown in brackets in the table are used before a word starting with a vowel, most words starting with **h**, or the French word **y**.

Subject pronoun	Reflexive pronoun	Meaning
je	me (m')	myself
tu	te (t')	yourself
il elle on	se (s')	himself herself itself oneself
nous	nous	ourselves
vous	vous	yourself (*singular*) yourselves (*plural*)
ils elles	se (s')	themselves

Je <u>me lève</u> tôt.	I get up early.
Elle <u>s'habille</u>.	She's getting dressed.
Ils <u>s'intéressent</u> beaucoup aux animaux.	They're very interested in animals.

➤ The present tense forms of a reflexive verb work in just the same way as an ordinary verb, except that the reflexive pronoun is used as well.

Reflexive forms	Meaning
je me lave	I wash (myself)
tu te laves	you wash (yourself)
il se lave elle se lave on se lave	he washes (himself) she washes (herself) it washes (itself) one washes (oneself)
nous nous lavons	we wash (ourselves)
vous vous lavez	you wash (yourself) (*singular*) you wash (yourselves) (*plural*)
ils se lavent elles se lavent	they wash (themselves)

➤ Some reflexive verbs, such as **s'asseoir** (meaning *to sit down*), are irregular. Some of these irregular verbs are shown in the **Verb tables**.

⇨ *For* **Verb tables***, see supplement.*

Where to put the reflexive pronoun

➤ In the present tense, the reflexive pronoun almost always comes <u>BEFORE</u> the verb.

Je <u>me</u> couche tôt.	I go to bed early.
Comment <u>t'</u>appelles-tu?	What's your name?

➤ When telling someone <u>NOT TO DO</u> something, you put the reflexive pronoun <u>BEFORE</u> the verb as usual.

Ne <u>te</u> lève pas.	Don't get up.
Ne <u>vous</u> habillez pas.	Don't get dressed.

➤ When telling someone <u>TO DO</u> something, you put the reflexive pronoun <u>AFTER</u> the verb and join the two words with a hyphen.

Lève-<u>toi</u>!	Get up!
Dépêchez-<u>vous</u>!	Hurry up!
Habillons-<u>nous</u>.	Let's get dressed.

Tip

When you are telling someone <u>TO DO</u> something, **te** or **t'** changes to **toi**.

Assieds-<u>toi</u>.   Sit down.

When you are telling someone <u>NOT TO DO</u> something, **te** or **t'** is used, not **toi**.

Ne te lève pas.   Don't get up.

⇨ *For more information on the* **Imperative***, see page 119.*

Each other and *one another*

➤ The French reflexive pronouns **nous**, **vous** and **se** can be used to translate the English phrase *each other* and *one another*.

Nous <u>nous</u> parlons tous les jours.	We speak to <u>each other</u> every day.
On <u>se</u> voit demain?	Shall we see <u>each other</u> tomorrow?
Les trois pays <u>se</u> ressemblent beaucoup.	The three countries are really like <u>one another</u>.

KEY POINTS

✔ A reflexive verb is made up of a reflexive pronoun and a verb.
✔ The reflexive pronouns are: **me**, **te**, **se**, **nous**, **vous**, **se** (**m'**, **t'**, **s'**, **nous**, **vous**, **s'** before a vowel, most words beginning with **h** and the French word **y**).
✔ The reflexive pronoun comes before the verb, except when you are telling someone to do something.

Test yourself

25 Fill the gap with the correct reflexive pronoun.

a Les enfants .... amusent dehors.

b Vous .... baignez tous les jours?

c Si on allait .... promener?

d Le train ne .... arrête pas ici.

e Comment tu .... appelles?

f Nous .... intéressons beaucoup à l'histoire.

g Tu .... rappelles son nom?

h Je suis fatiguée, je vais .... coucher.

i Qu'est-ce qui .... passe?

j Où .... trouve la poste?

26 Fill the gap with the correct form of the verb, and a reflexive pronoun if necessary.

a Il est malade, vous .... le docteur? **(appeler)**

b Je .... Nathalie. **(s'appeler)**

c Les bus ne .... pas là. **(s'arrêter)**

d Les garçons .... tout le temps. **(se battre)**

e Vous faites des bêtises: vous.................... ? **(arrêter)**

f Voulez-vous .... ? **(s'asseoir)**

g Je .... tard le week-end. **(se lever)**

h Elle .... son temps à lire. **(passer)**

i L'histoire .... en Allemagne. **(se passer)**

j .... , sinon tu vas rater le train. **(se dépêcher)**

Test yourself

27 Translate the sentences into French.

a The birds wake up early in summer...

b What's happening at school?...

c Are you going to bed now? (*Use **tu**.*)..

d I'm going for a walk. ....

e We're not here to enjoy ourselves. (*Use **on**.*)

....

f It's seven o'clock, are you getting up? (*Use **vous**.*)

....

g The hotel is situated near the golf club.

....

h The girls are getting dressed for the party.

....

i Are you interested in politics? (*Use **vous**.*) ....

j We're wondering how much that's going to cost.

....

28 Tell someone to do something (√) or not to do something (X) using the given elements.

a s'asseoir √/chérie ....

b se lever X/les enfants..

c se coucher √/tôt/Alain et Michèle ....

d s'amuser √/bien à la fête/ma petite..

e se dépêcher X/monsieur/on n'est pas pressés

....

f s'asseoir X /là/s'il vous plaît/madame ....

g se laver √/bien/Laurent...

h se calmer √/mesdames/il n'y a aucun danger

....

i s'inquiéter X/Gaston/tes parents vont venir

....

j se rappeler √/Julien/que les vélos coûtent cher

....

The imperfect tense

What is the imperfect tense?
The **imperfect tense** is one of the verb tenses used to talk about the past, especially in descriptions, and to say what used to happen, for example, I _used to walk_ to school; It _was_ sunny at the weekend.

Using the imperfect tense

➤ The imperfect tense is used:

- to describe what things were like and how people felt in the past
  I _was_ very sad when she left.
  It _was pouring_ with rain.

- to say what used to happen or what you used to do regularly in the past
  We _used to get up_ very early in those days.
  I never _used to like_ milk.

- to indicate things that were happening or something that was true when something else took place
  I _was watching_ TV when the phone rang.
  As we _were looking_ out of the window, we saw someone walk across the lawn.

  ⓘ Note that if you want to talk about an event or action that took place and was completed in the past, you use the perfect tense.

  ⇨ _For more information on the_ **Perfect tense**, _see page 151._

➤ You can often recognize an imperfect tense in English because it uses a form like _were looking_ or _was raining_. The words _used to_ also indicate an imperfect tense.

Tip
Remember that you <u>NEVER</u> use the verb **être** to translate _was_ or _were_ in forms like _was raining_ or _were looking_ and so on. You change the French verb ending instead.

Forming the imperfect tense of -er verbs

➤ To form the imperfect tense of **-er** verbs, you use the same stem of the verb as for the present tense. Then you add the correct ending, depending on whether you are referring to **je**, **tu**, **il**, **elle**, **on**, **nous**, **vous**, **ils** or **elles**.

Pronoun	Ending	Add to stem, e.g. donn-	Meanings
je (j')	-ais	je donn<u>ais</u>	I gave I was giving I used to give
tu	-ais	tu donn<u>ais</u>	you gave you were giving you used to give
il elle on	-ait	il donn<u>ait</u> elle donn<u>ait</u> on donn<u>ait</u>	he/she/it/one gave he/she/it/one was giving he/she/it/one used to give
nous	-ions	nous donn<u>ions</u>	we gave we were giving we used to give
vous	-iez	vous donn<u>iez</u>	you gave you were giving you used to give
ils elles	-aient	ils donn<u>aient</u> elles donn<u>aient</u>	they gave they were giving they used to give

Il <u>portait</u> toujours un grand chapeau noir.
He always wore a big black hat.

Nous <u>habitions</u> à Paris à cette époque.
We were living in Paris at that time.

Pour gagner un peu d'argent, je <u>donnais</u> des cours de français.
To earn a little money I used to give French lessons.

> *Tip*
> **je** changes to **j'** in front of a word starting with a vowel, most words starting with **h**, and the French word **y**.

Forming the imperfect tense of -ir verbs

➤ To form the imperfect tense of **-ir** verbs, you use the same stem of the verb as for the present tense. Then you add the correct ending, depending on whether you are referring to **je**, **tu**, **il**, **elle**, **on**, **nous**, **vous**, **ils** or **elles**.

Pronoun	Ending	Add to stem, e.g. fin	Meanings
je (j')	-issais	je fin<u>issais</u>	I finished I was finishing I used to finish
tu	-issais	tu fin<u>issais</u>	you finished you were finishing you used to finish
il elle on	-issait	il fin<u>issait</u> elle fin<u>issait</u> on fin<u>issait</u>	he/she/it/one finished he/she/it/one was finishing he/she/it/one used to finish
nous	-issions	nous fin<u>issions</u>	we finished we were finishing we used to finish
vous	-issiez	vous fin<u>issiez</u>	you finished you were finishing you used to finish
ils elles	-issaient	ils fin<u>issaient</u> elles fin<u>issaient</u>	they finished they were finishing they used to finish

Il <u>finissait</u> souvent ses devoirs avant le dîner.	He often finished his homework before dinner.
Cet après-midi-là ils <u>choisissaient</u> une bague de fiançailles.	That afternoon they were choosing an engagement ring.

Forming the imperfect tense of -re verbs

➤ To form the imperfect tense of **-re** verbs, you use the same stem of the verb as for the present tense. Then you add the correct ending, depending on whether you are referring to **je**, **tu**, **il**, **elle**, **on**, **nous**, **vous**, **ils** or **elles**. These endings are the same as for **-er** verbs.

Pronoun	Ending	Add to stem eg attend-	Meanings
je (j')	-ais	j'attend<u>ais</u>	I waited I was waiting I used to wait
tu	-ais	tu attend<u>ais</u>	you waited you were waiting you used to wait
il elle on	-ait	il attend<u>ait</u> elle attend<u>ait</u> on attend<u>ait</u>	he/she/it/one waited he/she/it/one was waiting he/she/it/one used to wait
nous	-ions	nous attend<u>ions</u>	we waited we were waiting we used to wait
vous	-iez	vous attend<u>iez</u>	you waited you were waiting you used to wait
ils elles	-aient	ils attend<u>aient</u> elles attend<u>aient</u>	they waited they were waiting they used to wait

For further explanation of grammatical terms, please see pages viii–xii.

| Christine m'**attendait** tous les soirs à la sortie. | Christine used to wait for me every evening at the exit. |
| Je **vivais** seule après mon divorce. | I was living alone after my divorce. |

Spelling changes in -er verbs

➤ As with the present tense, a few **-er** verbs change their spellings slightly when they are used in the imperfect tense. The forms with spelling changes have been <u>underlined</u> in the tables.

➤ With verbs such as **lancer** (meaning *to throw*), which end in **-cer**, **c** becomes **ç** before an **a** or an **o**. This is so that the letter **c** is still pronounced as in the English word *ice*.

Pronoun	Example verb: lancer
je	lançais
tu	lançais
il, elle, on	lançait
nous	lancions
vous	lanciez
ils, elles	lançaient

➤ With verbs such as **manger** (meaning *to eat*), which end in **-ger**, **g** becomes **ge** before an **a** or an **o**. This is so the letter **g** is still pronounced like the *s* in the English word *leisure*.

Pronoun	Example verb: manger
je	mangeais
tu	mangeais
il, elle, on	mangeait
nous	mangions
vous	mangiez
ils, elles	mangeaient

➤ These verbs follow the <u>1,2,3,6 pattern</u>. That is, they change in the first, second and third person singular, and in the third person plural.

Reflexive verbs in the imperfect tense

➤ The imperfect tense of reflexive verbs is formed just as for ordinary verbs, except that you add the reflexive pronoun (**me**, **te**, **se**, **nous**, **vous**, **se**).

Subject pronoun	Reflexive pronoun	Example with laver	Meaning
je	me (m')	lavais	I washed I was washing I used to wash
tu	te (t')	lavais	you washed you were washing you used to wash
il elle on	se (s')	lavait	he/she/it/one washed he/she/it/one was washing he/she/it/one used to wash
nous	nous	lavions	we washed we were washing we used to wash
vous	vous	laviez	you washed you were washing you used to wash
ils elles	se (s')	lavaient	they washed they were washing they used to wash

Tip

me changes to **m'**, **te** to **t'** and **se** to **s'** before a vowel, most words starting with **h** and the French word **y**.

Irregular verbs in the imperfect tense

➤ One of the most common verbs that is irregular in the imperfect tense is **être**.

Pronoun	être	Meaning
j'	étais	I was
tu	étais	you were
il, elle, on	était	he/she/it/one was
nous	étions	we were
vous	étiez	you were
ils, elles	étaient	they were

J'**étais** heureux.   I was happy.
Mon père **était** instituteur.   My father was a primary school teacher.

> **KEY POINTS**
> ✔ The imperfect tense endings for **-er** and **-re** verbs are:
>   **-ais**, **-ais**, **-ait**, **-ions**, **-iez**, **-aient**.
> ✔ The imperfect tense endings for **-ir** verbs are:
>   **-issais**, **-issais**, **-issait**, **-issions**, **-issiez**, **-issaient**.
> ✔ In verbs ending in **-cer** and **-ger**:
>   c → ç and g → ge in all but the **nous** and **vous** forms.
> ✔ **être** is irregular in the imperfect tense.

Test yourself

29 Fill the gap with the correct form of the imperfect.

a Les serveurs .... les verres des invités. **(remplir)**

b Mon frère et moi, nous .... chez nos grands-parents tous les étés. **(aller)**

c À cette époque je ne .... pas de viande. **(manger)**

d Quand tu étais enfant tu .... jouer avec des poupées? **(aimer)**

e C'était sept heures: tout le monde .... **(se lever)**

f Dans les années 1950 l'usine .... du travail à 2000 personnes. **(fournir)**

g Nous .... tous les jours. **(se parler)**

h Quand je vous ai vu vous .... le bus. **(attendre)**

i Elle .... trop vite: j'avais peur. **(rouler)**

j Mes sœurs .... à Paris en 2006. **(vivre)**

30 Match the sentences that are connected.

a C'était une serveuse.   On y passait les vacances.

b Ils étaient végétariens.   Je ne savais quoi dire.

c Elle était étudiante.   Elle travaillait à l'hôtel.

d On était à la campagne.   Elle lisait beaucoup.

e Je suis restée muette.   Ils ne mangeaient pas de viande.

31 Replace the highlighted present tense with the imperfect.

a Elle **finit** souvent avant les autres. ....

b J'**adore** me promener à la campagne. ....

c Tu **choisis** toujours le plat le plus cher. ....

d Ils **vendent** leurs produits au marché. ....

e Nous ne **savons** quoi faire. ....

f Il s'**entend** bien avec sa belle-mère. ....

g On **commence** toujours à neuf heures. ....

h Nous **avons** besoin d'aide. ....

i Il **joue** dehors avec ses copains. ....

j Il **pleut**. ....

32 Translate the sentence into French.

a I was thinking about you. ....

b What were you doing this afternoon? ....

c I went to the cinema often when I lived in Paris.

....

d We got on well when we were at school.

....

e She felt lonely and cried a lot. ....

f He was always losing his keys. ....

g I was wondering what to do. ....

h The teacher was nice: the children liked him a lot.

....

i It was raining and we were bored. ....

j Were you waiting for me? (*Use* **vous**.) ....

The future tense

> ### What is the future tense?
> The **future tense** is a verb tense used to talk about something that will happen or will be true.

Using the future tense

➤ In English the future tense is often shown by *will* or its shortened form *'ll*.
What <u>will</u> you do?
The weather <u>will</u> be warm and dry tomorrow.
He'<u>ll</u> be here soon.
I'<u>ll</u> give you a call.

➤ Just as in English, you can use the present tense in French to refer to something that is going to happen in the future.

Je <u>prends</u> le train de dix heures.	I'm taking the ten o'clock train.
Nous <u>allons</u> à Paris la semaine prochaine.	We're going to Paris next week.

➤ In English we often use *going to* followed by an infinitive to talk about something that will happen in the immediate future. You can use the French verb **aller** (meaning *to go*) followed by an infinitive in the same way.

Tu <u>vas tomber</u> si tu continues.	You're going to fall if you carry on.
Il <u>va manquer</u> le train.	He's going to miss the train.

> *Tip*
> Remember that French has no direct equivalent of the word *will* in verb forms like *will rain* or *will look* and so on. You change the French verb ending instead to form the future tense.

Forming the future tense

➤ To form the future tense in French, you use:

- the <u>infinitive</u> of **-er** and **-ir** verbs, for example, **donner, finir**

- the <u>infinitive without the final **e**</u> of **-re** verbs: for example, **attendr-**

➤ Then add the correct ending to the stem, depending on whether you are talking about **je**, **tu**, **il**, **elle**, **on**, **nous**, **vous**, **ils** or **elles**. The endings are the same for **-er**, **-ir** and **-re** verbs.

⟐ Note that apart from the **nous** and **vous** forms, the endings are the same as the present tense of **avoir**.

⟹ *For the present tense of **avoir**, see page 114.*

Pronoun	Ending	Add to stem, e.g. donner-, finir-, attendr-	Meaning
je (j')	-ai	je donnerai je finirai j'attendrai	I will give I will finish I will wait
tu	-as	tu donneras tu finiras tu attendras	you will give you will finish you will wait
il elle on	-a	il/elle/on donnera il/elle/on finira il/elle/on attendra	he/she/it/one will give he/she/it/one will finish he/she/it/one will wait
nous	-ons	nous donnerons nous finirons nous attendrons	we will give we will finish we will wait
vous	-ez	vous donnerez vous finirez vous attendrez	you will give you will finish you will wait
ils elles	-ont	ils/elles donneront ils/elles finiront ils/elles attendront	they will give they will finish they will wait

Elle te donnera mon adresse.
Le cours finira à onze heures.
Nous t'attendrons devant le cinéma.

She'll give you my address.
The lesson will finish at eleven o'clock.
We'll wait for you in front of the cinema.

Tip
je changes to **j'** in front of a word starting with a vowel, most words starting with **h**, and the French word **y**.

Spelling changes in -er verbs

➤ As with the present and imperfect tenses, a few **-er** verbs change their spellings slightly in the future tense. The forms with spelling changes have been underlined in the tables.

➤ With verbs such as **appeler** (meaning *to call*), which end in **-eler**, the **l** doubles throughout the future tense. The double consonant (**ll**) affects the pronunciation of the word. In **appeler**, the first **e** sounds like the vowel sound at the end of the English word *teacher*, but in **appellerai** the first **e** sounds like the one in the English word *pet*.

Pronoun	Example verb: appeler
j'	appellerai
tu	appelleras
il, elle, on	appellera
nous	appellerons
vous	appellerez
ils, elles	appelleront

➤ The exceptions to this rule are **geler** (meaning *to freeze*) and **peler** (meaning *to peel*), which change in the same way as **lever** (*see page* 111).

➤ With verbs such as **jeter** (meaning *to throw*), that end in **-eter**, the **t** doubles throughout the future tense. The double consonant (**tt**) affects the pronunciation of the word. In **jeter**, the first **e** sounds like the vowel sound at the end of the English word *teacher*, but in **jetterai** the first **e** sounds like the one in the English word *pet*.

Pronoun	Example verb: jeter
je	jetterai
tu	jetteras
il, elle, on	jettera
nous	jetterons
vous	jetterez
ils, elles	jetteront

➤ The exceptions to this rule include **acheter** (meaning *to buy*), which changes in the same way as **lever** (*see page* 111).

➤ With verbs such as **nettoyer** (meaning *to clean*), that end in **-yer**, the **y** changes to **i** throughout the future tense.

Pronoun	Example verb: nettoyer
je	nettoierai
tu	nettoieras
il, elle, on	nettoiera
nous	nettoierons
vous	nettoierez
ils, elles	nettoieront

➤ Verbs ending in **-ayer**, such as **payer** (meaning *to pay*) and **essayer** (meaning *to try*), can be spelled with either a **y** or an **i**. So **je paierai** and **je payerai**, for example, are both correct.

➤ With verbs such as **lever** (meaning *to raise*), **peser** (meaning *to weigh*) and **acheter** (meaning *to buy*), **e** changes to **è** throughout the future tense. In **lever** the first **e** sounds like the vowel sound at the end of the English word *teacher*, but in **lèverai** and so on the first **e** sounds like the one in the English word *pet*.

Pronoun	Example verb: lever
je	lèverai
tu	lèveras
il, elle, on	lèvera
nous	lèverons
vous	lèverez
ils, elles	lèveront

Reflexive verbs in the future tense

➤ The future tense of reflexive verbs is formed in just the same way as for ordinary verbs, except that you have to remember to give the reflexive pronoun (**me**, **te**, **se**, **nous**, **vous**).

Subject pronoun	Reflexive pronoun	Example with laver	Meaning
je	me (m')	laverai	I will wash
tu	te (t')	laveras	you will wash
il, elle, on	se (s')	lavera	he/she/it/one will wash
nous	nous	laverons	we will wash
vous	vous	laverez	you will wash
ils, elles	se (s')	laveront	they will wash

> *Tip*
> **me** changes to **m'**, **te** to **t'** and **se** to **s'** before a vowel, most words starting with **h** and the French word **y**.

Irregular verbs in the future tense

➤ There are some verbs that do not use their infinitives as the stem for the future tense, including **avoir**, **être**, **faire** and **aller**, which are shown in full in the Verb Tables.

➤ Other irregular verbs include:

Verb	Meaning	je	tu	il/elle/on	nous	vous	ils/elles
devoir	to have to, must	devrai	devras	devra	devrons	devrez	devront
pouvoir	to be able to, can	pourrai	pourras	pourra	pourrons	pourrez	pourront
savoir	to know	saurai	sauras	saura	saurons	saurez	sauront
tenir	to hold	tiendrai	tiendras	tiendra	tiendrons	tiendrez	tiendront
venir	to come	viendrai	viendras	viendra	viendrons	viendrez	viendront
voir	to see	verrai	verras	verra	verrons	verrez	verront
vouloir	to want	voudrai	voudras	voudra	voudrons	voudrez	voudront

➤ **il faut** becomes **il faudra** (meaning *it will be necessary to*).

➤ **il pleut** becomes **il pleuvra** (meaning *it will rain*).

➤ This is the future tense of **avoir**:

Pronoun	avoir	Meaning: *to have*
j'	aurai	I will have
tu	auras	you will have
il, elle, on	aura	he/she/it/one will have
nous	aurons	we will have
vous	aurez	you will have
ils, elles	auront	they will have

➤ This is the future tense of **être**:

Pronoun	être	Meaning: *to be*
je	serai	I will be
tu	seras	you will be
il, elle, on	sera	he/she/it/one will be
nous	serons	we will be
vous	serez	you will be
ils, elles	seront	they will be

➤ This is the future tense of **faire**:

Pronoun	faire	Meaning: *to do, to make*
je	ferai	I will do/make
tu	feras	you will do/make
il, elle, on	fera	he/she/it/one will do/make
nous	ferons	we will do/make
vous	ferez	you will do/make
ils, elles	feront	they will do/make

➤ This is the future tense of **aller**:

Pronoun	aller	Meaning: *to go*
j'	irai	I will go
tu	iras	you will go
il, elle, on	ira	he/she/it/one will go
nous	irons	we will go
vous	irez	you will go
ils, elles	iront	they will go

⇨ For **Verb tables**, *see supplement.*

KEY POINTS

✔ You can use a present tense in French to talk about something that will happen or be true in the future, just as in English.

✔ You can use **aller** with an infinitive to refer to things that will happen in the immediate future.

✔ The stem is the same as the infinitive for **-er**, **-ir** and **-re** verbs, except that the final **-e** of **-re** verbs is lost.

✔ The future tense endings are the same for **-er**, **-ir** and **-re** verbs: **-ai**, **-as**, **-a**, **-ons**, **-ez**, **-ont**.

✔ In verbs ending in **-eler** and **-eter**: l → **ll** and **t** → **tt** throughout the future tense.

✔ In verbs ending in **-yer**: **y** → **i** throughout the future tense (optional in **-ayer** verbs).

✔ Some verbs are irregular in the future tense. It is worth learning these in full.

Test yourself

33 Replace the highlighted verb with a future tense.

a Tu **participes** au marathon?...

b Nous **partons** en vacances demain..

c Je te le **prête**, si tu veux. ....

d Elles **passent** une semaine chez nous. ....

e Ils se **marient** l'année prochaine. ....

f Vous m'**offrez** ce cadeau?..

g Nous **nettoyons** la maison avant son arrivée...

h Vous **venez** avec nous? ....

i Peut-être que ce monsieur **peut** vous aider..

j Elle me **rend** l'argent la semaine prochaine. ....

34 Fill the gap with the correct form of the future tense.

a Il y .... beaucoup de problèmes. **(avoir)**

b Mes amis .... tous au match. **(être)**

c Où .... tu pendant les vacances? **(être)**

d Nous .... besoin d'une maison plus grande. **(avoir)**

e Tout le monde .... ravi de vous voir. **(être)**

f J'espère que demain il .... beau temps. **(faire)**

g Vous croyez que tout .... bien? **(aller)**

h Vous .... de votre mieux, n'est-ce pas? **(faire)**

i Ce gros chien lui .... peur. **(faire)**

j Vous .... enfin le temps de voyager. **(avoir)**

35 Match the consequence to the situation.

a **Sarah et Paul restent longtemps au soleil.**   Ils ne pourront pas la payer.

b **J'ai une bonne nouvelle pour eux.**   Ils iront bientôt au lit.

c **La facture est énorme.**   Ils seront ravis de le savoir.

d **Leur avion part à sept heures.**   Ils seront bronzés.

e **Les enfants sont très fatigués.**   Ils devront se lever tôt.

Test yourself

36 Translate the sentence into French.

a They'll be delighted to see her again. ....

b Sabine will be able to help them. ....

c You'll have to be careful. (*Use* **tu**.) ....

d I will be there at nine o'clock. ....

e I'll call you at the weekend, darling. ....

f She'll have time to read during the holidays. ....

g Marseille? It'll be hot! ....

h The children will want to go to the beach. ....

i We'll see the exhibition tomorrow. ....

j You'll be in London next week? (*Use* **vous**.) ....

The conditional

> ### What is the conditional?
> The **conditional** is a verb form used to talk about things that would happen or that would be true under certain conditions, for example, I _would help_ you if I could.
> It is also used to say what you would like or need, for example, _Could_ you _give_ me the bill?

Using the conditional

➤ You can often recognize a conditional in English by the word _would_ or its shortened form _'d_.
    I _would_ be sad if you left.
    If you asked him, he'_d_ help you.

➤ You use the conditional for:

- asking for something formally and politely, especially in shops
    I'_d like_ a kilo of pears, please.

- saying what you would like
    I'_d like_ to go to the United States.

- making a suggestion
    I _could come_ and pick you up.

- giving advice
    You _should say_ you're sorry.

> _Tip_
> There is no direct French translation of _would_ in verb forms like _would be_, _would like_, _would help_ and so on. You change the French verb ending instead.

Forming the conditional

➤ To form the conditional in French, you have to use:

- the infinitive of **-er** and **-ir** verbs, for example, **donner-**, **finir-**

- the infinitive without the final **e** of **-re** verbs, for example, **attendr-**

➤ Then add the correct ending to the stem, depending on whether you are talking about **je**, **tu**, **il**, **elle**, **on**, **nous**, **vous**, **ils** or **elles**. The endings are the same for all verbs. They are the same as the **-er** and **-re** endings for the IMPERFECT TENSE, but the stem is the same as that of the FUTURE TENSE.

⇨ _For more information on the **Imperfect tense** and the **Future tense**, see pages 128 and 136._

Pronoun	Ending	Add to stem, e.g. donner-, finir-, attendr-	Meanings
je (j')	-ais	je donner<u>ais</u> je finir<u>ais</u> j'attendr<u>ais</u>	I would give I would finish I would wait
tu	-ais	tu donner<u>ais</u> tu finir<u>ais</u> tu attendr<u>ais</u>	you would give you would finish you would wait
il elle on	-ait	il/elle/on donner<u>ait</u> il/elle/on finir<u>ait</u> il/elle/on attendr<u>ait</u>	he/she/it/one would give he/she/it/one would finish he/she/it/one would wait
nous	-ions	nous donner<u>ions</u> nous finir<u>ions</u> nous attendr<u>ions</u>	we would give we would finish we would wait
vous	-iez	vous donner<u>iez</u> vous finir<u>iez</u> vous attendr<u>iez</u>	you would give you would finish you would wait
ils elles	-aient	ils/elles donner<u>aient</u> ils/elles finir<u>aient</u> ils/elles attendr<u>aient</u>	they would give they would finish they would wait

J'<u>aimerais</u> aller aux États-Unis.   I'd like to go to the United States.

> *Tip*
> **je** changes to **j'** in front of a word starting with a vowel, most words starting with **h**, and the French word **y**.

[i] Note that you have to be careful not to mix up the future tense and the conditional. They look very similar.

FUTURE
je donnerai
je finirai
j'attendrai
j'aimerai
je voudrai
je viendrai
je serai

CONDITIONAL
je donnerais
je finirais
j'attendrais
j'aimerais
je voudrais
je viendrais
je serais

Spelling changes in -er verbs

➤ As with the future tense, a few **-er** verbs change their spellings slightly in the conditional. The forms with spelling changes have been <u>underlined</u> in the tables below.

➤ With verbs such as **appeler** (meaning *to call*), which end in **-eler**, the **l** doubles throughout the conditional. The double consonant (**ll**) affects the pronunciation of the word. In **appeler**, the first **e** sounds like the vowel sound at the end of the English word *teacher*, but in **appellerais** the first **e** sounds like the one in the English word *pet*.

Pronoun	Example verb: appeler
j'	appellerais
tu	appellerais
il, elle, on	appellerait
nous	appellerions
vous	appelleriez
ils, elles	appelleraient

➤ The exceptions to this rule are **geler** (meaning *to freeze*) and **peler** (meaning *to peel*), which change in the same way as **lever** (*see page 111*).

➤ With verbs such as **jeter** (meaning *to throw*), which end in **-eter**, the **t** doubles throughout the conditional. The double consonant (**tt**) affects the pronunciation of the word. In **jeter**, the first **e** sounds like the vowel sound at the end of the English word *teacher*, but in **jetterais** the first **e** sounds like the one in the English word *pet*.

Pronoun	Example verb: jeter
je	jetterais
tu	jetterais
il, elle, on	jetterait
nous	jetterions
vous	jetteriez
ils, elles	jetteraient

➤ The exceptions to this rule include **acheter** (meaning *to buy*), which changes in the same way as **lever** (*see page 111*).

➤ With verbs such as **nettoyer** (meaning *to clean*), that end in **-yer**, the **y** changes to **i** throughout the conditional.

Pronoun	Example verb: nettoyer
je	nettoierais
tu	nettoierais
il, elle, on	nettoierait
nous	nettoierions
vous	nettoieriez
ils, elles	nettoieraient

➤ Verbs ending in **-ayer**, such as **payer** (meaning *to pay*) and **essayer** (meaning *to try*), can be spelled with either a **y** or an **i**. So **je paierais** and **je payerais**, for example, are both correct.

➤ With verbs such as **lever** (meaning *to raise*), **peser** (meaning *to weigh*) and **acheter** (meaning *to buy*), **e** changes to **è** throughout the conditional. In **lever** the first **e** sounds like the vowel sound at the end of the English word *teacher*, but in **lèverais** and so on the first **e** sounds like the one in the English word *pet*.

Pronoun	Example verb: lever
je	<u>lèverais</u>
tu	<u>lèverais</u>
il, elle, on	<u>lèverait</u>
nous	<u>lèverions</u>
vous	<u>lèveriez</u>
ils, elles	<u>lèveraient</u>

Reflexive verbs in the conditional

➤ The conditional of reflexive verbs is formed in just the same way as for ordinary verbs, except that you have to remember to give the reflexive pronoun (**me**, **te**, **se**, **nous**, **vous**, **se**).

Subject pronoun	Reflexive pronoun	Example with laver	Meaning
je	me (m')	laverais	I would wash
tu	te (t')	laverais	you would wash
il, elle, on	se (s')	laverait	he/she/it would wash
nous	nous	laverions	we would wash
vous	vous	laveriez	you would wash
ils, elles	se (s')	laveraient	they would wash

> *Tip*
> **me** changes to **m'**, **te** to **t'** and **se** to **s'** before a vowel, most words starting with **h** and the French word **y**.

Irregular verbs in the conditional

➤ The same verbs that are irregular in the future tense are irregular in the conditional, including: **avoir**, **être**, **faire**, **aller**, **devoir**, **pouvoir**, **savoir**, **tenir**, **venir**, **voir**, **vouloir**.

⇨ *For more information on **Irregular verbs in the future tense**, see page 139.*

➤ To form the conditional of an irregular verb, use the same stem as for the future tense, for example:

    avoir → aur-
    être → ser-

➤ Then add the usual endings for the conditional.

Infinitive	Future stem	Conditional endings	Conditional form
avoir	aur-	-ais, -ais, -ait, -ions, -iez, -aient	j'aurais, tu aurais, il/elle/on aurait, nous aurions, vous auriez, ils/elles auraient
être	ser-	-ais, -ais, -ait, -ions, -iez, -aient	je serais, tu serais, il/elle/on serait, nous serions, vous seriez, ils/elles seraient
faire	fer-	-ais, -ais, -ait, -ions, -iez, -aient	je ferais, tu ferais, il/elle/on ferait nous ferions, vous feriez, ils/elles feraient
aller	ir-	-ais, -ais, -ait, -ions, -iez, -aient	j'irais, tu irais, il/elle/on irait, nous irions, vous iriez, ils/elles iraient

J'irais si j'avais le temps.
**Je voudrais un kilo de poires,
 s'il vous plaît.**
Tu devrais t'excuser.

I would go if I had time.
I'd like a kilo of pears, please.

You should say you're sorry.

KEY POINTS

✔ The conditional endings are the same for **-er**, **-ir** and **-re** verbs:
-ais, **-ais**, **-ait**, **-ions**, **-iez**, **-aient**.
✔ The conditional endings are the same as the endings for the imperfect tense of **-er** and **-re** verbs, but the stem is the same as the stem of the future tense.
✔ In verbs ending in **-eler** and **-eter**:
l → ll and **t → tt** throughout the conditional.
✔ In verbs ending in **-yer**:
y → i throughout the conditional (optional in **-ayer** verbs).
✔ The same verbs that are irregular in the future are irregular in the conditional. It is worth learning these in full.

For further explanation of grammatical terms, please see pages viii–xii.

Test yourself

37 Cross out the unlikely items.

a	On aurait besoin de ça à la piscine:	un maillot de bain/une raquette/une serviette/du shampooing
b	Les enfants aimeraient ça comme dessert:	des pâtes/de la glace/de la mousse au chocolat/du fromage
c	Ma petite amie m'offrirait ça pour mon anniversaire:	une chemise/un CD/de l'après-rasage/une cuillère
d	Ça coûterait moins cher:	l'auberge de jeunesse/la cantine/l'hôtel de luxe/une voiture d'occasion
e	Je voudrais y aller en vacances:	dans les banlieues/en Espagne/au pays de Galles/aux USA
f	Tu aurais peur si tu voyais ça:	ce film d'horreur/une grande araignée/un chaton/ses blessures
g	Vous trouveriez ça très intéressant:	ce film/ce parking/ce travail/cette exposition
h	Nous achèterions ça si nous étions riches:	un bic/une grande maison/une belle église/une belle voiture
i	Nous devrions visiter ça:	la gare routière/le musée/le château/le teinturier
j	Je le ferais si j'avais le temps:	de l'équitation/du chantage/du ski/de la natation

38 Replace the highlighted verb with a conditional.

a Je **veux** venir avec vous. ....

b Tu **dois** le faire tout de suite. ....

c Mon père **peut** nous donner des conseils. ....

d Nous **voulons** aller au cinéma demain soir. ....

e Ma femme **sera** enchantée de faire votre connaissance. ....

f Les employés **veulent** une augmentation de salaire. ....

g Qu'est-ce que vous nous **proposez**? ....

h Ils ne **savent** pas quoi dire. ....

i Ça ne **fait** aucune différence. ....

j Je n'**ose** pas le faire. ....

39 **Translate the sentence into French. To translate** *if* **use si. Use the imperfect for the past tense verb that goes with it.**

a If I had the money I'd buy it ....

b He'd come if she was there. ....

c How much would you give for that car? (*Use* **tu**.)

....

d If we started at seven o'clock we'd finish this afternoon.

....

e The children would have a good time here.

....

f We'd like a double room. ....

g She'd be furious if you said that. ....

h You ought to take some photos. (*Use* **vous**.)

....

i If it was good weather they'd go to the beach.

....

The perfect tense

> ## What is the perfect tense?
> The **perfect** is one of the verb tenses used in French to talk about the past, especially about actions that took place and were completed in the past.

Using the perfect tense

➤ In English there are two types of past tense: _I gave_, _I finished_, and _I have given_, _I have finished_. Both types are translated by the French perfect.

> _Tip_
> The perfect tense is the tense you will need most to talk about things that have happened or were true in the past. It is used to talk about actions that took place and WERE COMPLETED in the past.
> Use the imperfect tense for regular events and in most descriptions.
>
> ⇨ For more information on the **Imperfect tense**, see page 128.

Forming the perfect tense

➤ The present, imperfect, future and conditional tenses in French are made up of just <u>one</u> word, for example, **je donne**, **tu finissais**, **il attendra** or **j'aimerais**. The perfect tense has <u>TWO</u> parts to it:

- the <u>present</u> tense of the verb **avoir** (meaning _to have_) or **être** (meaning _to be_)

- a part of the main verb called the <u>past participle</u>, such as _given_, _finished_ and _done_ in English

➤ In other words, the perfect tense in French is like the form _I have done_ in English.

⇨ For more information on forming the present tense of **avoir** and **être**, see page 114.

Forming the past participle

➤ To form the past participle of regular verbs, you use the <u>infinitive</u> of the verb:

- For **-er** verbs, you replace the **-er** at the end of the infinitive with **é**.

Infinitive	Take off -er	Add -é
donner (_to give_)	donn-	donn<u>é</u>
tomber (_to fall_)	tomb-	tomb<u>é</u>

- For **-ir** verbs, you replace the **-ir** at the end of the infinitive with **-i**.

Infinitive	Take off -ir	Add -i
finir (to finish)	fin-	fini
partir (to leave, to go)	part-	parti

- For **-re** verbs, you replace the **-re** at the end of the infinitive with **-u**.

Infinitive	Take off -re	Add -u
attendre (to wait)	attend-	attendu
descendre (to go down, to come down, to get off)	descend-	descendu

Verbs that form their perfect tense with avoir

➤ Most verbs form their perfect tense with **avoir**, for example **donner**:

Pronoun	avoir	Past participle	Meaning
j'	ai	donné	I gave I have given
tu	as	donné	you gave you have given
il, elle, on	a	donné	he/she/it/one gave he/she/it/one has given
nous	avons	donné	we gave we have given
vous	avez	donné	you gave you have given
ils, elles	ont	donné	they gave they have given

Elle <u>a donné</u> son numéro de téléphone à Claude.	She gave Claude her phone number.
Il <u>a acheté</u> un ordinateur.	He's bought a computer.
Je n'<u>ai</u> pas <u>regardé</u> la télé hier.	I didn't watch TV yesterday.

> *Tip*
> **je** changes to **j'** in front of a word starting with a vowel, most words starting with **h**, and the French word **y**.

➤ The perfect tense of **-ir** verbs like **finir** is formed in the same way, except for the different ending of the past participle: **j'ai fini**, **tu as fini** and so on.

➤ The perfect tense of **-re** verbs like **attendre** is formed in the same way, except for the past participle: **j'ai attendu**, **tu as attendu** and so on.

avoir or être?

➤ <u>MOST</u> verbs form their perfect tense with **avoir**; these include **donner** as shown on page 152.

➤ There are two main groups of verbs which form their perfect tense with **être** instead of **avoir**:

- all reflexive verbs

⇨ *For more information on **Reflexive verbs**, see page 123.*

- a group of verbs that are mainly used to talk about movement or a change of some kind, including these ones:

aller	to go
venir	to come
arriver	to arrive, to happen
partir	to leave, to go
descendre	to go down, to come down, to get off
monter	to go up, to come up
entrer	to go in, to come in
sortir	to go out, to come out
mourir	to die
naître	to be born
devenir	to become
rester	to stay
tomber	to fall

Je <u>suis allé</u> au match de football hier.	I went to the football match yesterday.
Il <u>est sorti</u> acheter un journal.	He's gone out to buy a newspaper.
Vous <u>êtes descendu</u> à quelle station?	Which station did you get off at?

Grammar Extra!
Some of the verbs on the previous page take **avoir** when they are used with a direct object, for example:

descendre quelque chose	to get something down, to bring something down, to take something down
monter quelque chose	to go up something, to come up something
sortir quelque chose	to take something out
Est-ce que tu <u>as descendu</u> les bagages?	Did you bring the bags down?
Elle <u>a monté</u> les escaliers.	She went up the stairs.
Elle <u>a sorti</u> son porte-monnaie de son sac.	She took her purse out of her handbag.

⇨ *For more information on **Direct objects**, see page 61.*

Verbs that form their perfect tense with être

➤ When a verb takes **être**, the past participle <u>ALWAYS</u> agrees with the subject of the verb; that is, the endings change in the feminine and plural forms.

	Masculine endings	Examples	Feminine endings	Examples
Singular	-	tombé parti descendu	-e	tombé<u>e</u> parti<u>e</u> descendu<u>e</u>
Plural	-s	tombé<u>s</u> parti<u>s</u> descendu<u>s</u>	-es	tombé<u>es</u> parti<u>es</u> descendu<u>es</u>

Est-ce que ton frère est <u>allé</u> à l'étranger? Did your brother go abroad?
Elle est <u>venue</u> avec nous. She came with us.
Ils sont <u>partis</u> à six heures. They left at six o'clock.
Mes cousines sont <u>arrivées</u> hier. My cousins arrived yesterday.
  (*The cousins are female.*)

➤ Here are the perfect tense forms of **tomber** in full:

Pronoun	avoir	Past participle	Meaning
je	suis	**tombé** (*masculine*) **tombée** (*feminine*)	I fell/I have fallen
tu	es	**tombé** (*masculine*) **tombée** (*feminine*)	you fell/ you have fallen
il	est	**tombé**	he/it fell, he/it has fallen
elle	est	**tombée**	she/it fell, she/it has fallen
on	est	**tombé** (*singular*) **tombés** (*masculine plural*) **tombées** (*feminine plural*)	one fell/ one has fallen, we fell/ we have fallen
nous	sommes	**tombés** (*masculine*) **tombées** (*feminine*)	we fell/ we have fallen
vous	êtes	**tombé** (*masculine singular*) **tombée** (*feminine singular*) **tombés** (*masculine plural*) **tombées** (*feminine plural*)	you fell/ you have fallen
ils	sont	**tombés**	they fell/ they have fallen
elles	sont	**tombées**	they fell/ they have fallen

For further explanation of grammatical terms, please see pages viii–xii.

➤ The perfect tense of **-ir** verbs like **partir** is formed in the same way, except for the past participle: **je suis parti(e)**, **tu es parti(e)** and so on.

➤ The perfect tense of **-re** verbs like **descendre** is formed in the same way, except for the past participle: **je suis descendu(e)**, **tu es descendu(e)** and so on.

The perfect tense of reflexive verbs

➤ Here is the perfect tense of the reflexive verb **se laver** (meaning *to wash (oneself)*, *to have a wash*, *to get washed*) in full. Remember that all reflexive verbs take **être**, and so the past participle of reflexive verbs usually agrees with the subject of the sentence.

Subject pronoun	Reflexive pronoun	Present tense of être	Past participle	Meaning
je	me	suis	**lavé** (*masculine*) **lavée** (*feminine*)	I washed myself
tu	t'	es	**lavé** (*masculine*) **lavée** (*feminine*)	you washed yourself
il	s'	est	**lavé**	he washed himself
elle	s'	est	**lavée**	she washed herself
on	s'	est	**lavé** (*singular*) **lavés** (*masculine plural*) **lavées** (*feminine plural*)	one washed oneself we washed ourselves
nous	nous	sommes	**lavés** (*masculine*) **lavées** (*feminine*)	we washed ourselves
vous	vous	êtes	**lavé** (*masculine singular*) **lavée** (*feminine singular*) **lavés** (*masculine plural*) **lavées** (*feminine plural*)	you washed yourself (*singular*) you washed yourselves (*plural*)
ils	se	sont	**lavés**	they washed themselves
elles	se	sont	**lavées**	they washed themselves

Tip

When **on** means *we*, and masculine only or masculine and feminine are involved, the past participle has a masculine ending. You can use either the masculine singular or the masculine plural.

On s'est déjà lavé.
On s'est déjà lavés.   We've already washed.

Grammar Extra!
The past participle of reflexive verbs <u>DOES NOT</u> change if the direct object
(**la jambe** in the example below) <u>FOLLOWS</u> the verb.

Elle s'<u>est cassé</u> la jambe.   She's broken her leg.

Irregular verbs in the perfect tense

➤ Some past participles are irregular. There aren't too many, so try to learn them.

avoir (meaning *to have*)	→ **eu**
devoir (meaning *to have to, must*)	→ **dû**
dire (meaning *to say, to tell*)	→ **dit**
être (meaning *to be*)	→ **été**
faire (meaning *to do, to make*)	→ **fait**
mettre (meaning *to put*)	→ **mis**
pouvoir (meaning *to be able to, can*)	→ **pu**
prendre (meaning *to take*)	→ **pris**
savoir (meaning *to know*)	→ **su**
tenir (meaning *to hold*)	→ **tenu**
venir (meaning *to come*)	→ **venu**
voir (meaning *to see*)	→ **vu**
vouloir (meaning *to want*)	→ **voulu**

➤ **il pleut** becomes **il a plu** (*it rained*).

➤ **il faut** becomes **il a fallu** (*it was necessary*).

KEY POINTS

✔ The perfect tense describes things that happened and were completed in the past. It is not used for things that happened regularly or in descriptions.

✔ The perfect tense is formed with the present tense of **avoir** or **être** and a past participle.

✔ Most verbs take **avoir** in the perfect tense. All reflexive verbs and a small group of verbs referring to movement or change take **être**.

✔ The past participle ends in **-é** for **-er** verbs, in **-i** for **-ir** verbs, and in **-u** for **-re** verbs.

✔ With verbs that take **avoir**, the past participle does not usually change. With verbs that take **être**, including reflexive verbs, the past participle changes in the feminine and plural.

Test yourself

40 Fill the gap with the correct form of the past participle of the verb.

a Mes amies sont .... en vacances hier. **(partir)**

b La petite fille a trébuché et elle est .... **(tomber)**

c Nous avons tout de suite .... la police. **(appeler)**

d Sa réaction a .... ses collègues. **(étonner)**

e Tous mes copains sont .... au match. **(aller)**

f L'équipe a .... 4–1. **(perdre)**

g Quand je l'ai vu j'ai .... très peur. **(avoir)**

h Ma grand-mère est .... il y a deux ans. **(mourir)**

i Alain et Aurélie sont .... ensemble. **(arriver)**

j Quand ont-ils .... le travail? **(finir)**

41 Replace the highlighted present tense with the perfect tense.

a **Je rends** visite à des amis à Perpignan en mai. ....

b Où est-ce que tu **passes** tes vacances? ....

c Nos voisins **déménagent** à la mi-juin. ....

d Ça **prend** cinq minutes à préparer. ....

e Marlène **vient** me voir ce matin. ....

f Vous **vous amusez** au club, les enfants? ....

g Elle **m'écrit** de longs e-mails. ....

h Elles **descendent** au terminus. ....

i Qu'est-ce qui **se passe**? ....

j Tu **mets** le couvert? ....

Test yourself

42 Match the answer to the question.

a	Vous allez voir ce film?	Non, il ne nous l'a pas demandée.
b	Tu sais qu'ils se marient?	Oui, je me suis levée très tôt.
c	Tu es fatiguée, Caroline?	Non, je l'ai déjà vu.
d	Vous lui avez donné votre adresse?	Non, il ne pleut plus.
e	Il pleut encore?	Oui, ils me l'ont dit il y a une quinzaine de jours.

43 Translate the sentence into French.

a   She gave me her phone number.

   ....

b   I've lost my keys.

   ....

c   They won 2-1.

   ....

d   We stayed at home yesterday.

   ....

e   She's gone out to get some bread.

   ....

f   I took the dog out this morning.

   ....

g   He chose a yoghurt rather than an ice cream.

   ....

h   We had an accident on the way.

   ....

i   Anna has bought a new mobile.

   ....

j   The price of petrol has gone up.

   ....

Grammar Extra!

The pluperfect tense

> **What is the pluperfect tense?**
> The **pluperfect** is a verb tense which describes something that <u>had</u> happened or <u>had</u> been true at a point in the past, for example, *I'd forgotten to finish my homework.*

Using the pluperfect tense

➤ Examples of the pluperfect tense in English are *I had arrived, you'd fallen*.

Elle <u>avait essayé</u> des dizaines de pulls.	She <u>had tried on</u> dozens of jumpers.
Nous <u>avions</u> déjà <u>commencé</u> à manger quand il est arrivé.	We'd already <u>started</u> eating when he arrived.
J'<u>étais arrivée</u> la première.	I <u>had arrived</u> first.
Mes parents <u>s'étaient couchés</u> tôt.	My parents <u>had gone</u> to bed early.

Forming the pluperfect tense

➤ Like the perfect tense, the pluperfect tense in French has <u>two</u> parts to it:

- the <u>imperfect</u> tense of the verb **avoir** (meaning *to have*) or **être** (meaning *to be*)

- the past participle

➤ If a verb takes **avoir** in the perfect tense, then it will take **avoir** in the pluperfect too. If a verb takes **être** in the perfect, then it will take **être** in the pluperfect too.

> ⇨ For more information on the **Imperfect tense** and the **Perfect tense,** see pages 128 and 151.

Verbs taking avoir

➤ Here are the pluperfect tense forms of **donner** (meaning *to give*) in full.

Pronoun	avoir	Past participle	Meaning
j'	avais	donné	I had given
tu	avais	donné	you had given
il, elle, on	avait	donné	he/she/it/one had given
nous	avions	donné	we had given
vous	aviez	donné	you had given
ils, elles	avaient	donné	they had given

➤ The pluperfect tense of **-ir** verbs like **finir** (meaning *to finish*) is formed in the same way, except for the ending of the past participle: **j'avais fini**, **tu avais fini** and so on.

➤ The pluperfect tense of **-re** verbs like **attendre** (meaning *to wait*) is formed in the same way, except for the past participle: **j'avais attendu**, **tu avais attendu** and so on.

Verbs taking être

➤ Here are the pluperfect tense forms of **tomber** (meaning *to fall*) in full. When a verb takes **être** in the pluperfect tense, the past participle <u>always</u> agrees with the subject of the verb; that is, the endings change in the feminine and plural forms.

Pronoun	être	Past participle	Meaning
j'	étais	**tombé** (*masculine*) **tombée** (*feminine*)	I had fallen
tu	étais	**tombé** (*masculine*) **tombée** (*feminine*)	you had fallen
il	était	**tombé**	he/it had fallen
elle	était	**tombée**	she/it had fallen
on	était	**tombé** (*singular*) **tombés** (*masculine plural*) **tombées** (*feminine plural*)	one had fallen we had fallen
nous	étions	**tombés** (*masculine*) **tombées** (*feminine*)	we had fallen
vous	étiez	**tombé** (*masculine singular*) **tombée** (*feminine singular*) **tombés** (*masculine plural*) **tombées** (*feminine plural*)	you had fallen
ils	étaient	**tombés**	they had fallen
elles	étaient	**tombées**	they had fallen

➤ The pluperfect tense of **-ir** verbs like **partir** (meaning *to leave*, *to go*) is formed in the same way, except for the past participle: **j'étais parti(e)**, **tu étais parti(e)** and so on.

➤ The pluperfect tense of **-re** verbs like **descendre** (meaning *to come down*, *to go down*, *to get off*) is formed in the same way, except for the past participle: **j'étais descendu(e)**, **tu étais descendu(e)** and so on.

> *Tip*
> When **on** means *we*, the past participle can agree with the subject of the sentence, but it is optional.
>
> **On était <u>tombées</u>.** We had fallen. (*feminine*)

Reflexive verbs in the pluperfect tense

➤ Reflexive verbs in the pluperfect tense are formed in the same way as in the perfect tense, but with the imperfect tense of the verb **être** (*see page* 132).

⇨ For more information on the **Perfect tense of reflexive verbs,** *see page* 156.

Irregular verbs in the pluperfect tense

➤ Irregular past participles are the same as for the perfect tense (*see page* 157).

KEY POINTS

✔ The pluperfect tense describes things that had happened or were true at a point in the past before something else happened.
✔ It is formed with the imperfect tense of **avoir** or **être** and the past participle.
✔ The rules for agreement of the past participle are the same as for the perfect tense.

Test yourself

44 Match the connected sentences.

a	Marc n'avait plus d'argent.	On avait oublié de fermer la porte à clé.
b	Il était tout rouge.	Je ne savais pas qu'il était arrivé.
c	Les voleurs sont entrés sans difficulté.	On s'était couchés très tard.
d	Le lendemain on ne voulait pas se lever.	Il avait tout dépensé.
e	Quelle surprise!	Il avait couru cent mètres en moins de 20 secondes.

45 Fill the gap with the correct form of the pluperfect.

a   Malheureusement elle .... son appareil photo à la maison. **(oublier)**

b   Nous .... très tôt pour aller à l'aéroport. **(se lever)**

c   Je .... à quelque chose de meilleur. **(s'attendre)**

d   Mes amis .... quand je suis arrivée. **(partir)**

e   Nous les .... avant notre départ. **(appeler)**

f   Enfant, il .... être médecin, comme son père. **(vouloir)**

g   Vous .... le costume avant de l'acheter? **(essayer)**

h   Ils sont arrivés avec deux heures de retard: leur voiture .... en panne.
     (tomber)

i   Si j' .... je serais venue te voir. **(savoir)**

j   Elle m' .... la vérité juste avant sa mort. **(dire)**

Test yourself

46 Fill the gap with the past participle of the verb in brackets.

a   Si l'équipe avait mieux .... , elle aurait gagné. **(jouer)**

b   Si vous étiez .... plus tôt, vous seriez arrivés à temps. **(partir)**

c   Si je te l'avais .... , tu ne l'aurais pas cru. **(dire)**

d   Si tu t'étais .... avant deux heures du matin tu serais moins fatiguée.
(coucher)

e   L'accident n'aurait pas eu lieu si le temps n'avait pas .... si mauvais. **(être)**

f   Je leur avais dit que c'était dangereux — si seulement ils m'avaient .... !
(écouter)

g   Tu étais au courant? — Non, si seulement je l'avais .... ! **(savoir)**

h   Si j'avais .... les aider, je l'aurais fait. **(pouvoir)**

i   Si vous me l'aviez .... je vous l'aurais donné. **(demander)**

j   Si elles y étaient .... à pied ça aurait été très fatigant. **(aller)**

47 Translate the sentence into French. Put déjà between the two parts of the verb.

a   They'd already made up their minds. ....

b   He'd drunk a lot. ....

c   He'd already asked her twice. ....

d   I'd noticed her immediately. ....

e   She had felt fine during the day. ....

f   Perhaps you'd had enough of it?...

g   The girls had had to leave before dinner. ....

h   We had met in Paris. ....

i   She'd often seen him in the supermarket. ....

j   You had expected that?...

The passive

> ### What is the passive?
> The **passive** is a form of the verb that is used when the subject of the verb is the person or thing that is affected by the action, for example, *I was given, we were told, it had been made.*

Using the passive

➤ In a normal, or *active* sentence, the 'subject' of the verb is the person or thing that carries out the action described by the verb. The 'object' of the verb is the person or thing that the verb 'happens' to.

Ryan *(subject)* hit *(active verb)* me *(object)*.

➤ In English, as in French, you can turn an <u>active</u> sentence round to make a <u>passive</u> sentence.

I *(subject)* was hit *(passive verb)* by Ryan *(agent)*.

➤ Very often, however, you cannot identify who is carrying out the action indicated by the verb.

I was hit in the face.
The trees will be chopped down.
I've been chosen to represent the school.

> *Tip*
> There is a very important difference between French and English in sentences containing an <u>indirect object</u>. In English we can quite easily turn a normal (active) sentence with an indirect object into a passive sentence.
>
> **Active**
> Someone *(subject)* gave *(active verb)* me *(indirect object)* a book *(direct object)*.
>
> **Passive**
> I *(subject)* was given *(passive verb)* a book *(direct object)*.
> In French, an indirect object can <u>NEVER</u> become the subject of a passive verb.
>
> ⇨ *For more information on* **Direct** *and* **Indirect objects***, see pages* 61 *and* 65.

Forming the passive

➤ In English we use the verb *to be* with the past participle (*was hit, was given*) to form the passive. In French the passive is formed in exactly the same way, using **être** and the past participle. The past participle agrees with the subject of the passive verb; that is, the endings change in the feminine and plural forms.

Elle <u>est encouragée</u> par ses parents.	She is encouraged by her parents.
Vous <u>êtes</u> tous bien <u>payés</u>.	You are all well paid. (*'you' here is plural and refers to men, or men and women*)
Les portes <u>ont été fermées</u>.	The doors have been closed.

⇨ *For more information on the* **Past participle***, see page* 151–152.

➤ Here is the present tense of the **-er** verb **aimer** (meaning *to like, to love*) in its passive form.

Pronoun	Present tense of être	Past participle	Meaning
je	suis	**aimé** (*masculine*) **aimée** (*feminine*)	I am loved
tu	es	**aimé** (*masculine*) **aimée** (*feminine*)	you are loved
il	est	**aimé**	he/it is loved
elle	est	**aimée**	she/it is loved
on	est	**aimé** (*singular*) **aimés** (*masculine plural*) **aimées** (*feminine plural*)	one is loved we are loved
nous	sommes	**aimés** (*masculine*) **aimées** (*feminine*)	we are loved
vous	êtes	**aimé** (*masculine singular*) **aimée** (*feminine singular*) **aimés** (*masculine plural*) **aimées** (*feminine plural*)	you are loved
ils	sont	**aimés**	they are loved
elles	sont	**aimées**	they are loved

➤ The passive of **-ir** verbs is formed in the same way, except that the past participle is different. For example, **elle est remplie** (meaning *it is full*).

➤ The passive of **-re** verbs is formed in the same way, except that the past participle is different. For example, **il est défendu** (meaning *it is forbidden*).

Grammar Extra!
When **on** means *we*, the past participle can agree with the subject of the sentence, but it is optional.

On est <u>aimés</u> de tout le monde.   We're loved by everyone. (*masculine*)

➤ You can form other tenses of the passive by changing the tense of the verb **être**.
Imperfect: **j'étais aimé(e)** I was loved
Future: **tu seras aimé(e)** you will be loved
Perfect: **il a été aimé** he was loved

⇨ *For more information on the **Imperfect**, **future** and **perfect tenses**, see pages 128, 136 and 151.*

➤ Irregular past participles are the same as for the perfect tense (*see page 157*).

Avoiding the passive

➤ Passives are not as common in French as in English. There are <u>two</u> main ways that French speakers express the same idea.

- by using the pronoun **on** (meaning *someone* or *they*) with a normal, active verb

On leur a envoyé une lettre.	They were sent a letter. *(literally: Someone sent them a letter.)*
On m'a dit que tu ne venais pas.	I was told that you weren't coming. *(literally: They told me you weren't coming.)*

⇨ *For more information on **Pronouns,** see page* 55.

- by using a reflexive verb

Les melons <u>se vendent</u> 2 euros la pièce.	Melons are sold for 2 euros each.

⇨ *For more information on **Reflexive verbs**, see page* 123.

KEY POINTS
✔ The present tense of the passive is formed by using the present tense of **être** with the past participle.
✔ The past participle always agrees with the subject of the passive verb.
✔ You can sometimes avoid a passive construction by using a reflexive verb or the pronoun **on**.

Test yourself

48 Cross out the unlikely items.

a Le château a été construit — pour le roi/au quinzième siècle/pendant la nuit/ il y a trois cents ans

b Son roman sera publié — en 2009/en cinq langues/en septembre/bientôt

c Mon meilleur ami a été agressé — dans la rue/hier soir/demain matin/dans le métro

d Les matchs seront joués — la semaine dernière/cette semaine/ à Marseille/à bientôt

e Il était critiqué — par toute la presse/par jour/par l'Église/ par habitude

f Ce tableau a été peint — par le même peintre/il y a deux ans/par Picasso/ au crayon

g Les jeux électroniques sont vendus — en ligne/dans les magasins de meubles/ dans les boulangeries/dans les bibliothèques

h Les fraises se mangent — avec du sel/avec du sucre/en été/en dessert

i On m'a volé mon appareil photo — dans le bus/à Paris/quelquefois/samedi

j Tu es aimée — par tes ennemis/par tout le monde/ malgré tes défauts/pour tes défauts

49 Fill the gap with the correct form of the past participle.

a Cette maison a été .... par mon grand-père. **(construire)**

b Son portrait sera .... par un artiste célèbre. **(peindre)**

c Toutes ces broderies sont .... à la main. **(faire)**

d Ce match sera .... par des millions de téléspectateurs. **(regarder)**

e C'est une plante qui est .... par les lapins. **(adorer)**

f Ils sont .... par la police. **(rechercher)**

g Le questionnaire a été .... par tous les étudiants. **(remplir)**

h Trois suspects ont été .... **(arrêter)**

i Cette chanson est .... de tout le monde. **(connaître)**

j Ce roman a été .... en 2005. **(écrire)**

Test yourself

50 Translate the sentence into French.

a He had been killed. ....

b You had been warned, Sarah. (*Use **tu**.*)..

c The gîte will be cleaned before your arrival.

....

d America was discovered by Christopher Columbus.

....

e The door must be locked. ....

f The bridge will be finished next summer.

....

g Your bags have been found, sir. ....

h This photo was taken in 1995. ....

i The headlights have to be adjusted. ....

j I was made redundant in April. (*a woman*)

....

51 Match the active and passive sentences.

a Ils l'ont embauchée.   Il doit être refait.

b Il les a embauchés.   Il sera envoyé ce matin.

c Elle a envoyé ce SMS il y a une heure.   Ils ont été embauchés.

d Nous allons bientôt envoyer le document.   Elle a été embauchée.

e Tu dois refaire ce travail.   Il a été envoyé ce matin.

Grammar Extra!

The present participle

What is a present participle?
The **present participle** is a verb form ending in *-ing* which is used in English to form verb tenses, and which may be used as an adjective or a noun, for example,
What are you <u>doing</u>?; the <u>setting</u> sun; <u>Swimming</u> is easy!

Using the present participle

➤ Present participles are not as common in French as in English, because they are not used to form tenses. The main uses of the present participle in French are:

- as a verb, on its own, corresponding to the English *-ing* form. It <u>DOES NOT</u> agree with the subject of the verb when it is used in this way.

<u>Habitant</u> près de Paris, je vais assez souvent en ville.	Living close to Paris, I go into town quite often.
les voyageurs <u>descendant</u> à Périgueux	travellers getting off at Périgueux

- as a verb, after the preposition **en**. The present participle <u>DOES NOT</u> agree with the subject of the verb when it is used in this way. The subject of the two parts of the sentence is always the same. **en** can be translated in a number of different ways.

<u>En attendant</u> sa sœur, Richard s'est endormi.	While waiting for his sister Richard fell asleep.
Appelle-nous <u>en arrivant</u> chez toi.	Call us when you get home.
<u>En appuyant</u> sur ce bouton, on peut imprimer ses documents.	By pressing this button, you can print your documents.
Il s'est blessé <u>en essayant</u> de sauver un chat.	He hurt himself trying to rescue a cat.

  ⇨ *For more information on the preposition **en**, see page 232.*

- as an adjective, as in English. As with all adjectives in French, the ending <u>DOES</u> change in the feminine and plural forms.

le soleil <u>couchant</u>	the setting sun
l'année <u>suivante</u>	the following year
Ces enfants sont <u>énervants</u>.	Those children are annoying.
des chaises <u>pliantes</u>	folding chairs

Tip
The French present participle is <u>NEVER</u> used to translate English verb forms like *I was walking, we are leaving*.

⇨ *For more information on the **Imperfect tense** and the **Present tense**, see pages 128 and 98*

➤ English verbs describing movement that are followed by an adverb such as *out* or *down*, or a preposition such as *across* or *up* are often translated by a verb + **en** + present participle.

Il est sorti en courant.   He ran out. (*literally*: *He came out running*.)

J'ai traversé la rue en boîtant.   I limped across the street.
                                                  (*literally*: *I crossed the street limping*.)

Forming the present participle

➤ To form the present participle of regular **-er**, **-ir** and **-re** verbs, you use the **nous** form of the present tense and replace the **-ons** ending with **-ant**.

nous form of present tense	Take off -ons	Add -ant
donnons	donn-	donnant
lançons	lanç-	lançant
mangeons	mange-	mangeant
finissons	finiss-	finissant
partons	part-	partant
attendons	attend-	attendant
descendons	descend-	descendant

Irregular verbs

➤ Three verbs have an irregular present participle:

avoir (meaning *to have*)   → **ayant**

être (meaning *to be*)   → **étant**

savoir (meaning *to know*)   → **sachant**

KEY POINTS

✔ Present participles are never used to form tenses in French, but they can be used as verbs, either on their own or after **en**.

✔ They can also be used as adjectives, in which case they agree with the noun they describe.

✔ They are formed by taking the nous form of the present tense and replacing the **-ons** ending with **-ant**. The exceptions are **avoir**, **être** and **savoir**.

Test yourself

52 **Ces enfants sont énervants is another way of saying Ces enfants m'énervent. Change the sentences to this first pattern, replacing the highlighted verb with the same tense of être + a participle adjective.**

a   Ce problème **m'ennuie**. ....

b   Il **les amuse**, ce comique. ....

c   Leur offre **me tente**. ....

d   La promenade **nous a fatigués**. ....

e   Ça **me surprendrait**. ....

f   La situation **l'inquiétait**. ....

g   Leur comportement **me choque**. ....

h   Ses résultats **nous ont déçus**. ....

i   Le retard **l'a exaspéré**. ....

j   Ses idées **m'intéressent**. ....

53 **Using the elements provided make a sentence in the perfect tense, with en followed by a participle.**

a   le bébé/se réveiller/en/pleurer ....

b   les garçons/sortir/en/courir ....

c   mon amie/entrer/en/sourire ....

d   il/prendre/le cadeau/en/faire/semblant d'en être ravi

....

e   je/se couper/le doigt/en/ouvrir/une boîte de conserve

....

f   elle/rire/en/voir/cette image ....

g   l'enfant/s'endormir/en/regarder/la télé

....

h   je/envoyer/des SMS/en/attendre/mes amis

....

i   il/perdre/du poids/en/manger/un peu moins

....

j   il/traverser/la rue/en/courir/sans regarder

....

Test yourself

54 Fill the gap with the present participle of the verb.

a Ne .... pas quoi dire, je suis resté muet. **(savoir)**

b Le .... tout seul, elle est allée lui parler. **(voir)**

c .... chauffeur de taxi, je rencontre beaucoup de personnes. **(être)**

d .... des soucis financiers, il m'a demandé de l'argent. **(avoir)**

e Elle est montée dans la voiture .... que c'était un taxi. **(croire)**

f Nous avons invité vingt personnes, la plupart .... des collègues. **(être)**

g En.................... sa voix, j'ai raccroché. **(entendre)**

h Ne .... pas venir, elle a envoyé des fleurs. **(pouvoir)**

i Ne .... pas de place de stationnement, nous sommes partis. **(trouver)**

j En.................... notre clé, nous avons trouvé une bague. **(chercher)**

55 Match the two halves of the sentence

a En attendant ses copains   il a vu qu'il neigeait.

b En tombant dans l'escalier   il a tout de suite téléphoné à sa femme.

c En regardant par la fenêtre   il est devenu furieux.

d En lisant l'e-mail de son patron   il a bu une bière.

e En entendant la nouvelle   il s'est fait mal.

Impersonal verbs

> | **What is an impersonal verb?** |
> |---|
> | An **impersonal verb** is one that does not refer to a real person or thing and where the subject is represented by *it*, for example, *It's going to rain; It's ten o'clock.* |

➤ Impersonal verbs are only used with **il** (meaning *it*) and in the infinitive. They are called impersonal verbs because **il** does not really refer to a real person, animal or thing, just like *it* and *there* in English in the examples below.

Il pleut.	It's raining.
Il va pleuvoir.	It's going to rain.
Il y a un problème.	There's a problem.
Il pourrait y avoir un problème.	There could be a problem.

➤ There are also some very common verbs that can be used in this way in addition to their normal meanings, for example, **avoir**, **être** and **faire**.

Infinitive	Expression	Meaning
avoir + noun	**il y a**	there is (*singular*) there are (*plural*)
être + time	**il est**	it is
faire + noun	**il fait jour** **il fait nuit**	it's daylight it's dark
falloir + noun	**il faut**	we/you *etc.* need it takes
falloir + infinitive	**il faut**	we/you *etc.* have to
manquer	**il manque**	there is ... missing (*singular*) there are ... missing (*plural*)
paraître	**il paraît que**	people say that rumour has it that
rester + noun	**il reste**	there is ... left (*singular*) there are ... left (*plural*)
sembler	**il semble que**	it appears that it seems that
valoir mieux + infinitive	**il vaut mieux**	it would be better to

Il y a quelqu'un à la porte.	There's somebody at the door.
Il est deux heures.	It's two o'clock.
Il faut partir.	I've/We've *etc.* got to go.
Il manque cent euros.	100 euros are missing.
Il reste du pain.	There's some bread left.
Il vaut mieux ne rien dire.	It would be better to say nothing.

➤ Several impersonal verbs relate to the weather.

Infinitive	Expression	Meaning
faire + adjective	**il fait beau** **il fait mauvais**	the weather's lovely the weather's bad
faire + noun	**il fait du vent** **il fait du soleil**	it's windy it's sunny
geler	**il gèle**	it's freezing
neiger	**il neige**	it's snowing
pleuvoir	**il pleut**	it's raining

Grammar Extra!
There is another group of useful expressions that start with an impersonal **il**.
These are followed by a form of the verb called the <u>subjunctive</u>.

il faut que	
Il faut que je <u>parte</u>.	I've got to go.
il est nécessaire que	
Il est nécessaire que le comité <u>prenne</u> une décision rapidement.	The committee has to take a decision quickly.
il est possible que	
Il est possible qu'il <u>vienne</u>.	He might come.
il est dommage que	
Il est dommage que tu ne l'<u>aies</u> pas vu.	It's a shame you didn't see him.

⇨ *For more information on the **Subjunctive**, see page 178.*

KEY POINTS
✔ Impersonal verbs can only be used in the infinitive and the **il** form.
✔ **il faut**, **il y a**, **il est** and **il fait** with expressions relating to the weather are
   very common.

Test yourself

56 Translate the sentence into French.

a   There are five people in my family. ....

b   There is a factory near their house. ....

c   There has been an accident. ....

d   There was somebody at the door. ....

e   There will be lots to do. ....

f   There are some sandwiches left. ....

g   You've got to be careful. (*Use il faut*.) ....

h   Two bags are missing. ....

i   It would be better to tell the truth. ....

j   It seems that everything's going well. ....

57 Fill the gap with il + the verb shown in brackets.

a   Réveille-toi, ... huit heures!   **(être)**

b   Il est tard, ... aller au lit.   **(falloir)**

c   .... minuit quand nous nous sommes couchés.   **(être)**

d   Mince alors! .... encore du papier dans la photocopieuse.   **(manquer)**

e   Attendez, ... quelques détails à régler.   **(rester)**

f   .... nuit tôt en hiver.   **(faire)**

g   Hier nous avons fait une promenade parce qu' .... beau.   **(faire)**

h   .... que ce soit la faute de la direction.   **(sembler)**

i   Malheureusement tout n'est pas résolu. .... un gros problème.   **(rester)**

j   C'est une nette amélioration, ... le dire.   **(falloir)**

58 Match the related sentences.

a   **Je ne peux pas prendre une douche.**   Il y a des cafards dans mon appartement.

b   **Je déménage.**   Il n'y avait rien à voir.

c   **J'ai dû m'asseoir par terre.**   Il n'y avait pas de problèmes.

d   **Tout s'est très bien passé.**   Il n'y avait pas assez de chaises.

e   **Je me suis ennuyé au château.**   Il n'y a pas d'eau chaude.

Test yourself

59 Cross out phrases that could not complete the sentence.

a	Il faut	se dépêcher/neiger/sortir le chien/le voir
b	Il ne reste plus de	papier toilette/cerises/pluie/pain
c	Il y a	la grenouille/deux enfants à la porte/ un chien sous la table
d	Il est	trois heures/midi/nuit/minuit
e	Il fait	beau/froid/du vent/de la pluie
f	Il faisait déjà	33 degrés/nuit/très chaud/une heure
g	Il faut que tu	vas au bureau/ailles au bureau/rentres chez toi/ restes ici
h	Il est dommage qu'il ne	puisse pas venir/soit pas ici/fait pas beau/fasse pas beau
i	Il est possible qu'il	pleuve/pleut/neige/fasse du soleil
j	Il faut que je	le dis /le dise/le fais/le fasse

Grammar Extra!

The subjunctive

> ### What is the subjunctive?
> The **subjunctive** is a verb form that is used in certain circumstances to express some sort of feeling, or to show there is doubt about whether something will happen or whether something is true. It is only used occasionally in modern English, for example, *If I were you, I wouldn't bother.; So be it.*

Using the subjunctive

➤ In French the subjunctive is used after certain verbs and conjunctions when two parts of a sentence have different subjects.

I'm afraid <u>he</u> won't come back.
(The subject of the first part of the sentence is 'I'; the subject of the second part of the sentence is 'he'.)

➤ Sometimes, in a sentence like *We want her to be happy*, you use the infinitive of the verb in English (*to be*). This is <u>NOT</u> possible in French when there is a different subject in the two parts of the sentence (*we* and *her*). You have to use a subjunctive for the second verb.

Nous voulons être heureux. We want to be happy.
*(No change of subject, so you can just use an infinitive – **être** – in French.)*
Nous voulons qu'elle soit heureuse. We want her to be happy.
*(Subject changes from **nous** to **elle**, so you have to use a subjunctive – **soit** – in French.)*

➤ In the case of impersonal verbs, the infinitive can be used instead of the subjunctive.

Il faut que tu <u>viennes</u> à l'heure. → **Il faut <u>venir</u> à l'heure.**
  (using subjunctive)   *(using infinitive)*
You have to come on time.
Il vaut mieux que tu <u>restes</u> chez toi. → **Il vaut mieux <u>rester</u> chez toi.**
  (using subjunctive)   *(using infinitive)*
It's better that you stay at home.

Coming across the subjunctive

➤ The subjunctive has several tenses but you are mainly likely to come across the present subjunctive.

➤ You may see a subjunctive after certain verbs when you are:

- wishing something: **vouloir que** and **désirer que** (meaning *to wish that, to want*), **aimer mieux que** and **préférer que** (meaning *to prefer that*)

- fearing something: **avoir peur que** (meaning *to be afraid that*)

- giving your opinion in the negative: **ne croire que** (meaning *not to think that*)

- saying how you feel: **regretter que** (meaning *to be sorry that*), **être content que** (meaning *to be pleased that*), **être surpris que** (meaning *to be surprised that*) and so on
  Je suis content que vous les <u>aimiez</u>.   I'm pleased you like them.
  J'ai peur qu'il ne <u>revienne</u> pas.   I'm afraid he won't come back.

➤ You may see a subjunctive after certain verbal expressions starting with **il**, such as **il faut que** (meaning *it is necessary that*) and **il vaut mieux que** (meaning *it is better that*).
  Il faut que je <u>sois</u> prudent.   I need to be careful.

⇨ *For a list of some expressions requiring the subjunctive, see page 178.*

Forming the present subjunctive of -er verbs

➤ To form the stem of the present subjunctive you take the <u>infinitive</u> and chop off **-er**, just as for the present tense. Then you add the correct ending, depending on whether you are referring to **je**, **tu**, **il**, **elle**, **on**, **nous**, **vous**, **ils** or **elles**.

➤ For **-er** verbs the endings are the same as for the ordinary present tense, apart from the **nous** and **vous** forms, which have an extra **i**, as in the imperfect tense.

Pronoun	Ending	Add to stem, e.g. donn-	Meanings
je (j')	-e	je donn<u>e</u>	I give
tu	-es	tu donn<u>es</u>	you give
il elle on	-e	il donn<u>e</u> elle donn<u>e</u> on donn<u>e</u>	he/she/it/ one gives
nous	-ions	nous donn<u>ions</u>	we give
vous	-iez	vous donn<u>iez</u>	you give
ils elles	-ent	ils donn<u>ent</u> elles donn<u>ent</u>	they give

Tip
je changes to **j'** in front of a word starting with a vowel, most words starting with **h**, and the French word **y**.

Forming the present subjunctive of -ir verbs

➤ To form the stem of the present subjunctive you take the <u>infinitive</u> and chop off **-ir**, just as for the present tense. Then you add the correct ending, depending on whether you are referring to to **je**, **tu**, **il**, **elle**, **on**, **nous**, **vous**, **ils** or **elles**.

Pronoun	Ending	Add to stem, e.g. fin-	Meanings
je (j')	-isse	je fin<u>isse</u>	I finish
tu	-isses	tu fin<u>isses</u>	you finish
il elle on	-isse	il fin<u>isse</u> elle fin<u>isse</u> on fin<u>isse</u>	he/she/it/ one finishes
nous	-issions	nous fin<u>issions</u>	we finish
vous	-issiez	vous fin<u>issiez</u>	you finish
ils elles	-issent	ils fin<u>issent</u> elles fin<u>issent</u>	they finish

> *Tip*
> **je** changes to **j'** in front of a word starting with a vowel, most words starting with **h**, and the French word **y**.

Forming the present subjunctive of -re verbs

➤ To form the stem of the present subjunctive you take the <u>infinitive</u> and chop off **-re**, just as for the present tense. Then you add the correct ending, depending on whether you are referring to **je**, **tu**, **il**, **elle**, **on**, **nous**, **vous**, **ils** or **elles**.

Pronoun	Ending	Add to stem, e.g. attend-	Meanings
je (j')	-e	j'attend<u>e</u>	I wait
tu	-es	tu attend<u>es</u>	you wait
il elle on	-e	il attend<u>e</u> elle attend<u>e</u> on attend<u>e</u>	he/she/it/ one waits
nous	-ions	nous attend<u>ions</u>	we wait
vous	-iez	vous attend<u>iez</u>	you wait
ils elles	-ent	ils attend<u>ent</u> elles attend<u>ent</u>	they wait

> *Tip*
> **je** changes to **j'** in front of a word starting with a vowel, most words starting with **h**, and the French word **y**.

Irregular verbs in the subjunctive

➤ Some important verbs have irregular subjunctive forms.

Verb	Meaning	je (j')	tu	il/elle/on	nous	vous	ils/elles
aller	*to go*	aille	ailles	aille	allions	alliez	aillent
avoir	*to have*	aie	aies	ait	ayons	ayez	aient
devoir	*to have to, must*	doive	doives	doive	devions	deviez	doivent
dire	*to say, to tell*	dise	dises	dise	disions	disiez	disent
être	*to be*	sois	sois	soit	soyons	soyez	soient
faire	*to do, to make*	fasse	fasses	fasse	fassions	fassiez	fassent
pouvoir	*to be able to, can*	puisse	puisses	puisse	puissions	puissiez	puissent
prendre	*to take*	prenne	prennes	prenne	prenions	preniez	prennent
(apprendre and **comprendre** also behave like this – **j'apprenne, tu apprennes** and so on)							
savoir	*to know*	sache	saches	sache	sachions	sachiez	sachent
venir	*to come*	vienne	viennes	vienne	venions	veniez	viennent
vouloir	*to want to*	veuille	veuilles	veuille	voulions	vouliez	veuillent

KEY POINTS

✔ After certain verbs you have to use a subjunctive in French when there is a different subject in the two clauses. These verbs mostly relate to wishing, fearing, and saying what you think or what you feel or saying that you are uncertain. A subjunctive is also found after certain verbal expressions that start with **il**.

✔ The stem of the present tense subjunctive is the same as the stem used for the ordinary present tense.

✔ The present tense subjunctive endings for **-er** and **-re** verbs are:
-e, **-es**, **-e**, **-ions**, **-iez** and **-ent**.

✔ The present tense subjunctive endings for **-ir** verbs are:
-isse, **-isses**, **-isse**, **-issions**, **-issiez** and **-issent**.

60 Complete the sentence with the correct form of the present subjunctive.

a Il faut que vous lui .... **(parler)**

b Il vaut mieux que nous .... à l'hôtel. **(rester)**

c Il est nécessaire qu'elle .... avant nous. **(partir)**

d Il faut que je .... à temps. **(finir)**

e Ils veulent que je .... contente. **(être)**

f Je suis surprise qu'elle .... d'accord. **(être)**

g As-tu peur qu'il ne le .... pas? **(rendre)**

h Je ne veux pas que vous .... des bêtises. **(faire)**

i Nous sommes très contents qu'il .... venir. **(pouvoir)**

j Il faut que tu .... ici. **(attendre)**

61 Match the sentences that have the same meaning.

a **Je dois le lire.**   Je regrette qu'il pleuve.

b **Ils doivent partir maintenant.**   Il faut que je le lise.

c **Vous pouvez le faire? J'en suis**   Il faut qu'ils partent maintenant.
      contente.

d **Il pleut? C'est dommage.**   Il est possible qu'il soit déjà arrivé.

e **Il est peut-être déjà arrivé.**   Je suis contente que vous puissiez le faire.

Test yourself

62 Cross out the unlikely options.

a   Je regrette que ça te fasse   du bien/mal/peur/plaisir

b   Ils sont contents qu'elle soit   arrivée à l'heure/guérie/avec eux/dyslexique

c   Il faut que vous   fassiez attention/restiez là/
                                              conduire prudemment/rouliez moins vite

d   Il vaut mieux qu'il dise   des bêtises/la vérité/quelques mots/
                                              des mensonges

e   Je suis surprise que vous   le meilleur/le plus grand/le plus mauvais/
    n'ayez pas choisi   le plus ennuyant

f   Nous voulons que vous soyez   malades/fatigués/mécontents/satisfaits

g   Elle a peur qu'il   fasse mauvais temps/ne l'aime plus/
                                              soit sympathique/mente

h   Je préfère que vous   n'en parliez pas/soyez sincère/
                                              le gardiez pour vous/mentiez

i   Ils craignent que Luc n'aie pas   raison/tort/menti/peur

j   Il est dommage qu'il   soit parti/fasse beau temps/soit si bon/
                                              ne soit pas d'accord

63 Formulate a sentence using the elements provided

a   il faut/que/vous/revenir/l'année prochaine

    ....

b   il faut que/je/se coucher ....

c   je/être/content/que/il/être/ici ....

d   tu/être/surprise/que/je/avoir/peur? ....

e   ils/vouloir/que/nous/rester/chez nous

    ....

f   je/avoir/peur/que/elle/perdre/du temps

    ....

g   nous/craindre/que/elle/être/malade ....

h   il/vouloir/que/nous/payer/le...

i   tu/être/contente/que/on/finir/aujourd'hui?

    ....

j   je/regretter/que/il/faire/si mauvais temps

    ....

Verbs followed by an infinitive

Linking two verbs together

➤ Many verbs in French can be followed by another verb in the infinitive. The infinitive is the form of the verb that is found in the dictionary, such as **donner** (meaning *to give*), **finir** (meaning *to finish*) and **attendre** (meaning *to wait*).

➤ There are three main ways that verbs can be linked together:

- with no linking word
  Vous voulez attendre?　　　　　Would you like to wait?

- with the preposition **à**
  J'apprends <u>à</u> nager.　　　　　I'm learning to swim.

- with the preposition **de**
  Essayez <u>de</u> venir.　　　　　Try to come.

  ⇨ *For more information on **Prepositions after adjectives**, and on **Prepositions after verbs**, see pages 246 and 240.*

Verbs followed by an infinitive with no preposition

➤ A number of verbs and groups of verbs can be followed by an infinitive with no preposition. The following important group of verbs are all very irregular, but they crop up so frequently that they are worth learning in full:

- **devoir** (*to have to, must, to be due to*)
  Tu <u>dois être</u> fatiguée.　　　　　You must be tired.
  Elle <u>doit partir</u>.　　　　　She has to leave.
  Le nouveau centre commercial　　　The new shopping centre is due to
  　<u>doit ouvrir</u> en mai.　　　　　　open in May.

- **pouvoir** (*can, may*)
  Je <u>peux</u> t'<u>aider</u>, si tu veux.　　　I can help you, if you like.
  <u>Puis-je venir</u> vous voir samedi?　May I come and see you on Saturday?

- **savoir** (*to know how to, can*)
  Tu <u>sais conduire</u>?　　　　　Can you drive?
  Je <u>sais faire</u> les omelettes.　　I know how to make omelettes.

- **vouloir** (*to want*)
  Élise <u>veut rester</u> un jour de plus.　Élise wants to stay one more day.
  Ma voiture ne <u>veut</u> pas <u>démarrer</u>.　My car won't start.
  <u>Voulez</u>-vous <u>boire</u> quelque chose?　Would you like something to drink?
  Je <u>voudrais acheter</u> un ordinateur.　I'd like to buy a computer.

➤ **falloir** (meaning *to be necessary*) and **valoir mieux** (meaning *to be better*) are only used in the infinitive and with **il**.

Il faut prendre une décision.	We/you *etc*. have to make a decision.
Il vaut mieux téléphoner avant.	It's better to ring first.

⇨ *For more information on **Impersonal verbs**, see page 174.*

➤ The following common verbs can also be followed by an infinitive <u>without</u> a preposition:

adorer	to love
aimer	to like, to love
aimer mieux	to prefer
désirer	to want
détester	to hate
envoyer	to send
espérer	to hope
faire	to make
laisser	to let
préférer	to prefer
sembler	to seem

J'espère te voir la semaine prochaine.	I hope to see you next week.
Ne me fais pas rire!	Don't make me laugh!
Je préfère manger à la cantine.	I prefer to eat in the canteen.

➤ Some of these verbs combine with infinitives to make set phrases with a special meaning.

aller chercher quelque chose	to go and get something
laisser tomber quelque chose	to drop something
vouloir dire quelque chose	to mean something
faire faire quelque chose	to have something done

Va chercher ton papa!	Go and get your dad!
Paul a laissé tomber le vase.	Paul dropped the vase.
Qu'est-ce que ça veut dire?	What does that mean?
J'ai fait réparer mes chaussures.	I've had my shoes mended.

➤ Verbs that relate to seeing or hearing, such as **voir** (meaning *to see*), **regarder** (meaning *to watch, to look at*), **écouter** (meaning *to listen to*) and **entendre** (meaning *to hear*) can be followed by an infinitive.

Il nous a vus arriver.	He saw us arrive.
On entend chanter les oiseaux.	You can hear the birds singing.

➤ Verbs that relate to movement of some kind and do not have a direct object, such as **aller** (meaning *to go*) and **venir** (meaning *to come*), can be followed by an infinitive.

Je vais voir Nicolas ce soir.	I'm going to see Nicolas tonight.
Viens voir!	Come and see!

Verbs followed by à + infinitive

➤ There are some common verbs that can be followed by **à** and an infinitive.

s'amuser <u>à</u> faire quelque chose	to have fun doing something
apprendre <u>à</u> faire quelque chose	to learn to do something
commencer <u>à</u> faire quelque chose	to begin to do something
continuer <u>à</u> faire quelque chose	to go on doing something
s'habituer <u>à</u> faire quelque chose	to get used to doing something

J'apprends <u>à</u> skier.	I'm learning to ski.
Il a commencé <u>à</u> pleuvoir.	It began to rain.

➤ Some verbs can be followed by a person's name or by a noun relating to a person, and then by **à** and an infinitive. Sometimes you need to put **à** in front of the person too.

aider quelqu'un <u>à</u> faire quelque chose	to help someone do something
apprendre <u>à</u> quelqu'un <u>à</u> faire quelque chose	to teach someone to do something
inviter quelqu'un <u>à</u> faire quelque chose	to invite someone to do something

Verbs followed by de + infinitive

➤ There are some common verbs that can be followed by **de** and an infinitive.

arrêter <u>de</u> faire quelque chose, s'arrêter <u>de</u> faire quelque chose	to stop doing something
continuer <u>de</u> faire quelque chose	to go on doing something
décider <u>de</u> faire quelque chose	to decide to do something
se dépêcher <u>de</u> faire quelque chose	to hurry to do something
essayer <u>de</u> faire quelque chose	to try to do something
s'excuser <u>de</u> faire quelque chose	to apologize for doing something
finir <u>de</u> faire quelque chose	to finish doing something
oublier <u>de</u> faire quelque chose	to forget to do something
proposer <u>de</u> faire quelque chose	to suggest doing something
refuser <u>de</u> faire quelque chose	to refuse to do something
suggérer <u>de</u> faire quelque chose	to suggest doing something

J'<u>ai décidé de</u> lui écrire.	I decided to write to her.
Je leur <u>ai suggéré de</u> partir de bonne heure.	I suggested that they set off early.

➤ The following verbs meaning asking or telling are also followed by **de** and an infinitive. Sometimes you need to put **à** in front of the person you are asking or telling.

commander <u>à</u> quelqu'un <u>de</u> faire quelque chose	to order someone to do something
demander <u>à</u> quelqu'un <u>de</u> faire quelque chose	to ask someone to do something

For further explanation of grammatical terms, please see pages viii–xii.

dire <u>à</u> quelqu'un <u>de</u> faire quelque chose	to tell someone to do something
empêcher quelqu'un <u>de</u> faire quelque chose	to prevent someone from doing something
remercier quelqu'un <u>de</u> faire quelque chose	to thank someone for doing something
interdire <u>à</u> quelqu'un <u>de</u> faire quelque chose	to forbid someone to do something

---

Grammar Extra!

If it is important to emphasize that something is going on at a particular time, you can use the phrase **être en train de faire quelque chose**.

Il <u>est en train de travailler</u>. Est-ce que vous pouvez rappeler plus tard?	He's working. Can you call back later?

If you want to say you have just done something, you can use the phrase **venir de faire quelque chose**. In English you use the <u>PAST</u> tense, but in French you use the <u>PRESENT</u> tense.

Élisabeth <u>vient de partir</u>.	Élisabeth has just left.

> ### KEY POINTS
> ✔ Many French verbs can be followed by another verb in the infinitive.
> ✔ The two verbs may be linked by nothing at all, or by the prepositions à or **de**.
> ✔ The construction in French does not always match the English exactly. It's best to learn these constructions when you learn a new verb.

64 Translate the sentence into French.

a   The girls must be very disappointed. ....

b   I adore dancing. ....

c   He hates washing up. ....

d   Are you going to get some bread? (*Use tu*.)

     ....

e   She dropped her mobile phone. ....

f   We were watching the children playing in the garden.

     ....

g   I'm going to speak to Nicole. ....

h   She sent me to buy a paper. ....

i   What do you mean, sir? ....

j   He likes cooking. ....

65 Fill the gap with à or de.

a   Ma mère m'a appris .... lire.

b   J'essaye .... l'oublier.

c   Nous nous sommes habitués .... nous lever tôt.

d   Il a continué .... travailler jusqu'à minuit.

e   Nous avons oublié .... payer la facture.

f   Tu peux m'aider .... ranger la cuisine?

g   Ils ont décidé .... vendre leur voiture.

h   J'apprends .... conduire.

i   Alors, vous refusez .... nous aider?

j   Il nous a invités .... nous asseoir à sa table.

Test yourself

66 **Il est en train de travailler** is another way of saying **Il travaille**. Replace the highlighted verb with a phrase containing **en train de**.

a   Elle **parle** avec un client. ....

b   Les enfants **font** leurs devoirs. ....

c   Je **mets** le couvert. ....

d   Nous **buvons** un café. ....

e   **Je me lavais** les cheveux. ....

f   Ils **construisent** un nouveau garage. ....

g   Son père **lisait** son bulletin scolaire. ....

h   Elle **écrit** une carte postale à son petit ami. ....

i   Je lui **envoie** un SMS. ....

j   Il **repeint** la cuisine. ....

67 **Match the two halves of the sentence.**

a   **Le bruit**   m'a encouragé à demander une augmentation de salaire.

b   **Le professeur**   m'a demandé de laver sa voiture.

c   **La voisine**   m'a dit de me taire.

d   **Ma copine**   m'a empêché de dormir.

e   **Mon collègue**   m'a remercié d'avoir sorti son chien.

Other uses of the infinitive

➤ The infinitive can be used in many other ways:

- after certain adjectives

content de	happy to
prêt à	ready to

  Il est toujours <u>prêt à rendre</u> service. He's always ready to help.

- after certain prepositions

  <u>Pour aller</u> à la gare? How do you get to the station?
  Il est parti <u>sans dire</u> au revoir. He left without saying goodbye.

- after certain set phrases involving a verb plus a noun

avoir envie de <u>faire</u> quelque chose	to feel like doing something
avoir besoin de <u>faire</u> quelque chose	to need to do something
avoir peur de <u>faire</u> quelque chose	to be frightened of doing something

  J'ai besoin de <u>changer</u> de l'argent. I need to change some money.

- in instructions that are aimed at the general public – for example, on signs or in cookery books

  <u>Ajouter</u> le sel et le poivre, et bien <u>mélanger</u>. Add the salt and pepper, and mix well.
  <u>Conserver</u> au frais. Keep refrigerated.

- as the subject or object of a sentence, when the infinitive corresponds to the -*ing* form in English used as a noun

  <u>Fumer</u> n'est pas bon pour la santé. Smoking isn't good for your health.
  J'adore <u>lire</u>. I love reading.

Tip

You can use the verb **faire** with an infinitive to refer to something you are having done by someone else.

Je dois <u>faire réparer</u> ma voiture. I have to get my car repaired.

KEY POINTS

✔ Infinitives are found after certain adjectives, prepositions and set phrases, and in instructions to the general public.
✔ They can also function like nouns, as the subject or object of another verb.

Test yourself

68 Translate the sentence into French.

a I feel like going to the cinema. ....

b I need to buy some stamps. ....

c Don't cross the road without looking, Aurélie.

....

d We are ready to leave. ....

e They did it to help us. ....

f They like playing football. ....

g We've got to get the window mended.

....

h I want to get my hair cut. ....

i Push (*sign on a door*) ....

j Add the milk and the eggs. ....

69 Make a sentence with the elements provided.

a je/être/content de/pouvoir/aider/vous

....

b nous/être/désolé de/décevoir/te

....

c je/avoir/peur/de/faire/le/sans/demander/lui/la permission

....

d hier/tu/partir/sans/remercier/la

....

e elle/être/sûr de/comprendre/te

....

f vous/avoir/besoin/de/aller/y? ....

g nager/faire/du bien..

h la semaine prochaine/on/avoir/besoin/de/se détendre

....

i je/téléphoner/pour/savoir/à quelle heure/vous/arriver/demain

....

j peler/les tomates/c'est difficile

....

Negatives

What is a negative?

A **negative** question or statement is one which contains a word such as *not*, *never* or *nothing* and is used to say that something is not happening, is not true or is absent.

Using negatives

➤ In English we use words like *not*, *no*, *nothing* and *never* to show a negative.

I'm <u>not</u> very pleased.
Dan <u>never</u> rang me.
<u>Nothing</u> ever happens here!
There's <u>no</u> milk left.

➤ *Not* is often abbreviated and combined with certain English verbs – for example, *can't*, *won't*, *didn't*, *hasn't*.

He <u>isn't</u> joking.
She <u>didn't</u> say.

➤ In French, if you want to make something negative, you generally use a pair of words, for example, **ne ... pas** (meaning *not*). The verb goes in the middle.

ne ... pas	not
ne ... rien	nothing, not ... anything
ne ... personne	nobody, no one, not ... anybody, not ... anyone
ne ... jamais	never, not ... ever
ne ... plus	no longer, no more, not ... any longer, not ... any more

Je <u>ne</u> fume <u>pas</u>.	I don't smoke.
<u>Ne</u> changez <u>rien</u>.	Don't change anything.
Je <u>ne</u> vois <u>personne</u>.	I can't see anybody.
Elle <u>n'</u>arrive <u>jamais</u> à l'heure.	She never arrives on time.
Il <u>ne</u> travaille <u>plus</u> ici.	He's no longer working here.

Tip
ne changes to **n'** in front of a word that starts with a vowel, most words beginning with **h** and the French word **y**.

➤ In English, *didn't* is often used to make a statement negative.

I went to his party. → I did<u>n't</u> go to his party.
We saw David at the weekend. → We did<u>n't</u> see David at the weekend.

⚠ Note that the French verb **faire** is <u>NEVER</u> used in this way.

➤ **non plus** is the equivalent of English *neither* in phrases like *me neither*, *neither do I* and so on.

'Je n'aime pas les hamburgers.' —	'I don't like hamburgers.' — 'Me neither.'
'Moi <u>non plus</u>.'	
Il n'y va pas et moi <u>non plus</u>.	He isn't going and neither am I.

For further explanation of grammatical terms, please see pages viii–xii.

➤ The French word **ne** is missed out when negatives are used without a verb to answer a question.

'Qui a téléphoné?' — 'Personne.'	'Who rang?' — 'Nobody.'
'Qu'est-ce que tu fais cet après-midi?' — 'Rien.'	'What are you doing this afternoon?' — 'Nothing.'

> *Tip*
> In everyday conversation French native speakers often miss out the word **ne**. Be careful about doing this yourself in formal situations.
>
> | | |
> |---|---|
> | **Je peux pas venir ce soir.** | I can't come tonight. |
> | **Il me l'a pas dit.** | He didn't tell me. |

Grammar Extra!
Sometimes you will find two of these negative expressions combined.

Ils ne font jamais rien d'intéressant.	They never do anything interesting.
Je ne connais plus personne à Nice.	I don't know anyone in Nice any more.

Word order with negatives

➤ Negative expressions in French 'sandwich' the verb in the present tense and in other tenses that consist of just one word. **ne** goes before the verb and the other half of the expression comes after the verb.

Il _ne_ boit _jamais_ d'alcool.	He never drinks alcohol.
Il _ne_ pleuvait _pas_.	It wasn't raining.

➤ In the perfect tense and other tenses that consist of two or more words such as the pluperfect, there are two possibilities:

- **ne … pas**, **ne … rien**, **ne … plus** and **ne … jamais** follow the pattern: **ne (n')** + **avoir** or **être** + **pas/rien/plus/jamais** + past participle

Elle _n'a pas_ fait ses devoirs.	She hasn't done her homework.
Je _n'ai rien_ dit.	I didn't say anything.
Pierre _n'est pas_ encore arrivé.	Pierre isn't here yet.

- **ne … personne** follows the pattern: **ne (n')** + **avoir** + past participle + **personne**

Je _n'ai vu personne_.	I didn't see anybody.

⇨ *For more information on the **Perfect tense**, see page 151.*

➤ A negative sentence may also contain a pronoun such as **te**, **le**, **lui** and so on that is the direct or indirect object of the verb, or a reflexive pronoun. If so, **ne** comes before the pronoun.

Je _ne_ t'entends _pas_.	I can't hear you.
_Ne_ lui parle _pas_!	Don't speak to him/her!
Tu _ne_ te souviens _pas_ de lui?	Don't you remember him?
Il _ne_ se lève _jamais_ avant midi.	He never gets up before midday.

⇨ *For more information on **Direct** and **Indirect object pronouns** and on **Reflexive pronouns**, see pages 61, 65 and 124.*

➤ When a verb is in the infinitive, **ne ... pas**, **ne ... rien**, **ne ... plus** and **ne ... jamais** come together before the infinitive.

Il essayait de <u>ne pas</u> rire.	He was trying not to laugh.
J'ai peur de <u>ne pas</u> réussir.	I'm afraid of not succeeding.

Tip

After these negative expressions, **un**, **une** and **des** (the <u>indefinite article</u>) and **du**, **de la**, **de l'** and **des** (the <u>partitive article</u>) change to **de**.

Il ne reste plus <u>de</u> biscuits.	There aren't any biscuits left.

⇨ *For more information on the **Indefinite article** and the **Partitive article**, see pages 23 and 27*

---

non and pas

➤ **non** (meaning *no*) is the usual negative answer to a question. It can also correspond to *not* in English.

'Tu veux nous accompagner?' —	'Do you want to come with us?' —
'<u>Non</u>, merci.'	'<u>No</u> thanks.'
Tu viens ou <u>non</u>?	Are you coming or <u>not</u>?
J'espère que <u>non</u>.	I hope <u>not</u>.

➤ **pas** is generally used on its own when a distinction is being made, or for emphasis. It, too, often corresponds to *not* in English.

'Qui veut m'aider?' — '<u>Pas</u> moi!'	'Who wants to help me?' — '<u>Not</u> me!'
'Est-il de retour?' — '<u>Pas</u> encore.'	'Is he back?' — '<u>Not</u> yet.'
'Tu as froid?' — '<u>Pas</u> du tout.'	'Are you cold?' — '<u>Not</u> at all.'
<u>Pas</u> question!	<u>No</u> way!

KEY POINTS

✔ Negatives indicate when something is not happening or is not true. French uses set expressions or word pairs to indicate this.

✔ The two parts of these negative expressions 'sandwich' the verb in tenses consisting of only one word.

✔ **ne** comes before any object pronouns or reflexive pronouns.

✔ Before infinitives, **ne ... pas**, **ne ... rien**, **ne ... plus** and **ne ... jamais** come together.

✔ The articles **un**, **une**, **des**, **du**, **de la** and **de l'** change to **de** after negatives.

Test yourself

1   **Cross out the unlikely options.**

a   Il ne les aime pas.   les asperges/les professeurs/ses amis/fumer

b   Qu'est-ce que tu veux?   rien/jamais/un café/personne

c   Vous allez vous marier quand?   l'année prochaine/jamais/bientôt/
                                                                              moi non plus

d   Qui les accompagne?   je ne sais pas/rien/pas moi/personne

e   Je ne suis pas d'accord.   ce n'est pas mal/nous non plus/
                                                                              ça ne m'étonne pas/ne le regarde pas!

f   Qu'est-ce que vous avez fait   rien d'intéressant/je ne me rappelle plus/
        ce week-end?   rien du tout/rien de mieux

g   Combien tu l'as payée,   trop/ça ne te regarde pas/ne la regarde pas!/
        cette voiture?   dix mille euros

h   Tu utilises souvent ta machine   jamais/je ne l'ai plus/je n'ai plus le temps/
        à coudre?   je ne sais pas

i   Il a l'air en forme.   Il ne va plus à la gym/il ne fait jamais de sport/
                                                                              il ne mange pas de salade/il ne fume plus

j   Ils sont déjà allés en Provence?   ils n'y vont plus/jamais/non, je ne crois pas/
                                                                              moi non plus

2   **Make a negative sentence with the elements provided.**

a   je/voir/jamais/la ....

b   ça/intéresser/plus/me ....

c   s'inquiéter/pas/monsieur! ....

d   tu/avoir/rien/à faire? ....

e   ils/avoir/pas/finir/encore ....

f   elle/avoir/rien/dire/me ....

g   tu/devoir/pas/être/en retard ....

h   nous/manger/jamais/de viande ....

i   je/avoir/pas/voir/les/aujourd'hui ....

j   ce/être/pas/ma faute! ....

Test yourself

3 Translate the sentence into French.

a She doesn't live here any more. ....

b He doesn't understand me. ....

c We don't want to disturb you. ....

d He doesn't need to get up so early. ....

e I don't know anyone here. ....

f You never listen to me. ....

g I'd never liked her. ....

h Try not to spend too much, girls. ....

i There's nobody in the house. ....

j This chocolate – do you want it or not? ....

4 Match the response to the question.

a **La gym?**   Je n'y comprends rien.

b **Benoît?**   Pas question!

c **Du lait?**   Je ne le vois jamais.

d **L'informatique?**   Je n'y vais plus.

e **Te prêter de l'argent?**   Je n'en veux pas.

Questions

What is a question?
A **question** is a sentence which is used to ask someone about something and which normally has the verb in front of the subject. A question word such as *why*, *where*, *who*, *which* or *how* is used to ask a question.

How to ask a question in French

The basic rules

➤ There are four ways of asking questions in French:

- by making your voice go up at the end of the sentence

- by using the phrase **est-ce que**

- by changing round the order of words in a sentence

- by using a question word

Asking a question by making your voice go up

➤ If you are expecting the answer *yes* or *no*, there is a very straightforward way of asking a question. You can keep word order just as it would be in a normal sentence (subject then verb), but turn it into a question by making your voice go up at the end of the sentence. So to turn the sentence **Vous aimez la France** (meaning *You like France*) into a question, all you need to do is to add a question mark and make your voice go up at the end.

Vous (*subject*) **aimez** (*verb*) **la France?**	Do you like France?
On part tout de suite.	We're leaving right away.
On part tout de suite?	Are we leaving right away?
C'est vrai.	That's true.
C'est vrai?	Is that true?
Tes parents sont en vacances.	Your parents on holiday.
Tes parents sont en vacances?	Are your parents on holiday?

> *Tip*
> French speakers use this way of asking a question in ordinary, everyday conversations.

Asking a question by using est-ce que

➤ The phrase **est-ce que** is used to ask a question. Word order stays just the same as it would in an ordinary sentence. **Est-ce que** comes before the subject, and the verb comes after the subject. So to turn the sentence **Tu connais Marie** (meaning *You know Marie*) into a question, all you need to do is to add **est-ce que**.

Est-ce que tu (subject) **connais** (verb) **Marie?**	Do you know Marie?
Est-ce que vous allez en ville?	Are you going into town?
Est-ce que ta sœur est vraiment heureuse?	Is your sister really happy?

Asking a question by changing word order

➤ In ordinary sentences, the verb comes <u>AFTER</u> its subject. In this type of question, the verb is put <u>BEFORE</u> the subject. This change to normal word order is called <u>inversion</u>. You can do this when the subject is a pronoun such as **vous** or **il**. When you change the word order (or <u>invert</u>) in this way, you add a hyphen (-) between the verb and the pronoun.

Vous (subject) **aimez** (verb) **la France.**	You like France.
Aimez (verb)**-vous** (subject) **la France?**	Do you like France?
Il écrit bien.	He writes well.
Écrit-il bien?	Does he write well?
On part tout de suite.	We're leaving right away.
Partez-vous tout de suite?	Are you leaving right away?

⇨ *For more information on* **Pronouns**, *see page 55.*

> *Tip*
> This is quite a formal way of asking a question.

➤ In the perfect tense and other tenses that consist of two or more words such as the pluperfect, the part of the verb that comes from **avoir** or **être** is the one that goes before the pronoun.

As-tu vu mon sac?	Have you seen my bag?
Est-elle restée longtemps?	Did she stay long?

⇨ *For more information on the* **Perfect tense**, *see page 151.*

➤ When the verb ends in a vowel in the **il/elle** form, **-t-** is inserted before the pronoun to make the words easier to say.

Aime-t-il les chiens?	Does he like dogs?
A-t-elle assez d'argent?	Does she have enough money?

> *Tip*
> Unlike English there are two ways in French of answering *yes* to a question or statement. **oui** is the word you use to reply to an ordinary question.
>
> | | |
> |---|---|
> | **'Tu l'as fait?' — 'Oui.'** | 'Have you done it?' — 'Yes.' |
> | **'Elle est belle, n'est-ce pas?' — 'Oui.'** | 'She's beautiful, isn't she?' — 'Yes.' |
>
> **si** is the word you use to reply to a question or statement that contains a negative expression like **ne ... pas**.
>
> | | |
> |---|---|
> | **'Tu ne l'as pas fait?' — 'Si.'** | 'Haven't you done it?' — 'Yes (I have).' |
> | **'Elle n'est pas très belle.' — 'Mais si!'** | 'She isn't very beautiful.' — 'Yes, she is!' |

For further explanation of grammatical terms, please see pages viii–xii.

⇨ *For more information on **Negatives**, see page 192.*

Grammar Extra!

You can also form a question in this way with a noun or a person's name. If you do this, the noun or name comes first, then you add an extra pronoun after the verb and link them with a hyphen.

Jean-Pierre *(subject)* **est** *(verb)* **-il** *(pronoun)* **là?**	Is Jean-Pierre there?
La pièce dure-t-elle longtemps?	Does the play last long?

In less formal French, the pronoun may come before the verb, and the noun or name may come at the end of the sentence.

Il est là, Jean-Pierre?	Is Jean-Pierre there?
Elle dure longtemps, la pièce?	Does the play last long?

Asking a question by using a question word

➤ A question word is a word like *when* or *how* that is used to ask for information. The most common French question words are listed on pages 202–205.

➤ You can use a question word with one of the methods described above:

- you can make your voice go up at the end of the sentence. If you do this, the question word goes at the <u>END</u> of the sentence.

- you can use **est-ce que**. If you do this, the question word goes at the <u>START</u> of the sentence.

- you can change word order so that the verb comes before the subject. If you do this, the question word goes at the <u>START</u> of the sentence.

Vous arrivez <u>quand</u>?	
<u>Quand</u> est-ce que vous arrivez?	<u>When</u> do you arrive?
<u>Quand</u> arrivez-vous?	
Tu prends <u>quel</u> train?	
<u>Quel</u> train est-ce que tu prends?	<u>What</u> train are you getting?
<u>Quel</u> train prends-tu?	
Ils vont <u>où</u>?	
<u>Où</u> est-ce qu'ils vont?	<u>Where</u> are they going?
<u>Où</u> vont-ils?	

KEY POINTS

✔ You ask a question in French by making your voice go up at the end of the sentence, by using **est-ce que**, by changing normal word order, or by using a question word.

✔ When you put the verb in front of the subject, you join the two words with a hyphen. A **-t-** is used in the **il/elle** form if the verb ends in a vowel.

✔ You use **oui** to answer *yes* to an ordinary question, but **si** if there is a negative in the question or statement.

Test yourself

1   Change the order of the highlighted subject and verb, adding a t if necessary.

a   **Ils aiment** la plage, vos enfants? ....

b   À quelle heure **tu te lèves**? ....

c   **Vous vous appelez** Madame Blanc? ....

d   **Il parle** bien le français? ....

e   **Elle a** garé sa voiture dans le parking? ....

f   **Il a** gelé cette nuit? ....

g   **On va** au restaurant? ....

h   **Vous voulez** une chambre? ....

i   **Ils ont** fait leur choix? ....

j   **Il y a** un problème? ....

2   Fill the gap with a question word.

a   Claire est partie ce matin. — .... va-t-elle?

b   .... est-ce que les vacances commencent?

c   Vous prenez .... menu?

d   C'est de .... couleur?

e   .... est-ce que j'ai mis mon portable?

f   .... a fait ça?

g   Le bus part ....?

h   .... âge a-t-elle?

i   C'est .... , ce pull?

j   .... va ta mère depuis son opération?

Test yourself

3 **Cross out the unlikely answers.**

a Où va-t-elle? En France/À Paris/Au supermarché/Avec eux

b Est-ce que vous allez vendre votre appartement? Non/Peut-être/Si/Pas question

c Tu n'aimes pas les chats? Si/Jamais/Pas beaucoup/Pas du tout

d Ça coûte combien? Cinq ans/Trop/Plus que cinq mille euros/Très peu

e Qui appelles-tu? Ma mère/Le médecin/Personne/N'importe qui

f Il fait froid, n'est-ce pas? Oui/Tu as raison/Je ne sais pas/Ça dépend

g Comment vous appelez-vous? Mon patron/Mon ami/La direction/Cédric

h Tu ne l'as pas fait? Pas encore/Si/Peu importe/ Je suis en train de le faire

i Quand est-ce que le cours finit? Le lendemain/Demain/En septembre/ Dans une semaine

j Êtes-vous prêts à partir? Pas tout à fait/Presque/Ça va bien, merci/ Oui, bien sûr

Question words

Common question words

➤ Listed below are some very common question words. **que**, **quel**, **qui**, **quoi** and **lequel** are explained on pages 202–205.

- **combien** + *verb?* how much?, how many?
  combien de + *noun?* how much?, how many?

<u>**Combien**</u> **coûte cet ordinateur?**	How much does this computer cost?
C'est <u>**combien**</u>**, ce pantalon?**	How much are these trousers?
Tu en veux <u>**combien**</u>**? Deux?**	How many do you want? Two?
<u>**Combien de**</u> **personnes vas-tu inviter?**	How many people are you going to invite?

- **comment?** how?
<u>**Comment**</u> **va-t-elle?**	How is she?
<u>**Comment**</u> **tu t'appelles?**	What's your name?

  > *Tip*
  > **pardon** and **comment** are also used to ask someone to repeat something, and are the same as *Pardon?* in English. **quoi** can mean the same thing, but is informal, and is the same as *What?* in English.

- **où?** where?
<u>**Où**</u> **allez-vous?**	Where are you going?
<u>**D'où**</u> **viens-tu?**	Where are you from?

  > *Tip*
  > Be careful not to mix up **où**, which means *where*, and **ou** (without an accent), which means *or*.

- **pourquoi?** why?
<u>**Pourquoi**</u> **est-ce qu'il ne vient pas avec nous?**	Why isn't he coming with us?

- **quand?** when?
<u>**Quand**</u> **est-ce que tu pars en vacances?**	When are you going on holiday?
<u>**Depuis quand**</u> **est-ce que vous le connaissez?**	How long have you known him?

qui?, que? and quoi?

➤ In questions, **qui**, **que** and **quoi** are all pronouns. Which of them you choose depends on:

- whether you are referring to people or to things

- whether you are referring to the subject or object of the verb (the subject is the person or thing that is carrying out the action described by the verb; the object is the person or thing that 'receives' the action)

- whether the word you use will come after a preposition such as **à**, **de** or **en**

⇨ *For more information on **Pronouns** and **Prepositions**, see pages 55 and 227.*

➤ **qui?** and **que?** have longer forms, as shown in the table below. There is a difference in word order between the longer and shorter forms.

➤ **qui?** is used for talking about people, and means *who?* or *whom?* in English. You can use *whom?* in formal English to refer to the object of verb (though most people use *who?*). **qui?** can be used after a preposition.

Who? Whom?	Referring to people	Meaning	Examples	Meaning
Subject	qui? qui est-ce qui?	who?	**Qui vient? Qui est-ce qui vient?**	Who's coming?
Object	qui? qui est-ce que?	who? whom?	**Qui vois-tu? Qui est-ce que tu vois?**	Who/Whom can you see?
After prepositions	qui? qui est-ce que?	who? whom?	**De qui est-ce qu'il parle? Pour qui est ce livre? Ã qui avez-vous écrit?**	Who's he talking about? Who's this book for? Who did you write to?, To whom did you write?

Tip
que changes to **qu'** before a vowel, most words beginning with **h**, and the French word **y**.

⇨ *For more information on **que** and **qui**, see page 87.*

➤ **à qui** is the usual way of saying *whose* in questions.
  Ã qui est ce sac?   Whose is this bag?

⇨ *For more information on using **à** to show possession, see page 230.*

➤ **que?** and **quoi?** are used for talking about things, and mean *what?* in English. **que?** cannot be used after a preposition; you have to use **quoi?** instead.

What?	Referring to things	Meaning	Examples	Meaning
Subject	qu'est-ce qui?	what?	Qu'est-ce qui se passe? Qu'est-ce qui t'inquiète?	What's happening? What's worrying you?
Object	qu'est-ce que? que?	what?	Qu'est-ce que vous faites? Que faites-vous?	What are you doing?
After prepositions	quoi?	what?	À quoi penses-tu? De quoi parlez-vous?	What are you thinking about? What are you talking about?

> *Tip*
> It is possible to finish an English sentence with a preposition such as
> *about* or *of*.
> *Who did you write to?*
> *What are you talking about?*
> It is NEVER possible to end a French sentence with a preposition.

quel?, quelle?, quels? and quelles?

➤ **quel?** (meaning *who?*, *which?* or *what?*) can be used with a noun (as an adjective) or can replace a noun (as a pronoun). Compare this with **que?** (and its longer forms) and **quoi?**, which also mean *what?*, but are NEVER used with nouns.

⟹ *For more information on **Adjectives** and **Pronouns**, see pages 32 and 55.*

➤ **quel**, **quelle**, **quels** and **quelles** are all forms of the same word. The form that you choose depends on whether you are referring to something that is masculine or feminine, singular or plural.

	Masculine	Feminine	Meaning
Singular	quel?	quelle?	who? what? which?
Plural	quels?	quelles?	who? what? which?

Quel est ton chanteur préféré? — Who's your favourite singer?
Quel vin recommandez-vous? — Which wine do you recommend?
Quelle est ta couleur préférée? — What's your favourite colour?
Quelle heure est-il? — What time is it?
Quels sont tes chanteurs préférés? — Who are your favourite singers?
Vous jouez de quels instruments? — What instruments do you play?
Quelles sont tes couleurs préférées? — What are your favourite colours?
Quelles chaussures te plaisent le plus? — Which shoes do you like best?

⟹ *For more information on how **quel** in used in exclamations, see page 25.*

lequel?, laquelle?, lesquels? and lesquelles?

➤ In questions **lequel**, **laquelle**, **lesquels** and **lesquelles** (meaning *which one/ones?*) are all forms of the same pronoun, and are used to replace nouns. The form that you choose depends on whether you are referring to something that is masculine or feminine, singular or plural.

	Masculine	Feminine	Meaning
Singular	lequel?	laquelle?	which? which one?
Plural	lesquels?	lesquelles?	which? which ones?

'J'ai choisi un livre.' — **'Lequel?'**	'I've chosen a book.' — 'Which one?'
Laquelle de ces valises est à Bruno?	Which of these cases is Bruno's?
'Tu te souviens de mes amis?' — **'Lesquels?'**	'Do you remember my friends?' — 'Which ones?'
Lesquelles de vos sœurs sont mariées?	Which of your sisters are married?

⇨ For more information on **lequel**, see page 88.

n'est-ce pas? and non?

➤ English speakers often use an expression like *isn't it?*, *don't they?*, *weren't we?* or *will you?* tagged on to the end of a sentence to turn it into a question. French uses **n'est-ce pas?** instead. This useful little phrase never changes, so is very easy to use. You use it in questions when you expect the person you are talking to to agree with you.

Il fait chaud, n'est-ce pas?	It's warm, isn't it?
Tu parles français, n'est-ce pas?	You speak French, don't you?
Vous n'oublierez pas, n'est-ce pas?	You won't forget, will you?

➤ It is very common to use **non** (meaning *no*) in the same way in spoken French. **hein?** means the same as *eh?* in English, and is only used in very informal conversations.

Il fait chaud, non?	It's warm, isn't it?
Il fait chaud, hein?	It's warm, eh?

KEY POINTS

✔ In questions **qui?** means *who?*; **que?** and **quoi?** mean *what?*

✔ **qui est-ce qui?** (*subject*) and **qui est-ce que?** (*object*) are longer forms of **qui?** Both mean *who?* The word order is different from **qui**.

✔ **qu'est-ce qui?** (*subject*) and **qu'est-ce que?** (*object*) are longer forms of **que?** Both mean *what?* The word order is different from **que**.

✔ **qui?** (for people) and **quoi?** (for things) can be used after prepositions.

✔ **quel?** is both an adjective and a pronoun. It means *who?*, *what?* or *which?* in questions, and is used with a noun or replaces a noun.

✔ **lequel?** is a pronoun; it means *which?* or *which one?* in questions.

✔ **n'est-ce pas?** or **non?** can be tagged on to the end of sentences to turn them into questions.

Test yourself

4 **Fill the gap with qu'est-ce qui, qu'est-ce que, or quoi.**

a .... te fait peur?

b En .... consiste votre travail?

c .... tu en penses?

d Avec .... ont-ils payé leurs voitures de luxe?

e .... je peux vous offrir?

f .... a causé l'accident?

g Ils ne gagnent pas d'argent, alors .... les motive?

h Ça dépend de .... ?

i .... vous voulez dire?

j .... est arrivé à Ann?

5 **Fill the gap with the correct form of the adjective/pronoun quel or of the pronoun lequel.**

a On est .... jour, aujourd'hui?

b .... est l'adresse de l'hôpital?

c Il y a trois menus, ... vous allez prendre?

d .... piles est-ce qu'il faut que j'achète?

e À .... heure est-ce qu'on arrive?

f .... sont les châteaux les plus intéressants?

g La veste noire et la veste rouge, je les aime toutes les deux.
.... tu préfères?

h Vous nous faites voir vos photos? — .... ?

i Je viens de casser un vase. — .... ?

j Je voudrais voir les monuments. — .... ?

Test yourself

6 **Translate the question into French.**

a It's raining, isn't it?. ....

b Which is your favourite town, sir? ....

c Why are you crying, darling? (*Don't invert word order.*)

....

d How many people are going to come?

....

e Where's she from? (*Invert word order.*) ....

f Why did he say that? (*Don't invert word order.*)

....

g Whose is that big car? ....

h What time do you close? (*Don't invert word order.*)

....

i Which restaurant do you recommend? (*Invert word order.*)

....

j A headlight is broken. — Which one?

....

7 **Match the response to the question.**

a J'en veux.   Pourquoi?

b Pierre vient nous voir.   Lequel?

c Quelqu'un m'a donné cet argent.   Combien?

d Je n'aime pas cette fille.   Quand?

e J'ai choisi un parfum.   Qui?

Grammar Extra!

All the questions in the previous section are the actual words that someone uses when they are asking a question, and so they all end with a question mark. These are called <u>direct</u> questions. When you are telling someone else about a question that is being asked, you use an <u>indirect</u> question. Indirect questions never end with a question mark, and they are always introduced by a verb such as *to ask, to tell, to wonder, to know* and so on.

He asked me what the time was. (His actual question was *What is the time?*)
Tell me which way to go. (Your actual question was *Which way do I go?*)

Word order in indirect questions is generally the same as in English:
question word + subject + verb.

Dites-moi quel (*question word*) **autobus** (*subject*) **va** (*verb*) **à la gare.**	Tell me which bus goes to the station.
Il m'a demandé combien d'argent j'avais.	He asked me how much money I had.
Je me demande s'il viendra ou pas.	I wonder if he'll come or not.
Demande-lui qui est venu.	Ask him who came.

When the subject of the question is a noun and <u>NOT</u> a pronoun like **je** or **il**, the subject and verb that come after the question word are often swapped round.

Je me demande où (*question word*) **sont** (*verb*) **mes clés** (*subject*)**.**	I wonder where my keys are.

Adverbs

> **What is an adverb?**
> An **adverb** is a word usually used with verbs, adjectives or other adverbs that gives more information about when, how, where, or in what circumstances something happens, for example, *quickly, happily, now*.

How adverbs are used

➤ In general, adverbs are used together with:

- verbs (*act <u>quickly</u>, speak <u>strangely</u>, smile <u>cheerfully</u>*)

- adjectives (<u>*rather*</u> *ill, <u>a lot</u> better, <u>deeply</u> sorry*)

- other adverbs (<u>*really*</u> *fast, <u>too</u> quickly, <u>very</u> well*)

➤ Adverbs can also relate to the whole sentence; they often tell you what the speaker is thinking or feeling.
<u>Fortunately</u>, Jan had already left.
<u>Actually</u>, I don't think I'll come.

How adverbs are formed

The basic rules

➤ Adverbs in French <u>NEVER</u> change their form, no matter what they refer to.

Il est <u>très</u> beau.	He's very handsome.
Elles sont <u>très</u> belles.	They're very beautiful.
J'y vais <u>souvent</u>.	I often go there.
Nous y allons <u>souvent</u>.	We often go there.

> 🛈 Note that there is one exception to this rule. The word **tout** changes in certain phrases, for example, **tout seul** (meaning *all alone*).

Il est arrivé <u>tout seul</u>.	He arrived on his own.
Elle est souvent <u>toute seule</u>.	She's often on her own.

➤ Many English adverbs end in *-ly*, which is added to the end of the adjective (*quick* → *quickly*; *sad* → *sadly*; *frequent* → *frequently*). In French, many adverbs end in **-ment.** This is usually added to the end of the <u>feminine singular</u> form of the adjective.

Masculine adjective	Feminine adjective	Adverb	Meaning
heureux	heureuse	heureusement	fortunately
doux	douce	doucement	gently, slowly
seul	seule	seulement	only

➤ The adverb ending **-ment** is added to the <u>masculine</u> not the feminine form of the adjective if the masculine ends in **-é**, **-i** or **-u**.

Masculine adjective	Feminine adjective	Adverb	Meaning
désespéré	désespérée	désespérément	desperately
vrai	vraie	vraiment	truly
absolu	absolue	absolument	absolutely

➤ If the adjective ends in **-ant**, the adverb ends in **-amment**. If the adjective ends in **-ent**, the adverb ends in **-emment**. The first vowel in the **-emment** and **-amment** endings is pronounced in the same way in both – like the *a* in the English word *cat*.

    courant → **couramment** (*fluently*)
    récent → **récemment** (*recently*)

    ⚠ Note that an exception to this rule is the adverb **lentement** (meaning *slowly*), which comes from the adjective **lent** (meaning *slow*).

Irregular adverbs

➤ There are a number of common irregular adverbs.

Adjective	Meaning	Adverb	Meaning
bon	good	bien	well
gentil	nice, kind	gentiment	nicely, kindly
mauvais	bad	mal	badly
meilleur	better, best	mieux	better
petit	small	peu	little
pire	worse	pis	worse

    Elle travaille <u>bien</u>.   She works well.
    C'est un emploi très <u>mal</u> payé.   It's a very badly paid job.

Adjectives used as adverbs

➤ Certain adjectives are used as adverbs, mostly in set phrases:

- **bon** good
  sentir bon   to smell nice

- **cher** expensive
  coûter cher   to be expensive
  payer cher   to pay a lot

- **droit** straight
  aller tout droit   to go straight on

- **dur** hard
  travailler dur   to work hard

For further explanation of grammatical terms, please see pages viii–xii.

- **fort** loud
  parler plus fort   to speak up

- **mauvais** bad
  sentir mauvais   to smell

Adverbs made up of more than one word

➤ Adverbs can be made up of several words instead of just one. Here are some common ones:

bien sûr	of course
c'est-à-dire	that is
d'abord	first
d'habitude	usually
de temps en temps	from time to time
en général	usually
en retard	late
tout de suite	straight away

> ### KEY POINTS
> ✔ With the exception of **tout**, French adverbs do not change their form.
> ✔ The ending **-ment** is usually added to the feminine singular form of the corresponding adjective.
> ✔ If the masculine singular adjective ends in **-é**, **-i** or **-u**, the **-ment** ending is added to that.
> ✔ If the adjective ends in **-ant** or **-ent**, the adverb ends in **-amment** or **-emment** (apart from **lentement**).

Test yourself

1 **Fill the gap with an adverb made from the adjective shown.**

a .... nous ne pouvons pas venir. **(malheureux)**

b .... ils se connaissent déjà. **(apparent)**

c Tu es .... en retard! **(affreux)**

d Ils ont .... souffert. **(terrible)**

e Pour apprendre .... le français il faut aller en France. **(facile)**

f Je suis .... désolée. **(vrai)**

g Elle m'a .... parlé de ses projets d'avenir. **(long)**

h Il est .... plus grand que son frère. **(léger)**

i Elle se plaint .... **(constant)**

j Est-ce que vous pouvez parler plus ....? **(lent)**

2 **Cross out the unlikely options.**

a **D'habitude.** — Je me couche tard/Je vais au supermarché le samedi./Je le ferai tout de suite./J'aime ses films.

b **Tu veux venir à la fête?** — bien sûr!/vraiment/heureusement/de temps en temps

c **Ça sent mauvais!** — ce poisson/ce cendrier/cette chambre/ce fleur

d **Elle veut absolument** — se marier/voyager/se faire du souci/acheter une voiture

e **Ça coûte cher** — de faire une promenade/d'aller à l'université/de louer un appartement à Londres/d'assurer une voiture

f **Elle est vraiment gentille.** — ta mère/notre professeur/sa copine/ta maison

g **Nous avons travaillé dur** — avant les examens/lentement/d'abord/le trimestre dernier

h **Je lui parlerai** — récemment/tout de suite/doucement/en retard

i **Parlez plus fort!** — Il ne vous comprend pas./Il ne vous entend pas./Il est sourd./Le bébé dort.

j **Je les vois** — souvent/de temps en temps/rarement/gentiment

Test yourself

3   Translate the sentence into French.

a   Can I ask you something? — Of course!

   ....

b   We don't see her often. ....

c   Does he go to school by himself?

   ....

d   Fortunately nobody died. ....

e   I saw this film recently. ....

f   The letter was very badly written.

   ....

g   I'd like a better paid job. ....

h   They speak English very well. (*Put English at the end of the sentence.*)

   ....

i   Today I'm feeling even worse. ....

j   That soup smells nice! ....

Comparatives and superlatives of adverbs

Comparative adverbs

> ### What is a comparative adverb?
> A **comparative adverb** is one which, in English, has -er on the end of it or *more* or *less* in front of it, for example, *earlier, later, sooner, more/less frequently.*

➤ Adverbs can be used to make comparisons in French, just as they can in English. The comparative (*more often, faster*) of adverbs is formed using the same phrases as for adjectives.

- **plus ... (que)**   more ... (than)
  Tu marches <u>plus</u> vite <u>que</u> moi.   You walk faster than me.
  Elle chante <u>plus</u> fort <u>que</u> les autres.   She's singing louder than the others.

- **moins ... (que)**   less ... (than)
  Parle <u>moins</u> vite!   Don't speak so fast!
                                        (*literally: Speak less fast!*)
  Nous nous voyons <u>moins</u>   We see each other less often than before.
  souvent <u>qu'avant</u>.

- **aussi ... que**   as ... as
  Je parle français <u>aussi</u> bien <u>que</u> toi!   I can speak French as well as you!
  Viens <u>aussi</u> vite <u>que</u> possible.   Come as quickly as possible.

⇨ *For more information on **Comparative adjectives**, see page 43.*

Superlative adverbs

> ### What is a superlative adverb?
> A **superlative adverb** is one which, in English, has -est on the end of it or *most* or *least* in front of it, for example, *soonest, fastest, most/least frequently.*

➤ The superlative of adverbs (*the most, the fastest*) is formed using the same phrases as for adjectives, except that **le** <u>NEVER</u> changes to **la** or **les** in the feminine and plural with adverbs as it does with adjectives.

- **le plus ... (que)**   the most ... (that)
  Marianne parle <u>le plus</u> vite.   Marianne speaks fastest.

- **le moins ... (que)**   the least ... (that)
  C'est Gordon qui a mangé <u>le moins</u>.   Gordon ate the least.

⇨ *For more information on **Superlative adjectives**, see page 43.*

Adverbs with irregular comparatives and superlatives

➤ Some of the most common adverbs have irregular comparative and superlative forms.

Adverb	Meaning	Comparative	Meaning	Superlative	Meaning
beaucoup	a lot	**plus**	more	**le plus**	(the) most
bien	well	**mieux**	better	**le mieux**	(the) best
mal	badly	**pis** **plus mal**	worse	**le pis** **le plus mal**	(the) worst
peu	little	**moins**	less	**le moins**	(the) least

C'est lui qui danse <u>le mieux</u>.　　　　He dances best.

KEY POINTS

✔ Comparatives of adverbs are formed in the same way as comparatives of adjectives, using **plus ... (que)**, **moins ... (que)** and **aussi ... que**.

✔ Superlatives of adverbs are formed in the same way as superlatives of adjectives, using **le plus ... (que)** and **le moins ... (que)**.
le never changes in the feminine and plural.

✔ Unlike adjectives, adverbs do not change their form to agree with the verb, adjective or other adverb they relate to.

Test yourself

4 Fill the gap with a comparative adverb.

a Comment va votre mari? — Il va .... , merci.

b Elle est très sportive. Elle va à la gym .... que moi.

c Tu parles trop vite. Tu peux parler .... ?

d Je ne vous entends pas. Vous pouvez parler .... ?

e Si on veut maigrir il faut .... manger.

f Nous sommes en retard. Marchez .... !

g Ils sont riches. Ils gagnent .... que nous.

h Tu as mis de la sauce partout! Essaie de manger ....

i Pouah! Ce fromage sent encore .... !

j Son fils se comporte .... à l'école maintenant.

5 Make a sentence with the elements provided.

a mon copain/marcher/+vite/moi ....

b tu devrais/se comporter/+bien ....

c ils/avoir/joué/+intelligemment/nous ....

d Anne/travailler/+dur/les autres ....

e il/être/+gravement blessé/moi ....

f Sarah/lire/-bien/sa sœur ....

g nous/vouloir/vivre/+simplement ....

h pourquoi/tu/ne pas/venir/nous voir/+souvent?

....

i la grippe/se transmettre/+facilement/en hiver

....

6 **Match the sentences that mean the same.**

a   Elle est la meilleure joueuse.   Elle coûte le plus cher.

b   C'est la plus chère.   Elle vient le plus souvent.

c   C'est notre cliente la plus fidèle.   Elle parle moins.

d   Ses amis sont plus bavards qu'elle.   Elle joue le mieux.

e   Sauf elle, nous l'utilisons beaucoup.   Elle l'utilise moins.

7 **Cross out the unlikely options.**

a   Il joue le mieux.   Il est sage./Il est sympathique./Il est sportif./
                                             Il est doué.

b   C'est l'équipe qui joue   la nôtre/la leur/Lyon/le gardien de but
    le plus mal.

c   Il a mangé le moins.   Il n'avait pas soif./Il n'avait pas faim./
                                             Il n'aime pas le poisson./
                                             Il n'y avait rien à manger.

d   Essayez de l'expliquer aussi   cette théorie/le problème/
    simplement que possible.   la situation/l'invitation

e   Parle moins fort!   Personne ne t'entend./
                                             Nous ne sommes pas sourds./
                                             Tout le monde t'écoute./Je fais mes devoirs.

f   Viens aussi vite que   J'ai besoin de toi!/Les invités sont déjà arrivés./
    possible!   de mieux en mieux/Tu es en retard.

g   Paul a parlé le plus.   Il est bavard./Il sait de quoi il parle./
                                             Les autres l'ont écouté./Il est timide.

h   Nous nous voyons moins   Nous avons tous les deux beaucoup à faire./
    souvent qu'avant.   Nous ne travaillons plus ensemble./
                                             Maintenant tu habites à l'étranger./
                                             Tu habites à côté.

i   C'est elle qui a pleuré le plus.   Elle était très triste./Elle a beaucoup souffert./
                                             Elle avait très mal./Elle s'amusait beaucoup.

j   J'ai refermé la porte aussi   Il n'y avait personne./Le concert avait commencé./
    doucement que possible.   Le bébé dormait./Il était trois heures du matin.

Some common adverbs

➤ Here are some common adverbs that do not end in **-ment**:

alors	then, so, at that time
après	afterwards
après-demain	the day after tomorrow
aujourd'hui	today
assez	enough, quite
aussi	also, too, as
avant-hier	the day before yesterday
beaucoup	a lot, much
bientôt	soon
cependant	however
dedans	inside
dehors	outside
déjà	already, before
demain	tomorrow
depuis	since
derrière	behind
devant	in front
encore	still, even, again
enfin	at last
ensemble	together
ensuite	then
environ	about
hier	yesterday
ici	here
jamais	never, ever

> *Tip*
>
> **jamais** can sometimes be used without **ne** to mean *never* or *ever*.
>
> **'Est-ce que tu vas souvent au cinéma?' — 'Non, jamais.'**   'Do you go to the cinema a lot?' — 'No, <u>never</u>.'
>
> **As-tu <u>jamais</u> revu ton père?**   Did you <u>ever</u> see your father again?
>
> ⇨ *For more information on* **Negatives,** *see page 192.*

là	there, here
là-bas	over there
loin	far, far off, a long time ago
longtemps	a long time
maintenant	now, nowadays
même	even
moins	less
où	where
parfois	sometimes
partout	everywhere
peu	not much, not very

> **Tip**
>
> Be careful not to confuse **peu**, which means *not much* or *not very*, with **un peu**, which means *a little* or *a bit*.
>
> **Il voyage <u>peu</u>.**   He doesn<u>'t</u> travel <u>much</u>.
> **Elle est <u>un peu</u> timide.**   She's <u>a bit</u> shy.

peut-être	perhaps
plus	more
presque	nearly
puis	then
quelquefois	sometimes
si	so
soudain	suddenly
souvent	often
surtout	especially, above all
tard	late
tôt	early
toujours	always, still
tout	all, very
très	very
trop	too much, too
vite	quick, fast, soon

> **Tip**
>
> **vite** and **rapide** can both mean *fast* or *quick*. Remember, though, that **vite** is an <u>adverb</u> and **rapide** is an <u>adjective</u>.
>
> **une voiture <u>rapide</u>**   a fast car
> **Il roule trop <u>vite</u>.**   He drives too fast.

➤ Some of the adverbs listed on pages 218 and 219 can be followed by **de** and used in front of a noun to talk about quantities or numbers of things or people:

- **assez de** enough
  Nous n'avons pas <u>assez de</u> temps.   We don't have enough time.

- **beaucoup de** a lot of
  Elle fait <u>beaucoup de</u> fautes.   She makes a lot of mistakes.

- **trop de** too much, too many
  J'ai mangé <u>trop de</u> fromage.   I've eaten too much cheese.

➤ Several of the adverbs listed on pages 218 and 219 can also be used as prepositions: **après**, **avant**, **devant**, **derrière** and **depuis**.

⇨ *For more information on **Prepositions**, see page 227.*

➤ The question words **combien** (meaning *how much, how many*), **comment** (meaning *how*), **pourquoi** (meaning *why*) and **quand** (meaning *when*) are described on page 202.

➤ **pas**, **plus** and **jamais** are used in negative word pairs.

⇨ *For more information on **Negatives**, see page 192.*

> ### KEY POINTS
> ✔ Many very common adverbs do not end in **-ment**. They are worth learning.
> ✔ Several adverbs can be followed by **de** + noun and used to talk about quantities and numbers.

Test yourself

8 Cross out the unlikely answers.

a Quand est-ce que la cérémonie aura lieu?   Demain./Après-demain./Samedi./Déjà!

b Quand a-t-elle eu l'accident?   Avant./Avant-hier./Ensuite./ Le lendemain de son arrivée.

c Où sont les chiens?   Ensemble./Dehors./Là-bas./Ici.

d Combien de temps vous restez ici?   Environ trois jours./Quelquefois./ Pas longtemps./Presque un mois.

e Tu vas à la piscine?   Parfois./Souvent./Jamais./Ensuite.

f Quand va-t-elle au supermarché?   Soudain./Maintenant./Tard ce soir./ Tous les vendredis.

g Je l'ai fini!   Enfin!/Déjà?/Alors tu peux sortir avec tes amis./ Encore!

h Elle porte ses lunettes?   Jamais./Toujours./Demain./ Oui, surtout quand elle lit.

i Où est-ce que ça te fait mal?   Pas beaucoup./Partout./Surtout ici./Souvent.

j Elle aime les chats?   Beaucoup./Trop!/Moins./Énormément!

9 Fill the gap with an adverb.

a J'aime nager, ... en été.

b C'est .... la même chose: il la taquine et elle se met à pleurer!

c Il n'est pas rentré à la maison. Il est .... au bureau.

d Je ne vais pas au cinéma. J'ai .... vu ce film.

e Je pense que ça coûte .... cent euros.

f J'aime tous les animaux, ... les rats.

g Nous avons regardé le journal télévisé et nous sommes allés au lit aussitôt ....

h Ralentissez! Vous roulez .... vite.

i Il dort peu. Il se lève tôt et il se couche ....

j Nous avons dû attendre ....

Test yourself

10 Translate the sentence into French.

a It's quite nice weather today. ....

b It took quite a long time. ....

c Is there enough bread? (*Use* **Est-ce que**) ....

d It rains a lot. ....

e There's not a lot to see. ....

f He makes a lot of money. ....

g She drinks too much. ....

h I buy too many bags. ....

i You've lost too much weight. (*Use* **tu**) . ...

Word order with adverbs

Adverbs with verbs

➤ In English, adverbs can come in different places in a sentence.
   I'm <u>never</u> coming back.
   See you <u>soon</u>!
   <u>Suddenly</u> the phone rang.
   I'd <u>really</u> like to come.

➤ In French, the rules are more fixed. When an adverb goes with a verb that consists of just one word, such as a verb in the <u>present tense</u> or the <u>imperfect tense</u>, it generally goes <u>AFTER</u> that verb.

Il neige <u>toujours</u> en janvier.	It always snows in January.
Je pensais <u>souvent</u> à toi.	I often used to think about you.

➤ When an adverb goes with a verb that consists of more than one word, such as a verb in the <u>perfect tense</u>, it generally comes <u>BETWEEN</u> the part of the verb that comes from **avoir** or **être** and the past participle.

Il a <u>trop</u> mangé.	He's eaten too much.
Ils sont <u>déjà</u> partis.	They've already gone.

➪ *For more information on the **Perfect tense**, see page 151.*

➤ The rule above covers most adverbs that tell you about quantity or time (apart from a few listed later), and some very common ones telling you how something is done.

beaucoup	a lot, much
bien	well
bientôt	soon
déjà	already, before
encore	still, even, again
enfin	at last
mal	badly
mieux	better
peu	not much, not very
rarement	rarely
souvent	often
toujours	always, still
trop	too much, too
vraiment	really

➤ Some adverbs <u>FOLLOW</u> the past participle of verbs that consist of more than one word. This rule covers most adverbs that tell you how or where something is done, and a few adverbs that tell you about time.

aujourd'hui	today
demain	tomorrow
hier	yesterday
loin	far, far off, a long time ago
longtemps	a long time
partout	everywhere
quelquefois	sometimes

tôt	early
tard	late
vite	quick, fast, soon

On les a vus <u>partout</u>.   We saw them everywhere.
Elle est revenue <u>hier</u>.   She came back yesterday.

Adverbs with adjectives and other adverbs

➤ When an adverb goes with an <u>adjective</u>, it generally comes just <u>BEFORE</u> that adjective.
     Ils ont une <u>très</u> belle maison.   They have a very nice house.
     une femme <u>bien</u> habillée   a well-dressed woman

➤ When an adverb goes with another <u>adverb</u>, it generally comes just <u>BEFORE</u> that adverb.
     C'est <u>trop</u> tard.   It's too late.
     Fatima travaille <u>beaucoup</u> plus vite.   Fatima works much faster.

KEY POINTS

✔ Adverbs follow verbs that consist of just one word.
✔ They generally go before the past participle of verbs that consist of two words when they relate to quantity or time.
✔ They generally go after the past participle of verbs that consist of two words when they relate to how or where something is done.
✔ When used with an adjective or another adverb, they generally come just before it.

Test yourself

11 **Make a sentence with the elements provided, putting the adverb in the correct place.**

a je/beaucoup/admirer/ce professeur...

b je/toujours/avoir/voulu/aller en Inde...

c vous/bientôt/recevoir/
une lettre de confirmation ....

d ce/ne pas/encore/être/fini

e nous/rarement/se rencontrer...

f je/souvent/se demander/
pourquoi il l'a fait. ....

g tu/déjà/avoir/dit/me/ça ....

h elle/ne pas/aller/très bien ....

i tout/s'est passé/très bien ....

j nous/enfin/avoir réussi/
à joindre/le ....

12 **Cross out the adverbs that could not complete the sentence.**

a Ils sont partis   demain/aujourd'hui/hier/tôt.

b Elle les a faits   vite/rapidement/demain/avant-hier

c Nous les avons attendus   vite/longtemps/tôt/quelquefois

d Je me suis levée   tard/partout/tôt/vite

e Ça s'est passé   demain/vite/hier/aujourd'hui

f Ces puces! Le chat les a semées hier/partout/beaucoup/toujours

g L'hôtel n'était pas bien.
On aurait dû aller   ailleurs/loin/tout de suite/mieux

h Elle l'aurait fait   mieux/aujourd'hui/ailleurs/loin

i Nous sommes tombés
amoureux   tout de suite/enfin/très vite/petit à petit

j Ils ont joué   mal/beaucoup mieux/très bien/bientôt

Test yourself

13 Match the related sentences.

a	**Elle est élégante.**	Ils ont une très belle maison.
b	**Je les envie.**	Ils coûtent beaucoup moins cher.
c	**Je les plains.**	Elle est encore plus jolie.
d	**Je prends ceux-ci.**	Elle est toujours bien habillée.
e	**Je préfère celle-ci.**	Ils ont beaucoup souffert.

Prepositions

What is a preposition?
A **preposition** is a word such as *at*, *for*, *with*, *into* or *from*, which is usually followed
by a noun, pronoun or, in English, a word ending in *-ing*. Prepositions show how
people and things relate to the rest of the sentence, for example, *She's at home.*;
a tool for cutting grass; *it's from David*.

Using prepositions

➤ Prepositions are used in front of nouns and pronouns (such as *me*, *him*, *the man* and so on),
and show the relationship between the noun or pronoun and the rest of the sentence.
Some prepositions can be used before verb forms ending in *-ing* in English.
I showed my ticket <u>to</u> the inspector.
Come <u>with</u> me.
This brush is really good <u>for</u> cleaning shoes.

⇨ *For more information on **Nouns** and **Pronouns**, see pages 1 and 55.*

➤ Prepositions are also used after certain adjectives and verbs and link them to the rest of
the sentence.
Je suis très contente <u>de</u> te voir.	I'm very happy to see you.
Tu aimes jouer <u>au</u> tennis?	Do you like playing tennis?

➤ In English it is possible to finish a sentence with a preposition such as *for*, *about* or *on*, even
though some people think this is not good grammar. You can <u>NEVER</u> end a French sentence
with a preposition.
Le café au lait, c'est <u>pour</u> qui?	Who's the white coffee <u>for</u>?
<u>De</u> quoi parlez-vous?	What are you talking <u>about</u>?

Tip
The French preposition is not always the direct equivalent of the preposition
that is used in English. It is often difficult to give just one English equivalent
for French prepositions, as the way they are used varies so much between
the two languages.

à, de and en

à

➤ Be careful not to confuse the preposition **à** with the **il/elle/on** form of the verb **avoir**:
il a (meaning *he has*) and so on.

Tip

When **à** is followed by **le**, the two words become **au**. Similarly, when **à** is followed by **les**, the two words become **aux**.

⇨ *For more information on* **Articles***, see page* 14.

➤ à can mean *at*.

Les melons se vendent à 2 euros pièce.	Melons are selling <u>at</u> 2 euros each.
Nous roulions à 100 km à l'heure.	We were driving <u>at</u> 100 km an hour
J'ai lancé une pierre à Chantal.	I threw a stone <u>at</u> Chantal.
Je suis à la maison.	I'm <u>at</u> home.

ⓘ Note that **à la maison** can also mean *to the house*.

Je rentre à la maison.	I'm going back to the house *or* back home.

➤ à can mean *in*.

Nous habitons à la campagne.	We live <u>in</u> the country.
Mon père est à Londres.	My father is <u>in</u> London.
Restez au lit.	Stay <u>in</u> bed.
Jean est entré, un livre à la main.	Jean came in with a book <u>in</u> his hand.

Tip

à is used to mean *in* with the names of towns and cities, and **au** (*singular*) or **aux** (*plural*) are used to mean *in* with the names of countries that are masculine in French.

J'habite au Mexique.	I live <u>in</u> Mexico.
Elle est aux États-Unis.	She's <u>in</u> the States.

➤ à can mean *to*.

Je vais au cinéma ce soir.	I'm going <u>to</u> the cinema tonight.
Donne le ballon à ton frère.	Give the ball <u>to</u> your brother.

Tip

à is used to mean *to* with the names of towns and cities, and **au** (*singular*) or **aux** (*plural*) are used to mean *to* with the names of countries that are masculine in French.

Je vais assez souvent à Paris.	I go <u>to</u> Paris quite often.
Il va aux États-Unis la semaine prochaine.	He's going <u>to</u> the States next week.

➤ à is also used with **de** to mean *from ... to ...*

le trajet de Londres à Paris	the journey <u>from</u> London <u>to</u> Paris
La banque est ouverte de 9 heures à midi.	The bank is open <u>from</u> 9 <u>to</u> 12.
Je suis en vacances du 21 juin au 5 juillet.	I'm on holiday <u>from</u> 21 June <u>to</u> 5 July.

➤ **à** can mean *on*.

Il y a deux beaux tableaux <u>au</u> mur.	There are two beautiful paintings <u>on</u> the wall.
Le bureau se trouve <u>au</u> premier étage.	The office is <u>on</u> the first floor.
Qu'est-ce qu'il y a <u>à la</u> télé ce soir?	What's <u>on</u> TV tonight?

[*i*] Note that **à** and **sur** can both mean *on* in English. **sur** usually means on the top of something. **sur la télé** means *on top of the TV set*, but **à la télé** means *broadcast on TV*. **sur le mur** means *on top of the wall*, but **au mur** means *hanging on the wall*.

➤ **à** is often used to describe:

- what someone looks like or is wearing

la femme <u>au</u> chapeau vert	the woman in the green hat
un garçon <u>aux</u> yeux bleus	a boy with blue eyes

- how something is done

fait <u>à</u> la main	hand-made
laver <u>à</u> la machine	to machine-wash

- what a type of food is made of

une tarte <u>aux</u> poires	a pear tart
un sandwich <u>au</u> jambon	a ham sandwich

- how you travel

On y va <u>à</u> pied?	Shall we walk?
Il est venu <u>à</u> vélo.	He came on his bike.

> *Tip*
> Apart from **à vélo** and **à cheval** (meaning *on horseback*), the prepositions **en** and **par** are used with most other means of transport.

➤ **à** can also show what something is used for.

une boîte <u>aux</u> lettres	a letter box
une machine <u>à</u> laver	a washing machine
une tasse <u>à</u> café	a coffee cup

[*i*] Note that **une tasse à café** means a *coffee cup*, but **une tasse <u>de</u> café** means *a cup of coffee*. In the same way, **un verre <u>à</u> vin** means *a wine glass* but **un verre <u>de</u> vin** means *a glass of wine*.

➤ **à** is used with times, centuries and the names of festivals.

<u>à</u> trois heures	at three o'clock
<u>au</u> vingtième siècle	in the twentieth century
<u>à</u> Noël	at Christmas
<u>à</u> Pâques	at Easter

➤ **à** is used to talk about distances and rates.

La maison est <u>à</u> 6 kilomètres d'ici.	The house is 6 kilometres from here.
C'est <u>à</u> deux minutes de chez moi.	It's two minutes from my place.
Je suis payé <u>à</u> l'heure.	I'm paid by the hour.

➤ **à** shows who owns something, or whose turn it is.

Ce cahier est <u>à</u> Paul.	This notebook is Paul's.
C'est <u>à</u> toi?	Is this yours?
C'est <u>à</u> qui de nettoyer la salle de bains?	Whose turn is it to clean the bathroom?

➤ If you want to say where something hurts, you use **à**.

J'ai mal <u>à</u> la tête.	I've got a headache.
J'ai mal <u>aux</u> jambes.	My legs ache.
J'ai mal <u>à</u> la gorge.	I've got a sore throat.

➤ **à** is used with certain adjectives.

Son écriture est difficile <u>à</u> lire.	His/Her writing is difficult to read.
Je suis prêt <u>à</u> tout.	I'm ready for anything.

⇨ *For more information about **Prepositions after adjectives**, see page 246.*

➤ **à** is used with certain verbs.

s'intéresser <u>à</u> quelque chose	to be interested in something
penser <u>à</u> quelque chose	to think about something

⇨ *For more information about **Prepositions after verbs**, see page 240.*

➤ Finally, some common ways of saying goodbye contain **à**.

<u>À</u> bientôt!	See you soon!
<u>À</u> demain!	See you tomorrow!
<u>À</u> samedi!	See you Saturday!
<u>À</u> tout à l'heure!	See you later!

de

➤ **de** is used as part of the <u>partitive article</u>, which is usually the equivalent of *some* or *any* in English.

⇨ *For more information on the **Partitive article**, see page 27.*

> *Tip*
> When **de** is followed by **le**, the two words become **du.** Similarly, when **de** is followed by **les**, the two words become **des.**
>
> ⇨ *For more information on **Articles**, see page 14.*

➤ **de** can mean *from*.

Je viens <u>d'</u>Édimbourg.	I'm <u>from</u> Edinburgh.
une lettre <u>de</u> Rachid	a letter <u>from</u> Rachid
Je la vois <u>de</u> temps en temps.	I see her <u>from</u> time to time.

> *Tip*
> **de** changes to **d'** in front of a word starting with a vowel, most words starting with **h**, and the French word **y**.

➤ **de** is also used with **à** to mean *from … to …*

le trajet **de** Londres **à** Paris	the journey <u>from</u> London <u>to</u> Paris
La banque est ouverte **de** 9 heures **à** midi.	The bank is open <u>from</u> 9 <u>to</u> 12.
Je suis en vacances **du** 21 juin **au** 5 juillet.	I'm on holiday <u>from</u> 21 June <u>to</u> 5 July.

➤ **de** often shows who or what something belongs to.

un ami **de** la famille	a friend of the family
les fenêtres **de** la maison	the windows of the house
la voiture **de** Marie-Pierre	Marie-Pierre's car

➤ **de** can indicate what something contains, when it usually corresponds to *of* in English.

une boîte **d'**allumettes	a box <u>of</u> matches
deux bouteilles **de** vin	two bottles <u>of</u> wine
une tasse **de** café	a cup <u>of</u> coffee

☑ Note that **une tasse de café** means *a cup of coffee* but **une tasse à café** means *a coffee cup*. In the same way, **un verre à vin** means *a wine glass* but **un verre de vin** means *a glass of wine*.

➤ **de** can describe what material something is made of.

une robe **de** coton	a cotton dress
une porte **de** bois	a wooden door

> *Tip*
> **en** can also be used to say what something is made of, and is used when it is important to stress the material.
>
> **un bracelet en or**   a gold bracelet

➤ You can use **de** to say what something is used for.

un sac **de** couchage	a sleeping bag
un terrain **de** foot	a football pitch
un arrêt **de** bus	a bus stop

➤ **de** is found after superlatives (*the most…, the biggest, the least …* and so on).

la plus belle ville **du** monde	the most beautiful city in the world
le film le moins intéressant **du** festival	the least interesting film in the festival

⇨ *For more information on **Superlative adjectives**, see page 43.*

➤ **de** is used in phrases to talk about quantities.

Elle fait <u>beaucoup **de**</u> fautes.	She makes a lot of mistakes.
<u>Combien **de**</u> personnes as-tu invitées?	How many people have you invited?

➤ **de** is used with certain adjectives.

Je suis très surpris **de** te voir.	I'm very surprised to see you.
Il est triste **de** partir.	He's sad to be leaving.

⇨ *For more information on **Prepositions after adjectives**, see page 246.*

Grammar Extra!
If you want to use an adjective after **quelque chose**, **rien**, **quelqu'un** and **personne**, you link the words with **de**.

quelqu'un d'important	someone important
quelque chose d'intéressant	something interesting
rien d'amusant	nothing funny

➤ **de** is found after certain verbs.

dépendre **de** quelque chose	to depend on something
parler **de** quelque chose	to talk about something

⇨ *For more information on* **Prepositions after verbs**, *see page 240.*

en

ⓘ Note that **en** is never followed by an article such as **le**, **du** or **des**.

➤ **en** is used to talk about a place. It can be the equivalent of the English *to* or *in*.

Je vais **en** ville.	I'm going to town.
Il a un appartement **en** ville.	He has a flat in town.
Nous allons **en** France cet été.	We're going to France this summer.
Nous habitons **en** France.	We live in France.

> *Tip*
> **en** is used with the names of countries that are feminine in French. Use **à** with the names of towns and cities, and **au** or **aux** with masculine countries.

➤ **en** is used to talk about years and months, and to say how long something will take, when it is the equivalent of *in/within*:

en 1923	in 1923
en janvier	in January
Je le ferai **en** trois jours.	I'll do it in three days.

Grammar Extra!
en and **dans** can both be used in French to talk about a length of time, but the meaning is very different.

Je le ferai **dans** trois jours.	I'll do it in three days.
Je le ferai **en** trois jours.	I'll do it in three days.

Though both can be translated in the same way, the first sentence means that you'll do it in three days' time; the second means that it will take three days for you to do it.

➤ **en** is used with the names of the seasons, except for spring.

en été	in summer
en automne	in autumn
en hiver	in winter
BUT: **au printemps**	in spring

➤ **en** is used for most means of transport.

Je suis venu en voiture.	I came by car.
C'est plus rapide en train.	It's quicker by train.
Il est allé en Italie en avion.	He flew to Italy.

> *Tip*
> The prepositions **à** and **par** are also used with means of transport.

➤ Use **en** to say what language something is in.

une lettre écrite en espagnol	a letter written in Spanish
Dis-le en anglais.	Say it in English.

➤ **en** can be used to say what something is made of when you particularly want to stress the material.

un bracelet en or	a bracelet made of gold, a gold bracelet
un manteau en cuir	a coat made of leather, a leather coat

> *Tip*
> **de** can also be used to say what something is made of.
>
> **une porte de bois**   a wooden door

➤ **en** often describes the situation or state that something or someone is in.

Je suis en vacances.	I'm on holiday.
La voiture est en panne.	The car's broken down.
Tu es toujours en retard!	You're always late!

➤ **en** is found before present participles, the form of the verb that ends in *-ing* in English and *-ant* in French.

Je fais mes devoirs en regardant la télé.	I do my homework while watching TV.
Il m'a vu en passant devant la porte.	He saw me as he came past the door.

⇨ *For more information on the **Present participle**, see page 170.*

> **KEY POINTS**
> ✔ **à**, **de** and **en** are very frequent prepositions which you will use all the time.
> ✔ Each of them has several possible meanings, which depend on the context they are used in.

Test yourself

1 **Make a sentence with the elements provided.**

a avocats/se vendre/1 euro pièce ....

b nous/sommes rentrés/maison/minuit ....

c je/habiter/Portugal ....

d j'avais peur/il/rouler/160 km/h ....

e si tu/avoir mal/gorge/rester/lit! ....

f nous/être/en vacances/25 juillet-3 août ....

g la réception/se trouver/rez-de-chaussée ....

h il ne faut pas/laver/le/machine ....

i Tu/veux/tarte/pommes/ou/tarte/citron? ....

j il y a/3/grand/tasse/et/2/tasse/café ....

2 **Fill the gap with à, or à combined with an article.**

a Son grand-père était né .... dix-neuvième siècle.

b Le jardin n'est pas à nous, il est .... voisins.

c J'ai mal partout, surtout.................... genoux et .... pieds.

d L'auberge de jeunesse est .... 5 kilomètres de la gare.

e Il faut penser .... l'avenir.

f Son accent est difficile .... comprendre.

g Il va .... bureau à vélo.

h Laquelle? — Celle .... cheveux roux.

i Il n'y a rien .... télé ce soir.

j La bibliothèque est ouverte de 9 heures .... 18 heures.

Test yourself

3 **Translate the sentence into French.**

a We have booked a flight from London to Marseilles.

....

b You'll need a sleeping bag. (*Use* **tu**.)

....

c I'm going to buy bread, cheese and a bottle of wine.

....

d We're looking for the bus stop.

....

e We'd like to have a house in France.

....

f Have you got friends in England? (*Use* **Est-ce que vous**.)

....

g The garden is lovely in spring, but not in winter.

....

h I sometimes go to Paris by train.

....

i I don't know how to say it in French.

....

j Could you give me a plastic bag, please?

....

4 **Match the connected sentences.**

a **Je suis surprise de te voir.**   Je ne peux pas y aller à pied.

b **Il y a souvent des bouchons**   Il m'a ramené à la maison.
sur l'autoroute.

c **Je n'arrive pas à faire démarrer**   C'est plus rapide en train.
la voiture.

d **La maison est à dix kilomètres d'ici.**   Je croyais que tu étais aux États-Unis.

e **J'ai raté mon train.**   Je vais aller au centre en bus.

Some other common prepositions

ⓘ Note that some of these words are also adverbs, for example, **avant**, **depuis**.

⇨ *For more information on **Adverbs**, see page 209.*

➤ The following prepositions are also frequently used in French:

- **après** after

après le déjeuner	after lunch
après son départ	after he had left
la troisième maison après la mairie	the third house after the town hall
Après vous!	After you!

ⓘ Note that where English uses a verb in the perfect tense following *after*, French uses the infinitive **avoir** or **être** and a past participle.

Nous viendrons après avoir fait la vaisselle.	We'll come after we've done the dishes.

- **avant** before

Il est arrivé avant toi.	He arrived before you.
Tournez à gauche avant la poste.	Turn left before the post office.

ⓘ Note that where English uses a verb ending in *-ing* after *before*, French uses **de** followed by the infinitive.

Je préfère finir mes devoirs avant de manger.	I prefer to finish my homework before eating.

- **avec** with

avec mon père	with my father
une chambre avec salle de bain	a room with its own bathroom
Ouvre-la avec un couteau.	Open it with a knife.

- **chez**

Elle est chez Pierre.	She's at Pierre's house.
Elle va chez Pierre.	She's going to Pierre's house.
Je reste chez moi ce week-end.	I'm staying at home this weekend.
Je vais rentrer chez moi.	I'm going home.
Ils habitent près de chez moi.	They live near my house.

> *Tip*
> **chez** is also used with the name of jobs or professions to indicate a shop or place of business.
>
> **Je vais chez le médecin.** — I'm going to the doctor's.

- **contre** against

Ne mets pas ton vélo contre le mur.	Don't put your bike against the wall.

- **dans** in, into
  Il est <u>dans</u> sa chambre. He's in his bedroom.
  Nous passons une semaine We're spending a week in the Alps.
   <u>dans</u> les Alpes.
  <u>dans</u> deux mois in two months' time
  Il est entré <u>dans</u> mon bureau. He came into my office.

Grammar Extra!

dans and **en** can both be used in French to talk about a length of time, but the meaning is very different.

Je le ferai <u>dans</u> trois jours. I'll do it in three days.
Je le ferai <u>en</u> trois jours. I'll do it in three days.

Though both can be translated in the same way, the first sentence means that you'll do it in three days' time; the second means that it will take three days for you to do it.

- **depuis** since, for
  Elle habite Paris <u>depuis</u> 1998. She's been living in Paris since 1998.
  Elle habite Paris <u>depuis</u> cinq ans. She's been living in Paris for five years.

ⓘ Note that French uses the <u>present tense</u> with **depuis** to talk about actions that started in the past and are still going on.

 Il <u>est</u> en France <u>depuis</u> le mois He's been in France since September.
 de septembre. *(and he is still there)*

If you are saying how long something has <u>NOT</u> happened for, you use the <u>perfect tense</u> with **depuis**.

 Nous ne l'<u>avons</u> pas <u>vu</u> depuis un mois. We haven't seen him for a month.

⇨ *For more information on the **Present tense** and the **Perfect tense**, see pages 98 and 151.*

- **derrière** behind
  <u>derrière</u> la porte behind the door

- **devant** in front of
  Il est assis <u>devant</u> moi. He's sitting in front of me.

- **entre ... et** between ... and
  Il est assis <u>entre</u> son père <u>et</u> son oncle. He's sitting between his father and his uncle.
  Le bureau est fermé <u>entre</u> The office is closed between 1 and 2 p.m.
   13 <u>et</u> 14 heures.

- **jusque** as far as, until
  Je te raccompagne <u>jusque</u> chez toi. I'll go with you as far as your house.
  <u>Jusqu'où</u> vas-tu? How far are you going?
  <u>Jusqu'</u>ici nous n'avons pas eu Up to now we've had no problems.
   de problèmes.
  Je reste <u>jusqu'à</u> la fin du mois. I'm staying until the end of the month.

> **Tip**
> **jusque** changes to **jusqu'** before a word beginning with a vowel, most words starting with **h**, and the French word **y**.

- **par** by, with, per

deux **par** deux	two by two
par le train	by train
par la poste	by post
par e-mail	by email
Son nom commence **par** un H.	His name begins with H.
Prenez trois cachets **par** jour.	Take three tablets per day.
Le voyage coûte quatre cents euros **par** personne.	The trip costs four hundred euros per person.
Nous nous voyons une fois **par** mois.	We see each other once a month.
Il est tombé **par** terre.	He fell down.
Il y a beaucoup de touristes **par** ici.	There are a lot of tourists around here.

> **Tip**
> The prepositions **à** and **en** are also used with means of transport.

- **pendant** during, for

Ça s'est passé **pendant** l'été.	It happened during the summer.
Il n'a pas pu travailler **pendant** plusieurs mois.	He couldn't work for several months.

> **Tip**
> French uses the <u>perfect tense</u> with **pendant** to talk about actions in the past that are completed.
>
> | | |
> |---|---|
> | Nous <u>avons habité</u> pendant dix ans en Écosse. | We lived in Scotland for ten years. (*but don't any more*) |
>
> You can also miss out **pendant**.
>
> | | |
> |---|---|
> | Nous avons habité dix ans en Écosse. | We lived in Scotland for ten years. |
>
> **pendant** is also used to talk about something that will happen in the future.
>
> | | |
> |---|---|
> | Je <u>serai</u> à New York **pendant** un mois. | I'll be in New York for a month. |
>
> ⇨ *For more information on the* **Perfect tense**, *see page* 151.

- **pour** for (*who or what something is for, and where something or someone is going*)

C'est un cadeau **pour** toi.	It's a present for you.
Nous voudrions une chambre **pour** deux nuits.	We'd like a room for two nights.
le train **pour** Bordeaux	the train for Bordeaux

i Note that **pour** can also be used with infinitives, when it has the meaning of *in order to*.

Elle téléphone <u>pour savoir</u> à quelle heure on arrivera.	She's ringing to find out what time we'll get there.
<u>Pour aller</u> à Nice, s'il vous plaît?	Which way is it to Nice, please?

- **sans** without

Elle est venue <u>sans</u> son frère.	She came without her brother.
un café <u>sans</u> sucre	a coffee without sugar
un pull <u>sans</u> manches	a sleeveless sweater

i Note that **sans** can also be used before infinitives in French. In English a verb form ending in *-ing* is used after *without*.

Elle est partie <u>sans dire</u> au revoir.	She left <u>without saying</u> goodbye.

- **sauf** except

Tout le monde vient <u>sauf</u> lui.	Everyone's coming except him.

- **sous** under

<u>sous</u> la table	under the table
<u>sous</u> terre	underground

- **sur** on

Pose-le <u>sur</u> le bureau.	Put it down on the desk.
Ton sac est <u>sur</u> la table.	Your bag is on the table.
Vous verrez l'hôpital <u>sur</u> votre gauche.	You'll see the hospital on your left.
un livre <u>sur</u> la politique	a book on politics

i Note that **à** and **sur** can both mean *on* in English. **sur** usually means on the top of something. **sur la télé** means *on top of the TV set*, but **à la télé** means *broadcast on TV*. **sur le mur** means *on top of the wall*, but **au mur** means *hanging on the wall*.

> *Tip*
> With numbers and measurements **sur** can also mean *in*, *out of* and *by*.
>
> | | |
> |---|---|
> | **une personne <u>sur</u> dix** | one person <u>in</u> ten |
> | **J'ai eu quatorze <u>sur</u> vingt en maths.** | I got 14 <u>out of</u> 20 in maths. |
> | **La pièce fait quatre mètres <u>sur</u> deux.** | The room measures four metres <u>by</u> two. |

- **vers** towards (*a place*), at about

Il allait <u>vers</u> la gare.	He was going towards the station.
Je rentre chez moi <u>vers</u> cinq heures.	I go home at about 5 o'clock.

➤ **voici** (meaning *this is*, *here is*) and **voilà** (meaning *there is*, *that is*) are two very useful prepositions that French speakers often use to point things out.

<u>Voici</u> mon frère et <u>voilà</u> ma sœur.	This is my brother and that's my sister.
<u>Voici</u> ton sac.	Here's your bag.
Le <u>voici</u>!	Here he/it is!
Tiens! <u>Voilà</u> Paul.	Look! There's Paul.

Tu as perdu ton stylo?	Have you lost your pen?
En <u>voilà</u> un autre.	Here's another one.
Les <u>voilà</u>!	There they are!

Prepositions consisting of more than one word

➤ Prepositions can also be made up of several words instead of just one.

au bord de	at the edge of, at the side of
au bout de	after, at the end of
à cause de	because of
au-dessous de	below
au-dessus de	above
au fond de	at the bottom of, at the end of
au milieu de	in the middle of

<u>Au bout d</u>'un moment, il s'est endormi.	After a while, he fell asleep.
Nous ne pouvons pas sortir <u>à cause du</u> mauvais temps.	We can't go out because of the bad weather.
J'ai garé la voiture <u>au bord de</u> la route.	I parked the car by the side of the road.
Mon porte-monnaie est <u>au fond de</u> mon sac.	My purse is at the bottom of my bag.
Place le vase <u>au milieu de</u> la table.	Put the vase in the middle of the table.

Prepositions after verbs

➤ Some French verbs can be followed by an <u>infinitive</u> (the *to* form of the verb) and linked to it by either **de** or **à**, or no preposition at all. This is also true of verbs and their <u>objects</u>: the person or thing that the verb 'happens' to.

⇨ *For more information on* **Verbs followed by an infinitive**, *see page 243.*

> *Tip*
> The preposition that is used in French is not always the same as the one that is used in English. Whenever you learn a new verb, try to learn which preposition can be used after it too.

➤ The lists in this section concentrate on those French verbs that involve a different construction from the one that is used in English.

Verbs that are followed by à + object

➤ **à** is often the equivalent of the English word *to* when it is used with an indirect object after verbs like *send*, *give* and *say*.

dire quelque chose <u>à</u> quelqu'un	to say something <u>to</u> someone
donner quelque chose <u>à</u> quelqu'un	to give something <u>to</u> someone
écrire quelque chose <u>à</u> quelqu'un	to write something <u>to</u> someone

envoyer quelque chose <u>à</u> quelqu'un	to send something <u>to</u> someone
montrer quelque chose <u>à</u> quelqu'un	to show something <u>to</u> someone

⇨ *For more information on **Indirect objects**, see page 65.*

Tip

There is an important difference between French and English with this type of verb. In English, you can say either *to give something <u>to</u> someone* or *to give someone something*; *to show something <u>to</u> someone* or *to show someone something*. You can <u>NEVER</u> miss out **à** in French in the way that you can sometimes miss out *to* in English.

➤ Here are some verbs taking **à** in French that have a different construction in English.

croire <u>à</u> quelque chose	to believe <u>in</u> something
s'intéresser <u>à</u> quelqu'un/quelque chose	to be interested <u>in</u> someone/something
jouer <u>à</u> quelque chose	to play something (*sports, games*)
obéir <u>à</u> quelqu'un	to obey someone
penser <u>à</u> quelqu'un/quelque chose	to think <u>about</u> someone/something
répondre <u>à</u> quelqu'un	to answer someone
téléphoner <u>à</u> quelqu'un	to phone someone

Tip

When you are using **jouer** to talk about sports and games, you use **à**.
When you are using **jouer** to talk about musical instruments, you use **de**.

jouer <u>au</u> tennis	to play tennis
jouer <u>aux</u> échecs	to play chess
jouer <u>de</u> la guitare	to play the guitar
jouer <u>du</u> piano	to play the piano

➤ **plaire** followed by **à** is a common way of saying you like something.

plaire <u>à</u> quelqu'un	to please someone (*literally*)
Ton cadeau me plaît beaucoup.	I like your present a lot.
Ce film plaît beaucoup aux jeunes.	This film is very popular with young people.

Grammar Extra!

manquer à works quite differently from its English equivalent, *to miss*. The English object is the French subject, and the English subject is the French object.

manquer <u>à</u> quelqu'un	to be missed by someone (*literally*)
Tu (*subject*) **me** (*object*) **manques.**	I (*subject*) miss you (*object*).
Mon pays (*subject*) **me** (*object*) **manque beaucoup.**	I (*subject*) miss my country (*object*) very much.

➤ There are also some verbs where you can put a direct object before **à**. The verb **demander** is the most common.

demander quelque chose <u>à</u> quelqu'un	to ask someone something, to ask someone for something

⇨ *For more information on **Direct objects**, see page 61.*

ℹ️ Note that **demander** in French does <u>NOT</u> mean *to demand*. It means *to ask something* or *to ask for something*. If you want to say *demand* in French, use **exiger**.

Nous avons demandé notre chemin à un chauffeur de taxi.	We asked a taxi driver the way.
J'exige des excuses!	I demand an apology!

Verbs that are followed by de + object

➤ Here are some verbs taking **de** in French that have a different construction in English.

changer <u>de</u> quelque chose	to change something (*one's shoes and so on*)
dépendre <u>de</u> quelqu'un/quelque chose	to depend <u>on</u> someone/something
s'excuser <u>de</u> quelque chose	to apologize <u>for</u> something
jouer <u>de</u> quelque chose	to play something
parler <u>de</u> quelque chose	to talk <u>about</u> something
se servir <u>de</u> quelque chose	to use something
se souvenir <u>de</u> quelqu'un/ quelque chose	to remember someone/something

> *Tip*
> When you are using **jouer** to talk about sports and games, you use **à**.
> When you are using **jouer** to talk about musical instruments, you use **de**.
>
> | | |
> |---|---|
> | **jouer <u>au</u> tennis** | to play tennis |
> | **jouer <u>aux</u> échecs** | to play chess |
> | **jouer <u>de</u> la guitare** | to play the guitar |
> | **jouer <u>du</u> piano** | to play the piano |

➤ Some common phrases using **avoir** also contain **de**.

<u>avoir</u> besoin <u>de</u> quelque chose	to need something
<u>avoir</u> envie <u>de</u> quelque chose	to want something
<u>avoir</u> peur <u>de</u> quelque chose	to be afraid of something

➤ There are also some verbs where you can put a direct object before **de**. **remercier** is the most common.

remercier quelqu'un <u>de</u> quelque chose	to thank someone for something

⇨ *For more information on **Direct objects**, see page 61.*

Grammar Extra!
The verb **se tromper de quelque chose** is often the equivalent of *to get the wrong* ...

Je me suis trompé de numéro.	I got the wrong number.
Je me suis trompé de maison.	I got the wrong house.

Verbs taking a direct object in French but not in English

➤ In English there are a few verbs that are followed by *for, on, in, to* or *at* which, in French, are not followed by a preposition such as **à** or **de**. Here are the most common:

attendre quelqu'un/quelque chose	to wait <u>for</u> sb/sth
chercher quelqu'un/quelque chose	to look <u>for</u> sb/sth
demander quelqu'un/quelque chose	to ask <u>for</u> sb/sth
écouter quelqu'un/quelque chose	to listen <u>to</u> sb/sth
espérer quelque chose	to hope <u>for</u> sth
payer quelque chose	to pay <u>for</u> sth
regarder quelqu'un/quelque chose	to look <u>at</u> sb/sth

i Note that **attendre** does <u>NOT</u> mean *to attend* in English. It means *to wait for*. If you want to say that you attend something, use **assister à quelque chose**.

Je t'attends devant la gare.	I'll wait for you in front of the station.
Vous allez assister au concert?	Are you going to attend the concert?

➤ **habiter** can be used with or without a preposition:

- **habiter** is mostly used <u>without a preposition</u> when you are talking about living in a house, a flat and so on

Nous habitons un petit appartement en ville.	We live in a small flat in town.

- use **habiter** <u>with</u> **à** when you are talking about a town or city, and **au** (*singular*) or **aux** (*plural*) with the names of countries that are masculine in French

Nous habitons <u>à</u> Liverpool.	We live in Liverpool.
Nous habitons <u>aux</u> États-Unis.	We live in the United States.

- use **habiter** <u>with</u> **en** when you are talking about feminine countries

Nous habitons <u>en</u> Espagne.	We live in Spain.

KEY POINTS

✔ French prepositions after verbs are often not the ones that are used in English. French verbs often have a different construction from English verbs.

✔ French verbs are usually linked to their objects by **de**, **à** or nothing at all.

✔ You can never miss out **à** in French in the way that you can miss out *to* in English constructions like *to give someone something*.

5 **Cross out the unlikely options.**

a Où est le chat?

Sous la voiture./Sur le canapé./Dans le salon./À vélo.

b Vous restez ici pour combien de temps?

Depuis un mois./Pour un mois./Jusqu'à la fin du mois./ Un mois.

c Quand est-ce que tu me le rendras?

Dans cinq jours./Avant jeudi/Après le 15 août./ En quinze jours.

d Comment vous voulez payer?

Avec une carte de crédit./En liquide. / Avant la fin du mois./En plusieurs versements.

e Ne garez pas votre voiture

dans la rue./avant l'entrée./devant l'entrée./ sur le trottoir.

f Quand est-ce qu'ils sont arrivés?

Avant le dîner./Vers trois heures. /Depuis début mars./ Avec du retard.

g Prenez deux cachets

par e-mail./par jour./avec de l'eau./ pour faire baisser la fièvre.

h Il y a deux beaux tableaux

sur le mur./au mur./sur la table./au fond du sac.

i Nous ne pouvons pas sortir

sans eux./sous cette pluie./sans le savoir./ à cause de la pluie.

j Tu cherches tes clés?

Le voici!/Me voici!/Les voici!/Les voilà!

6 **Fill the gap with à or de, or with à or de combined with an article.**

a Elle n'a rien dit .... ses collègues.

b Je ne savais pas que tu jouais .... violon.

c Il était à la fête d'Alice, tu te souviens .... lui?

d Non, j'ai changé .... avis, je vais prendre l'autre.

e Les étudiants britanniques ne s'intéressent pas beaucoup .... la politique.

f Je remercie tout le monde .... leur participation.

g Je ne sais pas jouer .... échecs.

h Je vais envoyer ces photos .... laboratoire par e-mail.

i Il s'est excusé .... son retard.

j On va soit à la plage, soit au casino, ça dépend .... temps.

Test yourself

7 Translate the sentence into French.

a Everyone has to obey the rules.

....

b I didn't believe this story.

....

c I want to change direction.

....

d She advised me to telephone the doctor.

....

e Her books are very popular with girls. (*Use **plaire**.*)

....

f Can you play the piano? (*Use **Est-ce que vous**.*)

....

g I'm thinking about tomorrow.

....

h I asked the waiter for the bill.

....

i The children are afraid of dogs.

....

j Who's going to pay for the meal?

....

8 Match the related sentences.

a	**Espérons qu'il fera beau temps!**	Ils ont fréquenté la même école.
b	**Mes parents habitent un petit appartement en ville.**	Ils en seront ravis.
c	**Ils se souviennent de Matthieu.**	Hugo et Anna se marient demain.
d	**Bonjour, Stéphanie est là?**	Oh, pardon, je me suis trompée de numéro.
e	**Vous croyez que ces jeux vont plaire aux enfants?**	Ils n'ont pas de jardin.

Prepositions after adjectives

➤ Just like verbs, some French adjectives can be linked to what follows by either **à** or **de**.

➤ An adjective followed by **de** or **à** can be followed by a noun, a pronoun or an infinitive.

➤ Some adjectives that can be followed by **de** are used to say how you feel, that you are certain about something, or that it is necessary or important to do something. These are the most common:

certain	certain
content	happy
désolé	sorry
enchanté	delighted
heureux	happy
important	important
malheureux	unhappy
nécessaire	necessary
sûr	sure
triste	sad

Tu es <u>sûr de</u> pouvoir venir?	Are you sure you can come?
<u>Enchanté de</u> faire votre connaissance.	Delighted to meet you.
Il est <u>nécessaire de</u> réserver.	You have to book.

Grammar Extra!

➤ Some adjectives, such as **facile** (meaning *easy*), **intéressant** (meaning *interesting*) or **impossible** (meaning *impossible*), can be followed by either **à** or **de**. **de** tends to be used when you are saying something that is generally true. **à** tends to be used when you are saying something about someone or something in particular.

Il est difficile <u>de</u> prendre une décision.	It's difficult to make a decision.
Il est difficile <u>à</u> connaître.	He's difficult to get to know.
<u>Son accent</u> est difficile <u>à</u> comprendre.	His accent is difficult to understand.

For further explanation of grammatical terms, please see pages viii–xii.

Conjunctions

What is a conjunction?
A **conjunction** is a word such as *and*, *but*, *or*, *so*, *if* and *because*, that links two words
or phrases of a similar type, or two parts of a sentence, for example,
Diane <u>and</u> I have been friends for years; I left <u>because</u> I was bored.

---

et, mais, ou, parce que and si

➤ **et**, **mais**, **ou**, **parce que** and **si** are the most common conjunctions that you need to know
   in French.

- **et** and
  toi <u>et</u> moi   you <u>and</u> me
  Il pleut <u>et</u> il fait très froid.   It's raining <u>and</u> it's very cold.

- **mais** but
  C'est cher <u>mais</u> de très bonne qualité.   It's expensive, <u>but</u> very good quality.

  ⓘ Note that **mais** is also commonly found in front of **oui** and **si**.

  'Tu viens ce soir?' — '<u>Mais oui</u>!'   'Are you coming tonight?' — 'Definitely!'
  'Il n'a pas encore fini?' — '<u>Mais si</u>!'   'Hasn't he finished yet?' — 'He certainly has!'

- **ou** or
  Tu préfères le vert <u>ou</u> le bleu?   Do you like the green one <u>or</u> the blue one?
  Donne-moi ça <u>ou</u> je me fâche!   Give me that <u>or</u> I'll get cross!

  > *Tip*
  > Be careful not to confuse **ou** (meaning *or*) with **où** (meaning *where*).

- **parce que** because
  Je ne peux pas sortir <u>parce que</u>   I can't go out <u>because</u> I've still got
   j'ai encore du travail à faire.   work to do.

  > *Tip*
  > **parce que** changes to **parce qu'** before a word beginning with a vowel,
  > most words starting with **h**, and the French word **y**.
  >
  > **Il ne vient pas <u>parce qu'</u>il n'a**   He isn't coming because he
  > **pas de voiture.**   doesn't have a car.

- **si** if
  Je me demande <u>si</u> elle ment.   I wonder <u>if</u> she's lying.
  <u>Si</u> j'étais à ta place, je ne   <u>If</u> I were you, I wouldn't invite him.
      l'inviterais pas.

Tip

si changes to **s'** before **il** or **ils**.

<u>S'</u>il ne pleut pas, on mangera dehors.   If it doesn't rain, we'll eat outside.

Some other common conjunctions

➤ Here are some other common French conjunctions:
- **car** because
  Il faut prendre un bus pour y   You need to take a bus to get there
      accéder <u>car</u> il est interdit d´y   because cars are prohibited.
      monter en voiture.

🛈 Note that **car** is used in formal language or in writing. The normal way of saying *because* is **parce que**.

- **comme** as
  <u>Comme</u> il pleut, je prends la voiture.   <u>As</u> it's raining, I'm taking the car.

- **donc** so
  J'ai raté le train, <u>donc</u> je serai   I missed the train, <u>so</u> I'll be late.
      en retard.

- **lorsque** when
  J'allais composer ton numéro   I was about to dial your number
      <u>lorsque</u> tu as appelé.   <u>when</u> you called.

- **quand** when
  Je ne sors pas <u>quand</u> il pleut.   I don't go out <u>when</u> it rains.

🛈 Note that when **quand** and **lorsque** are used to talk about something that will happen in the future, the French verb has to be in the <u>future tense</u> even though English uses a verb in the <u>present tense</u>.

Quand je <u>serai</u> riche, j'achèterai   When <u>I'm</u> rich, I'll buy a nice house.
    une belle maison.

⇨ *For more information on the **Present tense** and the **Future tense**, see pages 98 and 136.*

➤ French, like English, also has conjunctions which have more than one part. Here are the most common:
- **ne ... ni ... ni** neither ... nor
  Je <u>n'</u>aime <u>ni</u> les lentilles <u>ni</u> les épinards.   I like <u>neither</u> lentils <u>nor</u> spinach.

🛈 Note that the **ne** part of this expression goes just before the verb.

- **ou ... ou, ou bien ... ou bien** either ... or
  Ou il est malade ou il ment.
  **Ou bien il m'évite ou bien il
    ne me reconnaît pas.**

Either he's sick or he's lying.
Either he's avoiding me or he
   doesn't recognize me.

The conjunction que

➤ When **que** is used to join two parts of a sentence, it means *that*.
  Il dit qu'il m'aime.
  Elle sait que vous êtes là.

He says that he loves me.
She knows that you're here.

> *Tip*
> In English you could say both *He says he loves me* and *He says that he loves me*,
> or *She knows you're here* and *She knows that you're here*.
> You can NEVER leave out **que** in French in the same way.

➤ **que** is also used when you are comparing two things or two people. In this case, it means
  as or *than*.
  **Ils n'y vont pas aussi souvent
    que nous.**
  **Les melons sont plus chers que
    les bananes.**

They don't go as often as us.

Melons are more expensive than bananas.

⇨ *For more information on **Comparative adjectives**, see page 43.*

➤ Some prepositions which give you information about when something happens, can also
  be conjunctions if you put **que** after them. **pendant que** (meaning *while*) is the most
  common of these.
  **Christian a téléphoné pendant
    que Chantal prenait son bain.**

Christian phoned while Chantal was
   in the bath.

ⓘ Note that when **pendant que** (meaning *while*), **quand** (meaning *when*) and **lorsque**
  (meaning *when*) are used to talk about something that will happen in the future,
  the French verb has to be in the future tense even though English uses a verb in the
  present tense.

  **Pendant que je serai en France,
    j'irai les voir.**

I'll go and visit them while I'm in France.

⇨ *For more information on the **Present tense** and the **Future tense**, see pages 98 and 136.*

Grammar Extra!
que can replace another conjunction to avoid having to repeat it.

**Quand tu seras plus grand et
  que tu auras une maison à toi, ...**
**Comme il pleut et que je n'ai
  pas de parapluie, ...**

When you're older and you have
  a house of your own, ...
As it's raining and I don't have an
  umbrella, ...

Numbers

1	**un (une)**
2	**deux**
3	**trois**
4	**quatre**
5	**cinq**
6	**six**
7	**sept**
8	**huit**
9	**neuf**
10	**dix**
11	**onze**
12	**douze**
13	**treize**
14	**quatorze**
15	**quinze**
16	**seize**
17	**dix-sept**
18	**dix-huit**
19	**dix-neuf**
20	**vingt**
21	**vingt et un (une)**
22	**vingt-deux**
30	**trente**
40	**quarante**
50	**cinquante**
60	**soixante**
70	**soixante-dix**
71	**soixante et onze**
72	**soixante-douze**
80	**quatre-vingts**
81	**quatre-vingt-un (-une)**
90	**quatre-vingt-dix**
91	**quatre-vingt-onze**
100	**cent**
101	**cent un (une)**
300	**trois cents**
301	**trois cent un (une)**
1000	**mille**
2000	**deux mille**
1,000,000	**un million**

1st	**premier (1er), première (1re)**
2nd	**deuxième (2e *or* 2ème) *or* second(e) ($2^{nd(e)}$)**
3rd	**troisième (3e *or* 3ème)**
4th	**quatrième (4e *or* 4ème)**
5th	**cinquième (5e *or* 5ème)**
6th	**sixième (6e *or* 6ème)**
7th	**septième (7e *or* 7ème)**
8th	**huitième (8e *or* 8ème)**
9th	**neuvième (9e *or* 9ème)**

For further explanation of grammatical terms, please see pages viii–xii.

10th	dixième (10e or 10ème)
11th	onzième (11e or 11ème)
12th	douzième (12e or 12ème)
13th	treizième (13e or 13ème)
14th	quatorzième (14e or 14ème)
15th	quinzième (15e or 15ème)
16th	seizième (16e or 16ème)
17th	dix-septième (17e or 17ème)
18th	dix-huitième (18e or 18ème)
19th	dix-neuvième (19e or 19ème)
20th	vingtième (20e or 20ème)
21st	vingt et unième (21e or 21ème)
22nd	vingt-deuxième (22e or 22ème)
30th	trentième (30e or 30ème)
100th	centième (100e or 100ème)
101st	cent unième (101e or 101ème)
1000th	millième (1000e or 1000ème)

1/2	un demi
1/3	un tiers
2/3	deux tiers
1/4	un quart
1/5	un cinquième
0.5	zéro virgule cinq (0,5)
3.4	trois virgule quatre (3,4)
10%	dix pour cent
100%	cent pour cent

EXEMPLES	**EXAMPLES**
Il habite au dix.	He lives at number ten.
à la page dix-neuf	on page nineteen
au chapitre sept	in chapter seven
Il habite au cinquième (étage).	He lives on the fifth floor.
Il est arrivé troisième.	He came in third.
échelle au vingt-cinq millième	scale one to twenty-five thousand

L'heure	**The time**
Quelle heure est-il?	What time is it?
Il est...	It's...
une heure	one o'clock
une heure dix	ten past one
une heure et quart	quarter past one
une heure et demie	half past one
deux heures moins vingt	twenty to two
deux heures moins le quart	quarter to two

À quelle heure?	At what time?
à minuit	at midnight
à midi	at midday, at noon
à une heure (de l'après-midi)	at one o'clock (in the afternoon)
à huit heures (du soir)	at eight o'clock (in the evening)
à 11h15 or onze heures quinze	at 11.15 or eleven fifteen
à 20h45 or vingt heures quarante-cinq	at 20.45 or twenty forty-five

La date	The date
Les jours de la semaine	**Days of the week**

lundi	Monday
mardi	Tuesday
mercredi	Wednesday
jeudi	Thursday
vendredi	Friday
samedi	Saturday
dimanche	Sunday

Quand?	**When?**
lundi	on Monday
le lundi	on Mondays
tous les lundis	every Monday
mardi dernier	last Tuesday
vendredi prochain	next Friday
samedi en huit	a week on Saturday
samedi en quinze	two weeks on Saturday

> ⓘ Note that days of the week are <u>NOT</u> written with a capital letter in French.

Les mois	**Months of the year**
janvier	January
février	February
mars	March
avril	April
mai	May
juin	June
juillet	July
août	August
septembre	September
octobre	October
novembre	November
décembre	December

Quand?	**When?**
en février	in February
le 1er décembre	on December 1st
le premier décembre	on December first
en 1998	in 1998
en mille neuf cent quatre-vingt-dix-huit	in nineteen ninety-eight

Quel jour sommes-nous?	**What day is it?**
Nous sommes le...	**It's...**
lundi 26 février *or*	Monday 26 February *or*
lundi vingt-six février	Monday twenty-sixth of February
dimanche 1er octobre *or*	Sunday 1st October *or*
dimanche premier octobre	Sunday the first of October

> ⓘ Note that months of the year are <u>NOT</u> written with a capital letter in French.

For further explanation of grammatical terms, please see pages viii–xii.

Vocabulaire	Useful vocabulary
Quand?	**When?**
aujourd'hui	today
ce matin	this morning
cet après-midi	this afternoon
ce soir	this evening
Souvent?	**How often?**
tous les jours	every day
tous les deux jours	every other day
une fois par semaine	once a week
deux fois par semaine	twice a week
une fois par mois	once a month
Ça s'est passé quand?	**When did it happen?**
le matin	in the morning
le soir	in the evening
hier	yesterday
hier soir	yesterday evening
avant-hier	the day before yesterday
il y a une semaine	a week ago
il y a quinze jours	two weeks ago
l'an dernier *or* **l'année dernière**	last year
Ça va se passer quand?	**When is it going to happen?**
demain	tomorrow
demain matin	tomorrow morning
après-demain	the day after tomorrow
dans deux jours	in two days
dans une semaine	in a week
dans quinze jours	in two weeks
le mois prochain	next month
l'an prochain *or* **l'année prochaine**	next year

Some common difficulties

General problems

➤ You can't always translate French into English and English into French word for word. While occasionally it is possible to do this, often it is not. For example:

- English <u>phrasal verbs</u> (verbs followed by a preposition or adverb), such as, *to run away*, *to fall down*, are often translated by <u>ONE</u> word in French.

continuer	to go on
tomber	to fall down
rendre	to give back

  ⇨ *For more information on **Verbs**, see pages 96.*

- Sentences which contain a verb and preposition in English, might <u>NOT</u> contain a preposition in French.

payer quelque chose	to pay <u>for</u> something
regarder quelqu'un/quelque chose	to look <u>at</u> somebody/something
écouter quelqu'un/quelque chose	to listen <u>to</u> somebody/something

- Similarly, sentences which contain a verb and preposition in French, might <u>NOT</u> contain a preposition in English.

obéir <u>à</u> quelqu'un/quelque chose	to obey somebody/something
changer <u>de</u> quelque chose	to change something
manquer <u>de</u> quelque chose	to lack something

- The same French preposition may be translated into English in different ways.

parler <u>de</u> quelque chose	to talk <u>about</u> something
sûr <u>de</u> quelque chose	sure <u>of</u> something
voler quelque chose <u>à</u> quelqu'un	to steal something <u>from</u> someone
croire <u>à</u> quelque chose	to believe <u>in</u> something

  ⇨ *For more information on **Prepositions**, see page 227.*

- A word which is singular in English may not be in French.

les bagages	luggage
ses cheveux	his/her hair

- Similarly, a word which is singular in French may not be in English.

un short	shorts
mon pantalon	my trousers

  ⇨ *For more information on **Nouns**, see page 1.*

- In English, you can use 's to show who or what something belongs to; in French, you have to use **de**.

la voiture de mon frère	my brother<u>'s</u> car
la chambre des enfants	the children<u>'s</u> bedroom

  ⇨ *For more information on the preposition **de**, see pages 230 and 231.*

Specific problems

-ing

➤ The -ing ending in English is translated in a number of different ways in French:

- to be ...-ing is translated by a verb consisting of one word.

Il **part** demain.	He's <u>leaving</u> tomorrow.
Je **lisais** un roman.	I <u>was reading</u> a book.

⇨ For more information on **Verbs**, see page 96.

☒ Note that when you are talking about somebody's or something's physical position, you use a <u>past participle</u>.

Elle est <u>assise</u> là-bas	She's <u>sitting</u> over there.
Il était <u>couché</u> par terre.	He was <u>lying</u> on the ground.

⇨ For more information on the **Past participle**, see page 151.

➤ -ing can also be translated by:

- an infinitive

J'aime <u>aller</u> au cinéma	I like <u>going</u> to the cinema.
Arrêtez de vous <u>disputer</u>!	Stop <u>arguing</u>!
Avant de <u>partir</u>...	Before <u>leaving</u>...

⇨ For more information on **Infinitives**, see page 184.

- a present participle

<u>Étant</u> plus timide que moi, elle...	Being shyer than me, she...

⇨ For more information on the **Present participle**, see page 170.

- a noun

<u>Le ski</u> me maintient en forme.	<u>Skiing</u> keeps me fit.

⇨ For more information on **Nouns**, see page 1.

to be

➤ The verb to be is generally translated by **être**.

Il <u>est</u> tard.	It's late.
Ce n'<u>est</u> pas possible!	It's not possible!

➤ When you are talking about the physical position of something, **se trouver** may be used.

Où <u>se trouve</u> la gare?	Where's the station?

➤ In certain set phrases which describe how you are feeling or a state you are in, the verb **avoir** is used.

avoir chaud	to be warm
avoir froid	to be cold
avoir faim	to be hungry
avoir soif	to be thirsty
avoir peur	to be afraid
avoir tort	to be wrong
avoir raison	to be right

➤ When you are describing what the weather is like, use the verb **faire**.

Quel temps <u>fait</u>-il?	What<u>'s</u> the weather like?
Il <u>fait</u> beau.	It<u>'s</u> lovely.
Il <u>fait</u> mauvais.	It<u>'s</u> miserable.
Il <u>fait</u> du vent.	It<u>'s</u> windy.

➤ When you are talking about someone's age, use the verb **avoir**.

Quel âge <u>as</u>-tu?	How old <u>are</u> you?
J'<u>ai</u> quinze ans.	I<u>'m</u> fifteen.

➤ When talking about your health, use the verb **aller**.

Comment <u>allez</u>-vous?	How <u>are</u> you?
Je <u>vais</u> très bien.	I<u>'m</u> very well.

it is, it's

➤ *it is* and *it's* are usually translated by **il est** or **elle est** when referring to a noun.

'Où est mon parapluie?' —	'Where's my umbrella?' — '<u>It's</u> there,
'<u>Il est</u> là, dans le coin.'	in the corner.'
Descends la valise si <u>elle</u> n'<u>est</u> pas trop lourde.	Bring the case down if <u>it is</u>n't too heavy.

➤ When you are talking about the time, use **il est**.

'Quelle heure <u>est-il</u>?' — **'<u>Il est</u> sept heures et demie.'**	'What time <u>is it</u>?' — '<u>It's</u> half past seven.'

➤ When you are describing what the weather is like, use the verb **faire**.

Il <u>fait</u> beau.	It<u>'s</u> lovely.
Il <u>fait</u> mauvais.	It<u>'s</u> miserable.
Il <u>fait</u> du vent.	It<u>'s</u> windy.

➤ If you want to say, for example, *it is difficult to do something* or *it is easy to do something*, use **il est**.

<u>Il est</u> difficile de répondre à cette question.	<u>It is</u> difficult to answer this question.

➤ In <u>ALL</u> other phrases and constructions, use **c'est**.

<u>C'est</u> moi qui ne l'aime pas.	<u>It's</u> me who doesn't like him.
<u>C'est</u> Charles qui l'a dit.	<u>It's</u> Charles who said so.
<u>C'est</u> ici que je les ai achetés.	<u>It's</u> here that I bought them.
<u>C'est</u> parce que la poste est fermée que...	<u>It's</u> because the post office is closed that...

For further explanation of grammatical terms, please see pages viii–xii.

there is, there are

➤ Both *there is* and *there are* are translated by **il y a**.

Il y a quelqu'un à la porte.	There is someone at the door.
Il y a cinq livres sur la table.	There are five books on the table.

can, to be able

➤ If you want to talk about someone's physical ability to do something, use **pouvoir**.

Pouvez-vous faire dix kilomètres à pied?	Can you walk ten kilometres?

➤ If you want to say that *you know how to do something*, use **savoir**.

Elle ne sait pas nager.	She can't swim.

➤ When *can* is used with verbs to do with what you can see or hear, you do NOT use **pouvoir** in French.

Je ne vois rien.	I can't see anything.
Il les entendait.	He could hear them.

to

➤ The preposition *to* is generally translated by **à**.

Donne le livre à Patrick.	Give the book to Patrick.

⇨ *For more information on the preposition à, see page 227–228.*

➤ When you are talking about the time, use **moins**.

dix heures moins cinq	five to ten
à sept heures moins le quart	at a quarter to seven

➤ If you want to say *(in order) to*, use **pour**.

Je l'ai fait pour vous aider.	I did it to help you.
Il va en ville pour acheter un cadeau.	He's going into town to buy a present.

The Alphabet

➤ The French alphabet is pronounced differently from the way it is pronounced in English. Use the list below to help you sound out the letters.

A, a	[a]	(ah)	like 'a' in 'la'
B, b	[be]	(bay)	
C, c	[se]	(say)	
D, d	[de]	(day)	
E, e	[ə]	(uh)	like 'e' in 'le'
F, f	[ɛf]	(eff)	
G, g	[ʒe]	(jay)	
H, h	[aʃ]	(ash)	
I, i	[i]	(ee)	
J, j	[ʒi]	(jee)	
K, k	[ka]	(ka)	
L, l	[ɛl]	(ell)	
M, m	[ɛm]	(emm)	
N, n	[ɛn]	(enn)	
O, o	[o]	(oh)	
P, p	[pe]	(pay)	
Q, q	[ky]	(ku)	like 'u' in 'une'
R, r	[ɛr]	(air)	
S, s	[ɛs]	(ess)	
T, t	[te]	(tay)	
U, u	[y]	(u)	like 'u' in 'une'
V, v	[ve]	(vay)	
W, w	[dubləve]	(doobla-vay)	
X, x	[iks]	(eex)	
Y, y	[igrɛk]	(ee-grek)	
Z, z	[zɛd]	(zed)	

For further explanation of grammatical terms, please see pages viii–xii.

Solutions

Nouns

1.
   a. princesse
   b. Anglaise
   c. employée
   d. reine
   e. vache
   f. chienne
   g. une Belge
   h. une camarade
   i. une serveuse
   j. une joueuse

2.
   a. un champignon, un chou, un citron
   b. un appartement, une maison, un jardin
   c. un tee-shirt, un chapeau, un mouchoir
   d. la main, le genou, la peau
   e. la patience, le silence, la chance
   f. une page, une image, un dessin
   g. un couteau, une fourchette, une cuillère
   h. un chat, un chien, une perruche
   i. une brosse à dents, une serviette, un shampooing
   j. une boulangerie, un café, un supermarché

3.
   a. **le lundi** = a day of the week: masculine noun
   b. **le français** = a language: masculine noun
   c. **un sandwich** = an English noun used in French: masculine noun
   d. **un gramme** = a metric weight: masculine noun
   e. **le printemps** = a season: masculine noun

4.
   a. un
   b. une
   c. une
   d. un
   e. une
   f. une
   g. un
   h. un
   i. une
   j. un

5.
   a. une veuve = **a widow**
   b. un veuf = **a widower**
   c. une lionne = **a lioness**
   d. une chanteuse = **a female singer**
   e. un étranger = **a foreign man**

6.
   a. une Anglaise
   b. une camarade
   c. une employée
   d. une reine
   e. une princesse
   f. une Belge
   g. une chienne
   h. une Française
   i. une fille
   j. une femme

7.
   a. un élève
   b. une élève
   c. une collègue
   d. le cadet
   e. la cadette
   f. une chanteuse
   g. une Anglaise
   h. la voisine
   i. le voisin
   j. une Belge

8.
   a. 1 voiture
   b. 3 fils
   c. 2 voix
   d. 2 hôtels
   e. 10 jeux
   f. 3 cailloux
   g. 1 chou
   h. 2 hiboux
   i. 3 journaux
   j. 1000 travaux

9.
   a. jardins
   b. amis
   c. femmes
   d. animaux
   e. bijoux
   f. fils
   g. chapeaux
   h. jeux
   i. choux
   j. genoux

10.
   a. 1
   b. 2
   c. 2
   d. 2
   e. 1
   f. 2
   g. 2
   h. 1
   i. 1
   j. 1

11.
   a. les cheveux et la peau
   b. les affaires et le tourisme
   c. un short et un tee-shirt
   d. un pantalon et un chapeau
   e. un travail et un appartement
   f. le nez et les genoux
   g. 8 champignons et 2 choux
   h. 2 fils et 1 neveu
   i. 1 printemps et 2 étés
   j. une réunion et des renseignements

Articles

1
- **a** la
- **b** le
- **c** le
- **d** les
- **e** l'
- **f** la
- **g** la
- **h** le
- **i** le
- **j** l'

2
- **a** l'homme et la femme
- **b** la maison et le jardin
- **c** les Belges et les Français
- **d** le Français et l'Anglaise
- **e** le cadet, Marc
- **f** la cadette, Marie
- **g** la vedette, Depardieu
- **h** les étudiants et le professeur
- **i** les souris et le fromage
- **j** le printemps et l'été

3
- **a** au
- **b** à la
- **c** de l'
- **d** à la
- **e** des
- **f** de l'
- **g** de l'
- **h** des
- **i** à l'
- **j** des

4
- **a** des fleurs
- **b** au Japon
- **c** des professeurs
- **d** de la piscine
- **e** à l'Europe
- **f** au monsieur
- **g** au port/au piscine
- **h** du court de tennis
- **i** aux hôpitaux

5
- **a** Je n'aime pas le football.
- **b** Je n'aime pas les souris.
- **c** Tu aimes le fromage?
- **d** Je n'aime pas les chiens.
- **e** Tu aimes les gâteaux?
- **f** Tu aimes la Bretagne?
- **g** Je n'aime pas les plages.
- **h** Tu aimes le français?
- **i** Tu aimes les champignons?
- **j** Je n'aime pas le vin.

6
- **a** aux
- **b** à la
- **c** au
- **d** à la
- **e** au

f à la
g à la
h au
i au
j à la

7
- **a** Mon sport préféré = **c'est le ski**
- **b** Ma région préférée = **c'est la Bretagne**
- **c** Ma saison préférée = **c'est le printemps**
- **d** Mon vin préféré = **c'est le champagne**
- **e** Mon fromage préféré = **c'est le brie**

8
- **a** la
- **b** du
- **c** l'
- **d** du
- **e** aux
- **f** au
- **g** aux
- **h** la
- **i** du
- **j** au

9
- **a** une
- **b** un
- **c** des
- **d** des
- **e** un
- **f** des
- **g** un
- **h** une
- **i** des
- **j** des

10
- **a** Je n'ai pas d'ordinateur.
- **b** Je n'ai pas de travail.
- **c** Je n'ai pas de voiture.
- **d** Je n'ai pas de problèmes.
- **e** Il n'y a pas de piscine.
- **f** Il n'y a pas de vin.
- **g** Il n'y a pas de miroir.
- **h** Je n'ai pas de chapeau.
- **i** Il n'y a pas de boulangerie.
- **j** Il n'y a pas d'hôpital.

11
- **a** Tu as des frères? = **Non, j'ai une sœur.**
- **b** Tu as des animaux? = **Oui, j'ai un chien.**
- **c** Avez-vous des enfants? = **Oui, j'ai un fils.**
- **d** Il y a des magasins? = **Oui, il y a une boulangerie.**
- **e** Tu as des joujoux? = **Oui, j'ai un ballon.**

12
- **a** est danseuse.
- **b** est un chanteur.
- **c** est acteur.
- **d** est serveuse.
- **e** est une chanteuse.
- **f** est médecin.
- **g** est chanteur.
- **h** est un professeur.
- **i** est coiffeuse.

13
- **a** du
- **b** des
- **c** des
- **d** de la
- **e** du
- **f** de l'
- **g** des
- **h** de la
- **i** de l'
- **j** du

14
- **a** du vin/du ciment
- **b** du tourisme/de l'eau
- **c** du café
- **d** du lait
- **e** du vin
- **f** du riz au lait
- **g** du beurre
- **h** du lait/du sucre
- **i** des oranges/des chips
- **j** de la glace

15
- **a** Je vais acheter du yaourt.
- **b** Je vais acheter du beurre et du lait.
- **c** Tu veux du miel?
- **d** Du lait et du sucre?
- **e** Est-ce qu'il y a du jus d'orange?
- **f** Est-ce qu'il y a du café pour moi?
- **g** Est-ce qu'il y a de la limonade?
- **h** Tu veux de la confiture?
- **i** Elle ne veut pas de margarine.
- **j** Je ne mange pas de fromage.

16
- **a** de
- **b** des
- **c** de
- **d** de
- **e** d'
- **f** d'
- **g** de
- **h** de
- **i** d'
- **j** des

Adjectives

1 **a** David Beckham = **un footballeur anglais**
b Serena et Venus Williams = **des joueuses de tennis américaines**
c Gérard Depardieu = **un acteur français**
d Thierry Henri et Zinedine Zidane = **des footballeurs français**
e Isabelle Huppert et Catherine Deneuve = **des actrices françaises**
f Amy Winehouse = **une chanteuse anglaise**
g Michael Schumacher = **un pilote de course allemand**
h Seve Ballesteros et Raquel Carriedo = **des joueurs de golf espagnols**
i Tom Jones = **un chanteur gallois**
j Rafael Nadal = **un joueur de tennis espagnol**

2 **a** américaine
b américain
c américaines
d américaines
e américains
f américaines
g américains
h américaine
i américain
j américaines

3 **a** un chapeau noir
b des tee-shirts noirs
c un pantalon noir
d une voiture noire
e un short noir
f une porte noire
g des étudiants noirs
h une collègue noire
i des amis noirs
j des chanteuses noires

4 **a** allemands
b française
c espagnoles
d allemande
e anglaises
f minérale
g lourds
h nette

i cruelle
j pareille

5 **a** une chemise = **blanche**
b ma cousine = **favorite**
c une phrase = **très longue**
d une histoire = **complètement fausse**
e une personne = **extrêmement gentille**

6 **a** une journée chaude
b une chemise blanche et une cravate noire
c des vins français et des fromages anglais
d une jolie fille et un beau garçon
e la bonne réponse
f une courte réunion
g un haut bâtiment
h un vieil homme et un petit garçon
i un mauvais choix
j une meilleure idée

7 **a** **Marie Vargas/ma cousine**
b **Max/Thomas/Paul**
c **une caravane/un skateboard**
d **Alice**
e **un cyclomoteur/un tracteur/un camion**
f **un jeu**
g **Delphine/Susanne**
h **un bébé**
i **Nicolas**
j **Isabelle/Thérèse**

8 **a** une vieille femme française
b un nouveau film américain
c une nouvelle idée intéressante
d une robe chère et élégante
e une jeune femme mince
f un bon repas indien
g un bon chocolat chaud
h une belle table ronde
i un enfant sage et intelligent
j une cravate rouge et noire

9 **a** prochaine
b dernières
c dernier
d dernière

e prochaine
f prochains
g prochaines
h derniers
i prochain
j derniers

10 **a** plus
b moins
c plus
d plus
e plus
f plus
g plus
h moins
i moins
j plus

11 **a** Lucien est plus intelligent que Serge.
b Serge est moins intelligent que Lucien.
c Lucien est plus grand que son frère.
d Élodie est plus petite que moi.
e Marie est moins sympathique que Chantal.
f Lucien est aussi sympathique que Chantal.
g Charles est plus optimiste que Xavier.
h Véronique est moins impatiente que Sébastien.
i Lucien est aussi inquiet que moi.
j Florent est plus sportif que son frère.

12 **a** le journal le plus intéressant
b la voiture la plus chère
c les hôtels les plus chers
d les chanteuses les plus populaires
e les jardins les plus petits
f les hôpitaux les plus grands
g la personne la moins optimiste
h les dessins les moins beaux
i les robes les moins belles
j le plus grand magasin de Londres

Adjectives

13 a la meilleure
b le meilleur
c les pires
d le plus mauvais
e les meilleurs
f la moindre
g le moindre
h le moindre
i les plus mauvaises
j le plus petit

14 a Cette
b Ce
c Ces
d Cette
e Cet
f cette
g ces
h cet
i ce
j ce

15 a Cette voiture est belle.
b Cette couleur est belle.
c Cet hôpital est grand.
d Ce jardin est beau.
e Ce pantalon est mieux.
f Ces champignons sont bons.
g Je vais acheter ce miroir.
h Tu veux ces roses?
i J'aime ce tee-shirt et ce short.

j Je vais acheter cette veste et ces chemises.
k J'ai ces sacs et cette valise.

16 a cette personne-là
b cette veste-ci
c ces enfants-ci
d ces femmes-là
e ce bouton-ci
f cet hôtel-là
g ce mot-ci
h ce guide-là
i ces pommes-ci
j ces gâteaux-là

17 a mes
b mon
c ta
d ta
e son
f sa
g son
h vos
i notre
j leurs

18 a Voilà son mari.
b Voilà ma voiture.
c Voilà votre journal, Monsieur.
d Voilà vos sacs, Madame.
e Voilà sa mère.
f Voilà tes jouets, Pierre.

g Voilà sa maison.
h Voilà mes affaires.
i Voilà notre train.
j Voilà son autre sœur.

19 a Marc/Matthieu
b le beurre/le rosbif
c Catherine
d l'Australie/la Seine
e le café
f les maths/la biologie
g les petits pois/les fraises
h Paul et Martin/Heinrich et Horst
i mon adresse
j la philosophie

20 a J'ai d'autres amis.
b J'ai quelques problèmes.
c J'y vais chaque mois.
d J'ai les mêmes chaussures.
e Il reste quelques pommes de terre.
f J'ai un autre pantalon.
g Il a le même problème.
h Il reste quelques billets.
i J'ai tout le travail.
j Voilà toutes les filles.

Pronouns

1
a mon amie
b mon pantalon/mon ami
c les autres
d mon mari et moi
e les souris/les personnes âgées
f tes examens
g sa Majesté la reine/tous les enfants de la classe
h une chaise/les affaires
i l'heure/le poivre et la moutarde/la circulation
j Sylvie et Christine

2
a Elle
b Ils
c Ils
d elles
e elles
f elle
g il
h elles
i ils
j ils

3
a l'addition = **elle**
b les personnes = **elles**
c les trains = **ils**
d mon frère et mes sœurs = **ils**
e l'appartement = **il**

4
a Où est Paul? — Il est à Paris.
b Prends du fromage, il est bon.
c J'aime ce vin, il est excellent.
d Il pleut.
e Où sont Pierre et Sonia? — Ils sont à Calais.
f Où est ta voiture? — Elle est à la maison.
g Prends des fraises, elles sont bonnes.
h On va au cinéma demain.
i Tu aimes ma veste? — Oui, elle est belle.
j Où sont les fourchettes? — Elles sont sur la table.

5
a la
b les
c t'
d m'
e t'
f les
g nous
h la
i le
j la

6
a -la
b -les
c -les
d -la
e -le
f -nous
g -le
h -la
i -nous

7
a Susanne est gentille. = **Elle va nous aider.**
b Tu es gentille. = **Tu vas m'aider.**
c J'aime ce pantalon. = **Je vais l'acheter.**
d Marie est jolie. = **Il voudrait la revoir.**
e J'aime ces chaussures. = **Je vais les acheter.**

8
a Tu aimes Sarah? — Non, je la déteste!
b Tu l'entends?
c Tu vois cet oiseau? — Oui, je le vois.
d Tu connais la réponse? — Non, je ne la connais pas.
e Henri et Sophie sont dans le jardin. — Oui, je les vois.
f Tu aimes ce vin? — Oui, je l'aime beaucoup.
g Le château est beau, on peut le visiter en été.
h Aidez-moi!
i J'aime cette photo. — Prends-la!
j Jonathon, où sont mes clés, les vois-tu or tu les vois?

9
a Bernard téléphone à ses parents tous les jours. = **Il leur téléphone tous les jours.**
b Laurent téléphone à son frère tous les jours. = **Il lui téléphone tous les jours.**
c Nathalie parle souvent à sa sœur. = **Elle lui parle souvent.**
d Paul écrit à mon mari et moi à Noël. = **Il nous écrit à Noël.**
e Pierre écrit à sa sœur à Noël. = **Il lui écrit à Noël.**

10
a Tu m'apportes un verre?
b Tu lui apportes du lait?
c Tu nous apportes ton cahier?
d Tu leur apportes des chaises?
e Tu me donnes la main?
f Tu lui donnes le ballon?
g Tu leur donnes les cadeaux?
h Tu nous donnes ce bâton?
i Tu leur téléphones ce soir?
j Tu me téléphones demain?

11
a lui
b leur
c lui
d leur
e lui
f me
g leur
h lui
i lui
j vous

12
a Elle m'a donné un verre de vin.
b Donne-lui du lait.
c Madame Reyer, Lise vous écrit une carte.
d Elle ne nous parle pas.
e Donne-moi les clés!
f Donne-lui l'argent!
g Tu me donnes l'argent?
h Je vais leur téléphoner ce soir.
i Il va leur dire la vérité.
j Elle ne veut pas me répondre.

13
a elle
b elle
c eux
d d'elles
e elles
f lui
g eux
h vous
i nous
j lui

14
a Tu es là, chérie? = **C'est toi, chérie?**
b Luc a cassé le joujou. = **C'est lui qui l'a cassé.**
c Lucie a cassé le vase. = **C'est elle qui l'a cassé.**
d Vous êtes là, Madame Ducasse? = **C'est vous, Madame?**

Pronouns

e Laurent a cassé les verres. = **C'est lui qui les a cassés.**

15 a Il est fatigué. — Moi aussi.
b Elle est optimiste. — Nous aussi.
c Je suis à l'hôtel, vous aussi?
d Elle est aussi inquiète que lui.
e Tu es aussi jolie qu'elle, Emma.
f Elle est plus petite que moi.
g Elle est gentille, lui non.
h Tu es riche, moi non.
i Ils sont plus riches que nous.
j Je pense souvent à lui. — Moi aussi.

16 a eux-mêmes
b elle-même
c nous-mêmes
d moi-même
e elles-mêmes
f toi-même
g soi-même
h moi-même
i eux-mêmes
j vous-même

17 a Tes chaussures sont plus belles. = **Je les préfère aux miennes.**
b Ton frère est plus gentil. = **Je le préfère au mien.**
c J'ai oublié mon guide. = **J'ai besoin du vôtre.**
d Je n'aime pas ma chambre. = **Je préfère la sienne.**
e Je n'ai pas de crème solaire. = **J'ai besoin de la tienne.**

18 a le mien
b la mienne
c la sienne
d la leur
e le sien
f la sienne
g les siens
h les siennes
i la leur
j le leur

19 a c'est la nôtre/c'est la leur
b ce sont les siennes
c c'est la mienne

d c'est le tien/ce n'est pas le tien/ce sont les leurs
e c'est le mien
f ce sont les siens
g c'est la mienne/c'est la vôtre
h ce sont les siens
i ce sont les miennes/ce sont les tiennes
j c'est le leur

20 a Ce n'est pas sa voiture, c'est la mienne.
b Sa maison est belle, je la préfère à la mienne.
c Leur professeur est bon, je le préfère au nôtre.
d Cette chambre est la sienne.
e Cette équipe est bonne. Elle est meilleure que la nôtre.
f Leur appartement est plus grand que le nôtre.
g Mon sac est plus lourd que le sien.
h Ces affaires sont les leurs.
i Je n'ai pas de shampooing, j'ai besoin du tien.
j Sa vie est plus difficile que la mienne.

21 a en as
b en veux
c m'en parler
d s'en servir
e m'en servir
f n'en veut pas
g en avez
h en voulez
i en goûter
j en acheter

22 a Elle aime beaucoup la France. = **Elle y passe tout l'été.**
b Tu peux me prêter de l'argent? = **J'en ai besoin.**
c Je n'ai pas de beurre. = **Je dois en acheter.**
d Il y a un problème? = **Tu peux m'en parler.**
e Quelle surprise! = **Je ne m'y attendais pas.**

23 a C'est très bon./Je suis fatiguée.

b Je ne l'aime pas.
c Sa maison est petite.
d C'est nul.
e Je suis dans le doute.
f Il est très petit./Il est lourd.
g C'est naturel./C'était prévisible.
h C'est important/C'est drôle./C'est de ta faute.
i C'est un secret.
j Comment fait-on pour y aller?

24 a Un dictionnaire? J'en ai trois.
b Je veux un chien. Non, j'en veux deux.
c Combien d'assiettes y a-t-il sur la table? – Il y en a quatre.
d Regarde sur la table, je pense que ton portable y est.
e Il y a de la glace? J'en veux!
f Je n'y pense plus.
g Tu as de l'argent – donnes-en à ta sœur!
h Nous avons besoin d''argent – donne-nous-en!
i J'ai besoin d'argent – donne-m'en!
j Comment fait-on pour y aller?

25 a le lui
b la lui
c les leur
d te le
e le lui
f vous en
g le leur
h t'en
i lui en
j vous le

26 a Ils veulent voir vos photos. = **Je vais les leur montrer.**
b Marie adore cette histoire. = **Je vais la lui lire.**
c J'adore les roses rouges. = **Je vais t'en envoyer.**
d Il demande du cognac. = **Ne lui en donne pas!**
e Nous avons besoin de l'adresse. = **Je vais vous l'envoyer.**

Pronouns

27 a quelque chose
b quelqu'un
c quelque chose
d quelqu'un
e quelqu'un
f quelque chose
g quelque chose
h quelqu'un
i quelque chose
j quelque chose

28 a Ici on est libre. = **Chacun fait ce qu'il veut.**
b Elle est malade. = **Elle ne veut voir personne.**
c La crise continue. = **Rien n'a changé.**
d On a fait une collecte. = **Nous avons donné 20 euros chacun.**
e C'est un beau quartier. = **Les maisons ont chacune leur grand jardin.**

29 a personne
b rien
c personne
d Personne
e rien
f Rien
g rien
h Personne
i rien
j Personne

30 a Je reste à la maison.
b C'est un collègue.
c Je suis inquiet./C'est le désastre.
d une nouvelle amie
e Elle est jolie.
f Le repas était très bon.
g Elle est sportive./Elle ne dit rien.
h Il pleut.
i tes cadeaux
j quelques

31 a qui
b que
c qui
d qui
e que
f que
g qui
h que
i qui
j que

32 a C'est le bus qui va au centre-ville.
b Ma sœur, qui est très intelligente, est à l'université.
c Voilà la voiture que je vais acheter.
d C'est le sport que j'aime le plus.
e Élodie est l'amie à qui j'écris.
f Qui est la personne à qui il parle?
g Qui est la fille avec qui il danse?
h Ce sont les enfants pour qui j'achète ce ballon.
i Voilà l'homme que j'adore!
j Voilà le modèle qui coûte le plus cher.

33 a sur lequel/sur que/sur qui
b pour lesquelles/pour qui
c sans qui
d avec qui/avec lequel
e auxquelles
f duquel
g desquels/auxquels
h duquel
i auxquelles
j sans laquelle

34 a les problèmes = **dont tu parles**
b l'argent = **dont j'ai besoin**
c le beau jardin = **dont elle est très fière**
d l'enfant = **dont le vélo disparu**
e la maladie = **dont elle souffre**

35 a C'est moi qui
b C'est lui qui
c Ce sont elles qui
d Ce sont eux qui
e C'est toi qui
f C'est moi qui
g Ce sont eux qui
h C'est vous qui
i c'est vous qui
j c'est toi qui

36 a Donne-moi ça! = **J'en ai besoin.**
b Ça te plaît de faire de longues promenades? = **Non, je préfère regarder la télé.**
c Ma robe n'est pas très élégante. = **Ça ne fait rien.**
d Écoute-moi ça! = **C'est vraiment ridicule.**
e Ce sont les enfants qui souffrent le plus. = **Oui, c'est très triste.**

37 a Celui
b Celles
c Ça
d celui
e celle
f celles-là
g ceux
h celles
i ceci
j Ceux

38 a Ceux de Pierre./Ceux qui sont les plus confortables.
b Celle à côté de la banque.
c Non, celui qui ne fait rien.
d Celui-là est mon frère.
e Oui, mais c'est petit.
f Non, celle-là est à mon frère./Regardez-moi ça!
g Écoute-moi ça!/Prenez celle-ci.
h Celle au milieu.
i Ça dépend.
j Ceci.

Verbs

1
a donnent
b parlez
c parles
d aime
e habitent
f chante
g marches
h regarde
i commence
j admirons

2
a C'est un médecin. = **Il travaille à l'hôpital.**
b Ils sont végétariens. = **Ils ne mangent pas de viande.**
c Elle est factrice. = **Elle marche beaucoup.**
d Nous sommes parisiens. = **Nous habitons près de la Seine.**
e Je suis jardinière. = **J'aime beaucoup les plantes.**

3
a Nous l'utilisons souvent.
b Vous lui donnez beaucoup d'argent.
c Marie l'adore.
d En ce moment il lui parle au téléphone.
e Maintenant ils jouent mieux.
f Je lui demande demain.
g Sa petite amie le regarde.
h Nous y arrivons à deux heures.
i Vous y restez longtemps?
j Mes amies passent un mois à Lille.

4
a Tu l'aimes?
b Il joue dehors en ce moment.
c Les enfants adorent notre chien.
d Nous aimons beaucoup Paris.
e Tu le lui donnes?
f Nous passons un mois en France avec eux.
g Elle reste à la maison aujourd'hui.
h Tu manges ça?
i Vous cherchez vos clés?
j Pourquoi tu pleures?

5
a choisissent
b finissons
c remplis
d établit
e finit
f choisis
g bâtissent
h finissez
i ralentit
j remplissons

6
a Le concert dure deux heures. = **Il finit à vingt heures quinze.**
b Ils sont végétariens. = **Ils choisissent toujours les salades.**
c Il y a une voiture de police. = **Je ralentis tout de suite.**
d Elle ne boit pas de vin. = **Je remplis son verre d'eau.**
e Le fromage n'est pas bon. = **Nous choisissons un dessert.**

7
a Elles finissent leurs devoirs.
b Nous investissons dans l'immobilier.
c En ce moment il en finit l'introduction.
d Ton verre est vide, je le remplis?
e Aujourd'hui nous en finissons la plupart.
f Celles-ci sont jolies, vous les choisissez?
g J'en choisis les meilleures.
h On voit la police, on ralentit.
i Laure a de l'argent, elle l'investit dans la boutique.
j Ils ont leurs formulaires, ils les remplissent.

8
a Ils finissent leur jeu.
b Elle choisit toujours du poisson?
c Le cours finit à midi?
d Nous finissons le travail demain.
e Ils choisissent l'équipe aujourd'hui.
f Vous investissez dans son avenir.

g Tu finis à six heures ce soir?
h Je remplis la piscine.
i Pourquoi vous ralentissez?
j Je les paye, je les choisis.

9
a attends
b vendent
c vendez
d entends
e entend
f attendent
g défend
h attendons
i entendent
j vends

10
a Le service n'est pas bon. = **On attend longtemps.**
b Mes amis ont besoin d'argent. = **Ils vendent leur voiture.**
c Ma cousine attend un enfant. = **Elle ne fume pas.**
d Je n'entends pas ta question. = **Tu la répètes.**
e Tu es mon amie. = **Je te défends.**

11
a Je t'entends bien.
b Tu l'attends longtemps?
c Voilà sa voiture, il la vend.
d Vous les défendez?
e Elle lui tend la main.
f Les lionnes défendent leurs petits.
g Anne est en retard, nous l'attendons.
h Ces meubles, vous les vendez?
i Ça dépend du temps.
j On en entend beaucoup.

12
a Vous l'attendez?
b Ma voiture est trop petite, je la vends.
c Nous entendons leur télé.
d Ça dépend du prix.
e Il défend ses amis.
f Tu m'entends?
g Les filles attendent le bus.
h L'ordinateur est nul, ils le vendent.
i Ils entendent les cloches tous les matins.
j Elle attend un enfant.

Verbs

13
  a lance
  b lançons
  c manges
  d mangeons
  e appelez
  f appellent
  g jette
  h nettoies
  i gèle
  j espère

14
  a de la glace
  b de l'argent/de l'eau
  c les cerises
  d le mauvais temps
  e Marc
  f quand il gèle
  g se casser le bras
  h Il mange peu./Il n'aime pas manger.
  i Je n'aime pas le ménage./Tu m'aides à la nettoyer?
  j Nous nous levons.

15
  a Nous mangeons avec eux?
  b Elle s'appelle Alice.
  c Mes voisins jettent beaucoup.
  d Je jette ces vieilles baskets.
  e Je pèle les oignons, vous deux pelez les pommes de terre.
  f Tu leur envoies une carte?
  g Il mange trop.
  h Je préfère les pays chauds.
  i Nous espérons les revoir.
  j En hiver ils règlent le thermostat.

16
  a Les examens commencent jeudi. = **J'espère avoir de bons résultats.**
  b Ils m'envoient toujours un beau cadeau pour mon anniversaire. = **Je les considère comme mes meilleurs amis.**
  c Ce restaurant est très cher. = **Nous mangeons ailleurs.**
  d Cette jupe est jolie. = **Tu l'essaies?**
  e Mes parents adorent le fromage. = **Ils en achètent beaucoup.**

17
  a ont
  b avons
  c Allez
  d as
  e faites
  f est
  g font
  h pars
  i sommes
  j va

18
  a Tu pleures. = **Qu'est-ce qu'il y a?**
  b J'ai deux frères. = **Comment s'appellent-ils?**
  c Il fait très chaud aujourd'hui. = **On va à la piscine?**
  d Demain c'est son anniversaire. = **On lui fait un gâteau?**
  e Les enfants font beaucoup de bruit. = **Est-ce qu'ils se battent?**

19
  a Tu as les yeux
  b Ils ont les cheveux
  c Elle a les hanches
  d Vous avez les cheveux
  e Nous avons les mains
  f J'ai les mains
  g Elle a le bras
  h J'ai le cœur
  i Il a les pieds
  j Elles ont les jambes

20
  a Qu'est-ce qu'ils font ce week-end?
  b Mes parents vont bien, merci.
  c Jeanne est très jeune: elle a cinq ans.
  d Nous allons toujours en France: cette année nous y allons avec des amis.
  e Qu'est-ce qu'il y a? — Rien.
  f Lisa est dentiste: elle gagne beaucoup d'argent.
  g Il fait froid, je vais allumer le chauffage.
  h Il est tard: je vais au lit.
  i Nous n'avons pas de billets. — Ça ne fait rien.
  j Le train part du quai numéro cinq.

21
  a Regarde-moi, Martin!
  b Écoutez-moi, les enfants!
  c Donnes-en à ta sœur, Pierre!
  d Si tu en as besoin, demande-lui!
  e Attendez-nous, Monsieur!
  f Suivez-moi, Madame!
  g Goûtes-en un peu!
  h Finissez vos devoirs avant le dîner!
  i Aidez-nous!
  j Excuse-moi!

22
  a Pars
  b Restez
  c Prends
  d Fais-le
  e Réveillez-moi
  f Prêtez-leur
  g Parles-en
  h appelle-la
  i pensez-y
  j attendons-la

23
  a vos places
  b l'omelette
  c l'échec/cette bonne nouvelle
  d les réunions
  e ces peintures
  f l'appartement
  g de la chaise
  h de la pluie/de l'examen
  i ton fils
  j la question

24
  a Soyez sages, les enfants! = **Ne faites pas de bêtises.**
  b Sois tranquille! = **Il ne va rien lui arriver.**
  c Ayez de la patience! = **Ça va prendre du temps.**
  d Veuillez les attendre ici. = **Ils arrivent bientôt.**
  e Soyons réalistes. = **Ce n'est pas une idée pratique.**

25
  a s'
  b vous
  c se
  d s'
  e t'
  f nous
  g te
  h me
  i se
  j se

Verbs

26 a appelez
b m'appelle
c s'arrêtent
d se battent
e arrêtez
f vous asseoir
g me lève
h passe
i se passe
j Dépêche-toi

27 a Les oiseaux se réveillent tôt en été.
b Qu'est-ce qui se passe à l'école?
c Tu te couches maintenant?
d Je vais me promener.
e On n'est pas ici pour s'amuser.
f Il est sept heures, vous vous levez?
g L'hôtel se trouve près du club de golf.
h Les filles s'habillent pour la fête.
i Vous vous intéressez à la politique?
j Nous nous demandons combien ça va coûter.

28 a Assieds-toi, chérie!
b Ne vous levez pas, les enfants!
c Couchez vous tôt, Alain et Michèle!
d Amuse-toi bien à la fête, ma petite!
e Ne vous dépêchez pas, monsieur, on n'est pas pressés!
f Ne vous asseyez pas là, s'il vous plaît, madame!
g Lave-toi bien, Laurent!
h Calmez-vous, mesdames, il n'y a aucun danger!
i Ne t'inquiète pas, Gaston, tes parents vont venir!
j Rappelle-toi, Julien, que les vélos coûtent cher.

29 a remplissaient
b allions
c mangeais
d aimais
e se levait
f fournissait

g nous parlions
h attendiez
i roulait
j vivaient

30 a C'était une serveuse. = **Elle travaillait à l'hôtel.**
b Ils étaient végétariens. = **Ils ne mangeaient pas de viande.**
c Elle était étudiante. = **Elle lisait beaucoup.**
d On était à la campagne. = **On y passait les vacances.**
e Je suis restée muette. = **Je ne savais quoi dire.**

31 a finissait
b adorais
c choisissais
d vendaient
e savions
f entendait
g commençait
h avions
i jouait
j pleuvait

32 a Je pensais à toi.
b Qu'est-ce que tu faisais cet après-midi?
c J'allais souvent au cinéma quand je vivais à Paris.
d Nous nous entendions bien quand nous étions à l'école.
e Elle se sentait seule et pleurait beaucoup.
f Il perdait toujours ses clés.
g Je me demandais quoi faire.
h Le professeur était sympathique: les enfants l'aimaient beaucoup.
i Il pleuvait et nous nous ennuyions.
j Vous m'attendiez?

33 a participeras
b partirons
c prêterai
d passeront
e marieront
f offrirez
g nettoierons
h viendrez

i pourra
j rendra

34 a aura
b seront
c seras
d aurons
e sera
f fera
g ira
h ferez
i fera
j aurez

35 a Sarah et Paul restent longtemps au soleil. = **Ils seront bronzés.**
b J'ai une bonne nouvelle pour eux. = **Ils seront ravis de le savoir.**
c La facture est énorme. = **Ils ne pourront pas la payer.**
d Leur avion part à sept heures. = **Ils devront se lever tôt.**
e Les enfants sont très fatigués. = **Ils iront bientôt au lit.**

36 a Ils seront ravis de la revoir.
b Sabine pourra les aider.
c Tu devras faire attention.
d Je serai là à neuf heures.
e Je t'appellerai ce week-end, chérie.
f Elle aura du temps pour lire pendant les vacances.
g Marseille? Il fera chaud!
h Les enfants voudront aller à la plage.
i Nous verrons l'exposition demain.
j Vous serez à Londres la semaine prochaine?

37 a une raquette
b des pâtes/du fromage
c une cuillère
d l'hôtel de luxe
e dans les banlieues
f un chaton
g ce parking
h un bic/une belle église
i la gare routière/le teinturier
j du chantage

Verbs

38 a voudrais
b devrais
c pourrait
d voudrions
e serait
f voudraient
g proposeriez
h sauraient
i ferait
j oserais

39 a Si j'avais l'argent, je l'achèterais.
b Il viendrait si elle était là.
c Combien tu donnerais pour cette voiture?
d Si nous commencions à sept heures nous finirions cet après-midi.
e Les enfants s'amuseraient bien ici.
f Nous voudrions une chambre pour deux personnes.
g Elle serait furieuse si tu disais ça.
h Vous devriez faire des photos.
i S'il faisait beau ils iraient à la plage.

40 a parties
b tombée
c appelé
d étonné
e allés
f perdu
g eu
h morte
i arrivés
j fini

41 a J'ai rendu
b as passé
c ont déménagé
d a pris
e est venue
f vous êtes amusés
g m'a écrit
h sont descendues
i s'est passé
j a mis

42 a Vous allez voir ce film? = **Non, je l'ai déjà vu.**
b Tu sais qu'ils se marient? = **Oui, ils me l'ont dit il y a une quinzaine de jours.**
c Tu es fatiguée, Caroline? = **Oui, je me suis levée très tôt.**
d Vous lui avez donné votre adresse? = **Non, il ne nous l'a pas demandée.**
e Il pleut encore? = **Non, il ne pleut plus.**

43 a Elle m'a donné son numéro de téléphone.
b J'ai perdu mes clés.
c Ils ont gagné 2-1.
d Nous sommes restés à la maison hier.
e Elle est sortie chercher du pain.
f J'ai sorti le chien ce matin.
g Il a choisi un yaourt plutôt qu'une glace.
h Nous avons eu un accident en chemin.
i Anna a acheté un nouveau portable.
j Le prix de l'essence a augmenté.

44 a Marc n'avait plus d'argent. = **Il avait tout dépensé.**
b Il était tout rouge. = **Il avait couru cent mètres en moins de 20 secondes.**
c Les voleurs sont entrés sans difficulté. = **On avait oublié de fermer la porte à clé.**
d Le lendemain on ne voulait pas se lever. = **On s'était couchés très tard.**
e Quelle surprise! = **Je ne savais pas qu'il était arrivé.**

45 a avait oublié
b nous étions levés
c m'étais attendu
d étaient partis
e avions appelés/appelées
f avait voulu
g aviez essayé
h était tombée
i avais su
j avait dit

46 a joué
b partis
c dit
d couchée
e été
f écouté/écoutée
g su
h pu
i demandé
j allées

47 a Ils s'étaient déjà décidés.
b Il avait beaucoup bu.
c Il lui avait déjà demandé deux fois.
d Je l'avais remarquée immédiatement.
e Elle s'était sentie bien pendant la journée.
f Peut-être que vous en aviez eu assez?
g Les filles avaient dû partir avant le dîner.
h Nous nous étions rencontrés à Paris.
i Elle l'avait souvent vu au supermarché.
j Tu t'étais attendu à ça?

48 a pendant la nuit
b en 2009
c demain matin
d la semaine dernière/ à bientôt
e par jour/par habitude
f au crayon
g dans les magasins de meubles/dans les boulangeries/dans les bibliothèques
h avec du sel
i quelquefois
j par tes ennemis/pour tes défauts

49 a construite
b peint
c faites
d regardé
e adorée
f recherchés
g rempli
h arrêtés
i connue
j écrit

50 a Il avait été tué.
b Tu avais été prévenue, Sarah.
c Le gîte sera nettoyé avant votre arrivée.
d L'Amérique a été découverte par Christophe Colomb.

Verbs

e La porte doit être fermée à clé.

f Le pont sera terminé l'été prochain.

g Vos sacs ont été retrouvés, monsieur.

h Cette photo a été prise en 1995.

i Les phares doivent être réglés.

j J'ai été licenciée en avril.

51 a Ils l'ont embauchée. = **Elle a été embauchée.**

b Il les a embauchés. = **Ils ont été embauchés.**

c Elle a envoyé ce SMS il y a une heure. = **Il a été envoyé ce matin.**

d Nous allons bientôt envoyer le document. = **Il sera envoyé ce matin.**

e Tu dois refaire ce travail. = **Il doit être refait.**

52 a est ennuyant

b est amusant

c est tentante

d a été fatigante

e serait surprenant

f était inquiétante

g est choquant

h ont été décevants

i a été exaspérant

j sont intéressantes

53 a Le bébé s'est réveillé en pleurant.

b Les garçons sont sortis en courant.

c Mon amie est entrée en souriant.

d Il a pris le cadeau en faisant semblant d'en être ravi.

e Je me suis coupé le doigt en ouvrant une boîte de conserve.

f Elle a ri en voyant cette image.

g L'enfant s'est endormi en regardant la télé.

h J'ai envoyé des SMS en attendant mes amis.

i Il a perdu du poids en mangeant un peu moins.

j Il a traversé la rue en courant, sans regarder.

54 a sachant

b voyant

c Étant

d Ayant

e croyant

f étant

g entendant

h pouvant

i trouvant

j cherchant

55 a En attendant ses copains = il a bu une bière.

b En tombant dans l'escalier = il s'est fait mal.

c En regardant par la fenêtre = il a vu qu'il neigeait.

d En lisant l'e-mail de son patron = il est devenu furieux.

e En entendant la nouvelle = il a tout de suite téléphoné à sa femme.

56 a Il y a cinq personnes dans ma famille.

b Il y a une usine près de leur maison.

c Il y a eu un accident.

d Il y avait quelqu'un à la porte.

e Il y aura beaucoup à faire.

f Il reste des sandwichs.

g Il faut faire attention.

h Il manque deux sacs.

i Il vaudrait mieux dire la vérité.

j Il semble que tout aille bien.

57 a il est

b il faut

c Il était

d Il manque

e il reste

f Il fait

g il faisait

h Il paraît *or* Il semble

i Il reste

j il faut

58 a Je ne peux pas prendre une douche. = **Il n'y a pas d'eau chaude.**

b Je déménage. = **Il y a des cafards dans mon appartement.**

c J'ai dû m'asseoir par terre. = **Il n'y avait pas assez de chaises.**

d Tout s'est très bien passé. = **Il n'y avait pas de problèmes.**

e Je me suis ennuyé au château. = **Il n'y avait rien à voir.**

59 a neiger

b pluie

c la grenouille

d nuit

e de la pluie

f une heure

g vas au bureau

h fait pas beau

i pleut

j le dis/le fais

60 a parliez

b restions

c parte

d finisse

e sois

f soit

g rende

h fassiez

i puisse

j attendes

61 a Je dois le lire. = **Il faut que je le lise.**

b Ils doivent partir maintenant. = **Il faut qu'ils partent maintenant.**

c Vous pouvez le faire? J'en suis contente. = **Je suis contente que vous puissiez le faire.**

d Il pleut? C'est dommage. = **Je regrette qu'il pleuve.**

e Il est peut-être déjà arrivé. = **Il est possible qu'il soit déjà arrivé.**

62 a du bien/plaisir

b dyslexique

c conduire prudemment

d des bêtises/des mensonges

e le plus mauvais/le plus ennuyant

f malades/fatigués/mécontents

g soit sympathique

h mentiez

i peur

j fasse beau temps/soit si bon

Verbs

63 a Il faut que vous reveniez l'année prochaine.
b Il faut que je me couche.
c Je suis content qu'il soit ici.
d Tu es surprise que j'aie peur?
e Ils veulent que nous restions chez nous.
f J'ai peur qu'elle perde du temps.
g Nous craignons qu'elle ne soit malade.
h Il veut que nous le payions.
i Tu es contente qu'on finisse aujourd'hui?
j Je regrette qu'il fasse si mauvais temps.

64 a Les filles doivent être très déçues.
b J'adore danser.
c Il déteste faire la vaisselle.
d Tu vas chercher du pain?
e Elle a laissé tomber son portable.
f Nous regardions les enfants jouer dans le jardin.
g Je vais parler à Nicole.
h Elle m'a envoyé acheter un journal.
i Qu'est-ce que vous voulez dire, Monsieur?
j Il aime faire la cuisine.

65 a à
b de
c à
d à *or* de
e de
f à
g de
h à
i de
j à

66 a est en train de parler
b sont en train de faire
c suis en train de mettre
d sommes en train de boire
e J'étais en train de me laver
f sont en train de construire
g était en train de lire
h est en train d'écrire
i suis en train de lui envoyer
j est en train de repeindre

67 a Le bruit = **m'a empêché de dormir.**
b Le professeur = **m'a dit de me taire.**
c La voisine = **m'a remercié d'avoir sorti son chien.**
d Ma copine = **m'a demandé de laver sa voiture.**
e Mon collègue = **m'a encouragé à demander une augmentation de salaire.**

68 a J'ai envie d'aller au cinéma.
b J'ai besoin d'acheter des timbres.
c Ne traverse pas la rue sans regarder, Aurélie.
d Nous sommes prêts à partir.
e Ils l'ont fait pour nous aider.
f Ils aiment jouer au foot.
g Nous devons faire réparer la fenêtre.
h Je veux me faire couper les cheveux.
i Pousser
j Ajouter le lait et les œufs.

69 a Je suis content de pouvoir vous aider.
b Nous sommes désolés de te décevoir.
c J'ai peur de le faire sans lui demander la permission.
d Hier tu es parti *or* partie sans la remercier.
e Elle est sûre de te comprendre.
f Vous avez besoin d'y aller?
g Nager fait du bien.
h La semaine prochaine on aura besoin de se détendre.
i Je téléphone pour savoir à quelle heure vous arrivez demain.
j Peler les tomates, c'est difficile.

Negatives

1 a ses amis/fumer
   b jamais/personne
   c moi non plus
   d rien
   e ce n'est pas mal/ne le regarde pas!
   f rien de mieux
   g ne la regarde pas!
   h je ne sais pas
   i Il ne va plus à la gym/ il ne fait jamais de sport/ il ne mange pas de salade
   j ils n'y vont plus/moi non plus

2 a Je la vois jamais.
   b Ça ne m'intéresse plus.
   c Ne vous inquiétez pas, monsieur!

   d Tu n'as rien à faire?
   e Ils n'ont pas encore fini.
   f Elle ne m'a rien dit.
   g Tu ne dois pas être en retard.
   h Nous ne mangeons jamais de viande.
   i Je ne les ai pas vus or vues aujourd'hui.
   j Ce n'est pas ma faute!

3 a Elle n'habite plus ici.
   b Il ne me comprend pas.
   c Nous ne voulons pas vous déranger.
   d Il n'a pas besoin de se lever si tôt.
   e Je ne connais personne ici.
   f Tu ne m'écoutes jamais.

   g Je ne l'avais jamais aimée.
   h Essayez de ne pas trop dépenser, les filles.
   i Il n'y a personne à la maison.
   j Ce chocolat, tu le veux ou non?

4 a La gym? = **Je n'y vais plus.**
   b Benoît? = **Je ne le vois jamais.**
   c Du lait? = **Je n'en veux pas.**
   d L'informatique? = **Je n'y comprends rien.**
   e Te prêter de l'argent? = **Pas question!**

Questions

1 a Aiment-ils
   b te lèves-tu?
   c Vous appelez-vous
   d Parle-t-il
   e A-t-elle
   f A-t-il
   g Va-t-on
   h Voulez-vous
   i Ont-ils
   j Y a-t-il

2 a Où
   b Quand
   c quel
   d quelle
   e Où
   f Qui
   g quand
   h Quel
   i combien
   j Comment

3 a Avec eux
   b Si
   c Jamais
   d Cinq ans
   e N'importe qui
   f Je ne sais pas/Ça dépend

   g **Mon patron/Mon ami/ La direction**
   h **Peu importe**
   i **Le lendemain**
   j **Ça va bien, merci**

4 a Qu'est-ce qui
   b quoi
   c Qu'est-ce que
   d quoi
   e Qu'est-ce que
   f Qu'est-ce qui
   g qu'est-ce qui
   h quoi
   i Qu'est-ce que
   j Qu'est-ce qui

5 a quel
   b Quelle
   c lequel
   d Quelles
   e quelle
   f Quels
   g Laquelle
   h Lesquelles
   i Lequel
   j Lesquels

6 a Il pleut, n'est-ce pas or non?
   b Quelle est votre ville préférée, monsieur?
   c Pourquoi tu pleures, chérie?
   d Combien de personnes vont venir?
   e D'où vient-elle?
   f Pourquoi il a dit ça?
   g À qui est cette grosse voiture?
   h À quelle heure vous fermez?
   i Quel restaurant recommandez-vous?
   j Un phare est cassé. — Lequel?

7 a J'en veux. = **Combien?**
   b Pierre vient nous voir. = **Quand?**
   c Quelqu'un m'a donné cet argent. = **Qui?**
   d Je n'aime pas cette fille. = **Pourquoi?**
   e J'ai choisi un parfum. = **Lequel?**

Adverbs

1
a Malheureusement
b Apparemment
c affreusement
d terriblement
e facilement
f vraiment
g longuement
h légèrement
i constamment
j lentement

2
a **Je le ferai tout de suite.**
b **vraiment/ heureusement/de temps en temps**
c **ce fleur**
d **se faire du souci**
e **de faire une promenade**
f **ta maison**
g **lentement/d'abord**
h **récemment/en retard**
i **Il ne vous comprend pas./ Le bébé dort.**
j **gentiment**

3
a Je peux vous demander quelque chose? – Bien sûr!
b Nous ne la voyons pas souvent.
c Il va à l'école tout seul?
d Heureusement personne n'est mort.
e J'ai vu ce film récemment.
f La lettre était très mal écrite.
g Je voudrais un emploi mieux payé.
h Ils parlent très bien l'anglais.
i Aujourd'hui je me sens encore moins bien.
j Cette soupe sent bon!

4
a mieux
b plus souvent
c plus lentement
d plus fort
e moins
f plus vite
g plus
h plus proprement
i plus mauvais
j mieux

5
a Mon copain marche plus vite que moi.
b Tu devrais mieux te comporter.
c Ils ont joué plus intelligemment que nous.
d Anne travaille plus dur que les autres.
e Il est plus gravement blessé que moi.
f Sarah lit moins bien que sa sœur.
g Nous voulons vivre plus simplement.
h Pourquoi tu ne viens pas nous voir plus souvent?
i La grippe se transmet plus facilement en hiver.

6
a Elle est la meilleure joueuse. = **Elle joue le mieux.**
b C'est la plus chère. = **Elle coûte le plus cher.**
c C'est notre cliente la plus fidèle. = **Elle vient le plus souvent.**
d Ses amis sont plus bavards qu'elle. = **Elle parle moins.**
e Sauf elle, nous l'utilisons beaucoup. = **Elle l'utilise moins.**

7
a **Il est sage./Il est sympathique.**
b **le gardien de but**
c **Il n'avait pas soif./Il n'y avait rien à manger.**
d **l'invitation**
e **Personne ne t'entend.**
f **de mieux en mieux**
g **Il est timide.**
h **Tu habites à côté.**
i **Elle s'amusait beaucoup.**
j **Il n'y avait personne.**

8
a **Déjà!**
b **Avant./Ensuite.**
c **Ensemble.**
d **Quelquefois.**
e **Ensuite.**
f **Soudain.**
g **Encore!**
h **Demain.**
i **Pas beaucoup./Souvent.**
j **Moins.**

9
a surtout
b toujours
c encore
d déjà
e environ
f même
g après
h trop
i tard
j longtemps

10
a Il fait assez beau aujourd'hui.
b Cela a pris assez longtemps.
c Est-ce qu'il y a assez de pain?
d Il pleut beaucoup.
e Il n'y a pas beaucoup de choses à voir.
f Il gagne beaucoup d'argent.
g Elle boit trop.
h J'achète trop de sacs.
i Tu as perdu trop de poids.

11
a J'admire beaucoup ce professeur.
b J'ai toujours voulu aller en Inde.
c Vous recevrez bientôt une lettre de confirmation.
d Ce n'est pas encore fini.
e Nous nous rencontrons rarement.
f Je me demande souvent pourquoi il l'a fait.
g Tu m'as déjà dit ça.
h Elle ne va pas très bien.
i Tout s'est très bien passé.
j Nous avons enfin réussi à le joindre.

12
a demain
b demain
c vite/tôt/quelquefois
d partout
e demain
f hier/beaucoup/toujours
g loin/tout de suite/mieux
h loin
i enfin
j bientôt

13
a Elle est élégante. = **Elle est toujours bien habillée.**
b Je les envie. = **Ils ont une très belle maison.**
c Je les plains. = **Ils ont beaucoup souffert.**
d Je prends ceux-ci. = **Ils coûtent beaucoup moins cher.**
e Je préfère celle-ci. = **Elle est encore plus jolie.**

Prepositions

1
a Les avocats se vendent un euro pièce.
b Nous sommes rentrés à la maison à minuit.
c J'habite au Portugal.
d J'avais peur, il roulait à 160 km/h.
e Si tu as mal à la gorge, reste au lit!
f Nous sommes en vacances du 25 juillet au 3 août.
g La réception se trouve au rez-de-chaussée.
h Il ne faut pas le laver en machine.
i Tu veux une tarte aux pommes ou une tarte au citron?
j Il y a trois grandes tasses et deux tasses à café.

2
a au
b aux
c aux, aux
d à
e à
f à
g au
h aux
i à la
j à

3
a Nous avons réservé un vol de Londres à Marseille.
b Tu auras besoin d'un sac de couchage.
c Je vais acheter du pain, du fromage et une bouteille de vin.
d Nous cherchons l'arrêt de bus.
e Nous aimerions avoir une maison en France.

f Est-ce que vous avez des amis en Angleterre?
g Le jardin est beau au printemps, mais pas en hiver.
h Je vais parfois à Paris en train.
i Je ne sais pas comment le dire en français.
j Pourriez-vous me donner un sac en plastique, s'il vous plaît?

4
a Je suis surprise de te voir. = **Je croyais que tu étais aux États-Unis.**
b Il y a souvent des bouchons sur l'autoroute. = **C'est plus rapide en train.**
c Je n'arrive pas à faire démarrer la voiture. = **Je vais aller au centre en bus.**
d La maison est à dix kilomètres d'ici. = **Je ne peux pas y aller à pied.**
e J'ai raté mon train. = **Il m'a ramené la maison.**

5
a À vélo.
b Depuis un mois.
c En quinze jours.
d Avant la fin du mois.
e avant l'entrée.
f Depuis début mars./Avec du retard.
g par e-mail.
h sur le mur./au fond du sac.
i sans le savoir.
j Le voici!/Me voici!

6
a à
b du

c de
d d'
e à
f de
g aux
h au
i de
j du

7
a Tout le monde doit obéir aux règles.
b Je n'ai pas cru à cette histoire.
c Je veux changer de direction.
d Elle m'a conseillé de téléphoner au médecin.
e Ses livres plaisent beaucoup aux filles.
f Est-ce que vous savez jouer du piano?
g Je pense à demain.
h J'ai demandé l'addition au serveur.
i Les enfants ont peur des chiens.
j Qui va payer le repas?

8
a Espérons qu'il fera beau temps! = **Hugo et Anna se marient demain.**
b Mes parents habitent un petit appartement en ville. = **Ils n'ont pas de jardin.**
c Ils se souviennent de Matthieu. = **Ils ont fréquenté la même école.**
d Bonjour, Stéphanie est là? = **Oh, pardon, je me suis trompée de numéro.**
e Vous croyez que ces jeux vont plaire aux enfants? = **Ils en seront ravis.**

Index

VERB TABLES

Introduction

This section is designed to help you find all the verb forms you need in French.

From pages 2–7 you will find a list of 93 regular and irregular verbs with a summary of their main forms, followed on pages 8–28 by some very common regular and irregular verbs shown in full, with example phrases.

French verb forms

INFINITIVE	PRESENT	PERFECT	IMPERFECT	FUTURE	PRESENT SUBJUNCTIVE
1 acheter -er verb with a spelling change	j'ach**è**te tu ach**è**tes il ach**è**te nous achetons vous achetez ils ach**è**tent	j'ai acheté	j'achetais	j'ach**è**terai	j'ach**è**te
2 acquérir	see full verb table page 8				
3 aller	see full verb table page 9				
4 appeler -er verb with a spelling change	j'appe**ll**e tu appe**ll**es il appe**ll**e nous appelons vous appelez ils appe**ll**ent	j'ai appelé	j'appelais	j'appe**ll**erai	j'appe**ll**e
5 arriver similar to **donner** [28], apart from the perfect tense	j'arrive	je suis arrivé(e)	j'arrivais	j'arriverai	j'arrive
6 s'asseoir	see full verb table page 10				
7 attendre similar to **vendre** [88]	j'attends	j'ai attendu	j'attendais	j'attendrai	j'attende
8 avoir	see full verb table page 11				
9 battre	je bats	j'ai battu	je battais	je battrai	je batte
10 boire	je bois nous b**uv**ons ils boivent	j'ai bu	je b**uv**ais	je boirai	je boi**v**e
11 bouillir	je bous nous bouillons	j'ai bouilli	je bouillais	je bouillirai	je bouille
12 commencer -er verb with a spelling change	je commence nous commen**ç**ons vous commencez ils commencent	j'ai commencé	je commen**ç**ais nous commencions ils commen**ç**aient	je commencerai	je commence
13 conclure	je conclus nous concluons	j'ai conclu	je concluais	je concluerai	je conclue
14 connaître	je connais il connaît nous connaissons	j'ai connu	je connaissais	je connaîtrai tu connaîtras	je connaisse
15 coudre	je couds nous cou**s**ons ils cou**s**ent	j'ai cou**s**u	je cou**s**ais	je coudrai	je cou**s**e
16 courir	je cours nous courons	j'ai couru	je courais	je courrai	je coure
17 craindre	je crains nous crai**gn**ons	j'ai craint	je crai**gn**ais	je craindrai	je crai**gn**e

INFINITIVE	PRESENT	PERFECT	IMPERFECT	FUTURE	PRESENT SUBJUNCTIVE
18 **créer** similar to **donner** [28]	je crée	j'ai cr**éé**	je créais	je créerai	je crée
19 **crier** similar to **donner** [28]	je crie	j'ai crié	je criais nous cr**ii**ons vous cr**ii**ez	je crierai	je crie
20 **croire**	see full verb table page 12				
21 **croître**	je croîs nous croi**ss**ons	j'ai cr**û**	je croi**ss**ais	je croîtrai	je croi**ss**e
22 **cueillir**	je cueille nous cueillons	j'ai cueilli	je cueillais	je cueillerai	je cueille
23 **cuire**	je cuis nous cuisons ils cuisent	j'ai cuit	je cuisais	je cuirai	je cuise
24 **descendre** similar to **vendre** [88], apart from the perfect tense	je descends	je suis descendu(e)	je descendais	je descendrai	je descende
25 **devenir** similar to **venir** [89]	je deviens	je suis devenu(e)	je devenais	je deviendrai	je devienne
26 **devoir**	see full verb table page 13				
27 **dire**	see full verb table page 14				
28 **donner**	see full verb table page 15				
29 **dormir**	je dors nous dormons	j'ai dormi	je dormais	je dormirai	je dorme
30 **écrire**	j'écris nous écri**v**ons	j'ai écrit	j'écri**v**ais	j'écrirai	j'écri**v**e
31 **émouvoir**	j'ém**eu**s nous émouvons ils ém**eu**vent	j'ai ému	j'émouvais	j'émouvrai	j'ém**eu**ve
32 **entrer** similar to **donner** [28], apart from the perfect tense	j'entre	je suis entré(e)	j'entrais	j'entrerai	j'entre
33 **envoyer** -**er** verb with a spelling change	j'envoie nous envoyons ils envo**i**ent	j'ai envoyé	j'envoyais	j'env**err**ai	j'envoie
34 **espérer** -**er** verb with a spelling change	j'esp**è**re tu esp**è**res il esp**è**re nous espérons vous espérez ils esp**è**rent	j'ai espéré	j'espérais	j'espérerai	j'esp**è**re

INFINITIVE	PRESENT	PERFECT	IMPERFECT	FUTURE	PRESENT SUBJUNCTIVE
35 **être**	see full verb table page 16				
36 **faire**	see full verb table page 17				
37 **falloir**	il f**aut**	il a fallu	il fallait	il f**aud**ra	il fa**ill**e
38 **finir**	see full verb table page 18				
39 **fuir**	je fuis nous fu**y**ons vous fu**y**ez ils fuient	j'ai fui	je fu**y**ais nous fu**y**ions vous fu**y**iez	je fuirai	je fuie
40 **haïr**	je hais tu hais il hait nous haïssons vous haïssez ils haïssent	j'ai haï	je haïssais	je haïrai	je haïsse
41 **jeter** -**er** verb with a spelling change	je je**tt**e tu je**tt**es il je**tt**e nous jetons vous jetez ils je**tt**ent	j'ai jeté	je jetais	je je**tt**erai	je je**tt**e
42 **joindre**	je joins nous joi**gn**ons	j'ai joint	je joi**gn**ais	je joindrai	je joi**gn**e
43 **lever** -**er** verb with a spelling change	je l**è**ve tu l**è**ves il l**è**ve nous levons vous levez ils l**è**vent	j'ai levé	je levais	je l**è**verai	je l**è**ve
44 **lire**	je lis nous lisons	j'ai lu	je lisais	je lirai	je lise
45 **manger** -**er** verb with a spelling change	je mange nous mang**e**ons vous mangez ils mangent	j'ai mangé	je mang**e**ais nous mangions vous mangiez ils mang**e**aient	je mangerai	je mange
46 **maudire**	je maudis nous maudi**ss**ons	j'ai maudit	je maudi**ss**ais	je maudirai	je maudi**ss**e
47 **mettre**	see full verb table page 19				
48 **monter** similar to **donner** [28], apart from the perfect tense	je monte	je suis monté(e)	je montais	je monterai	je monte
49 **mordre** similar to **vendre** [88]	je mords	j'ai mordu	je mordais	je mordrai	je morde
50 **moudre**	je mouds nous moulons ils moulent	j'ai moulu	je moulais	je moudrai	je moule

INFINITIVE	PRESENT	PERFECT	IMPERFECT	FUTURE	PRESENT SUBJUNCTIVE
51 **mourir**	je m**eu**rs nous mourons ils m**eu**rent	je suis mort(e)	je mourais	je mourrai	je m**eu**re
52 **naître**	je nais il naît nous nai**ss**ons	je suis né(e)	je nai**ss**ais	je naîtrai	je nai**ss**e
53 **nettoyer** -**er** verb with a spelling change	je netto**ie** nous nettoyons ils netto**ie**nt	j'ai nettoyé	je nettoyais	je netto**ie**rai	je netto**ie** nous nettoyions ils netto**ie**nt
54 **offrir** similar to **ouvrir** [55]	j'offre	j'ai offert	j'offrais	j'offrirai	j'offre
55 **ouvrir**	see full verb table page 20				
56 **paraître**	je parais il paraît nous parai**ss**ons	j'ai paru	je parai**ss**ais	je paraîtrai tu paraîtras	je parai**ss**e
57 **partir** similar to **sentir** [77], apart from the perfect tense	je pars nous partons ils partent	je suis parti(e)	je partais	je partirai	je parte
58 **passer** similar to **donner** [28], apart from the perfect tense	je passe	je suis passé(e)	je passais	je passerai	je passe
59 **payer** -**er** verb with a spelling change	je pa**ie** *or* paye nous payons ils pa**ie**nt *or* payent	j'ai payé	je payais	je pa**ie**rai *or* payerai	je pa**ie** *or* paye
60 **peindre**	je peins nous pei**gn**ons ils pei**gn**ent	j'ai peint	je pei**gn**ais	je peindrai	je pei**gn**e
61 **perdre**	je perds	j'ai perdu	je perdais	je perdrai	je perde
62 **plaire**	je plais nous plaisons	j'ai plu	je plaisais	je plairai	je plaise
63 **pleuvoir**	il pleut	il a plu	il pleuvait	il pleuvra	il pleuve
64 **pouvoir**	see full verb table page 21				
65 **prendre**	je prends nous prenons ils pre**nn**ent	j'ai pris	je prenais	je prendrai	je pre**nn**e
66 **protéger** -**er** verb with a spelling change	je prot**è**ge tu prot**è**ges il prot**è**ge nous protég**e**ons vous protégez ils prot**è**gent	j'ai protégé	je protég**e**ais nous protégions ils protég**e**aient	je protégerai	je prot**è**ge

INFINITIVE	PRESENT	PERFECT	IMPERFECT	FUTURE	PRESENT SUBJUNCTIVE
67 **recevoir**	je reçois nous recevons ils reçoivent	j'ai reçu	je recevais	je recevrai	je reçoive
68 **rentrer** similar to **donner** [28], apart from the perfect tense	je rentre	je suis rentré(e)	je rentrais	je rentrerai	je rentre
69 **répondre**	je réponds	j'ai répondu	je répondais	je répondrai	je réponde
70 **résoudre**	je résous tu résous il résout nous résolvons vous résolvez ils résolvent	j'ai résolu	je résolvais	je résoudrai	je résolve
71 **rester** similar to **donner** [28], apart from the perfect tense	je reste	je suis resté(e)	je restais	je resterai	je reste
72 **retourner** similar to **donner** [28], apart from the perfect tense	je retourne	je suis retourné(e)	je retournais	je retournerai	je retourne
73 **revenir** similar to **venir** [89]	je reviens	je suis revenu(e)	je revenais	je reviendrai	je revienne
74 **rire**	je ris il rit nous rions ils rient	j'ai ri	je riais nous ri**i**ons ils riaient	je rirai	je rie nous ri**i**ons
75 **rompre**	je romps	j'ai rompu	je rompais	je romprai	je rompe
76 **savoir**	see full verb table page 22				
77 **sentir**	see full verb table page 23				
78 **servir**	je sers nous servons ils servent	j'ai servi	je servais	je servirai	je serve
79 **sortir** similar to **sentir** [77], apart from the perfect tense	je sors	je suis sorti(e)	je sortais	je sortirai	je sorte

INFINITIVE	PRESENT	PERFECT	IMPERFECT	FUTURE	PRESENT SUBJUNCTIVE
80 suffire	je suffis nous suffisons	j'ai suffi	je suffisais	je suffirai	je suffise
81 suivre	je suis nous suivons ils suivent	j'ai suivi	je suivais	je suivrai	je suive
82 se taire	see full verb table page 24				
83 tenir similar to **venir** [89], apart from the perfect tense	je tiens	j'ai tenu	je tenais	je tiendrai	je tienne
84 tomber similar to **donner** [28], apart from the perfect tense	je tombe	je suis tombé(e)	je tombais	je tomberai	je tombe
85 traire	je trais nous tra**y**ons ils traient	j'ai trait	je tra**y**ais	je trairai	je traie nous tra**y**ions ils traient
86 vaincre	je vaincs tu vaincs il vainc nous vain**qu**ons vous vain**qu**ez ils vain**qu**ent	j'ai vaincu	je vain**qu**ais	je vaincrai	je vain**qu**e
87 valoir	je v**aux** il v**aut** nous valons ils valent	j'ai valu	je valais	je v**aud**rai	je va**ill**e nous valions vous valiez ils va**ill**ent
88 vendre	see full verb table page 25				
89 venir	see full verb table page 26				
90 vêtir	je vêts	j'ai vêtu	je vêtais	je vêtirai	je vête
91 vivre	je vis nous vivons ils vivent	j'ai vécu	je vivais	je vivrai	je vive
92 voir	see full verb table page 27				
93 vouloir	see full verb table page 28				

acquérir (to acquire)

PRESENT

j'	**acquiers**
tu	**acquiers**
il/elle/on	**acquiert**
nous	**acquérons**
vous	**acquérez**
ils/elles	**acquièrent**

PRESENT SUBJUNCTIVE

j'	**acquière**
tu	**acquières**
il/elle/on	**acquière**
nous	**acquérions**
vous	**acquériez**
ils/elles	**acquièrent**

PERFECT

j'	**ai acquis**
tu	**as acquis**
il/elle/on	**a acquis**
nous	**avons acquis**
vous	**avez acquis**
ils/elles	**ont acquis**

IMPERFECT

j'	**acquérais**
tu	**acquérais**
il/elle/on	**acquérait**
nous	**acquérions**
vous	**acquériez**
ils/elles	**acquéraient**

FUTURE

j'	**acquerrai**
tu	**acquerras**
il/elle/on	**acquerra**
nous	**acquerrons**
vous	**acquerrez**
ils/elles	**acquerront**

CONDITIONAL

j'	**acquerrais**
tu	**acquerrais**
il/elle/on	**acquerrait**
nous	**acquerrions**
vous	**acquerriez**
ils/elles	**acquerraient**

PRESENT PARTICIPLE

acquérant

PAST PARTICIPLE

acquis

IMPERATIVE

acquiers / acquérons / acquérez

EXAMPLE PHRASES

Elle **a acquis** la nationalité française en 2003.   She acquired French nationality in 2003.

je/j' = I **tu** = you **il** = he/it **elle** = she/it **on** = we/one **nous** = we **vous** = you **ils/elles** = they

aller (to go)

PRESENT

je	**vais**
tu	**vas**
il/elle/on	**va**
nous	**allons**
vous	**allez**
ils/elles	**vont**

PRESENT SUBJUNCTIVE

j'	**aille**
tu	**ailles**
il/elle/on	**aille**
nous	**allions**
vous	**alliez**
ils/elles	**aillent**

PERFECT

je	**suis allé(e)**
tu	**es allé(e)**
il/elle/on	**est allé(e)**
nous	**sommes allé(e)s**
vous	**êtes allé(e)(s)**
ils/elles	**sont allé(e)s**

IMPERFECT

j'	**allais**
tu	**allais**
il/elle/on	**allait**
nous	**allions**
vous	**alliez**
ils/elles	**allaient**

FUTURE

j'	**irai**
tu	**iras**
il/elle/on	**ira**
nous	**irons**
vous	**irez**
ils/elles	**iront**

CONDITIONAL

j'	**irais**
tu	**irais**
il/elle/on	**irait**
nous	**irions**
vous	**iriez**
ils/elles	**iraient**

PRESENT PARTICIPLE

allant

PAST PARTICIPLE

allé

IMPERATIVE

va / allons / allez

EXAMPLE PHRASES

Vous **allez** au cinéma?   Are you going to the cinema?
Je **suis allé** à Londres.   I went to London.
Est-ce que tu **es** déjà **allé** en Allemagne?   Have you ever been to Germany?

je/j' = I **tu** = you **il** = he/it **elle** = she/it **on** = we/one **nous** = we **vous** = you **ils/elles** = they

s'asseoir (to sit down)

PRESENT

je	**m'assieds/m'assois**
tu	**t'assieds/t'assois**
il/elle/on	**s'assied/s'assoit**
nous	**nous asseyons/ nous assoyons**
vous	**vous asseyez/ vous assoyez**
ils/elles	**s'asseyent/s'assoient**

PRESENT SUBJUNCTIVE

je	**m'asseye**
tu	**t'asseyes**
il/elle/on	**s'asseye**
nous	**nous asseyions**
vous	**vous asseyiez**
ils/elles	**s'asseyent**

PERFECT

je	**me suis assis(e)**
tu	**t'es assis(e)**
il/elle/on	**s'est assis(e)**
nous	**nous sommes assis(es)**
vous	**vous êtes assis(e(s))**
ils/elles	**se sont assis(es)**

IMPERFECT

je	**m'asseyais**
tu	**t'asseyais**
il/elle/on	**s'asseyait**
nous	**nous asseyions**
vous	**vous asseyiez**
ils/elles	**s'asseyaient**

FUTURE

je	**m'assiérai**
tu	**t'assiéras**
il/elle/on	**s'assiéra**
nous	**nous assiérons**
vous	**vous assiérez**
ils/elles	**s'assiéront**

CONDITIONAL

je	**m'assiérais**
tu	**t'assiérais**
il/elle/on	**s'assiérait**
nous	**nous assiérions**
vous	**vous assiériez**
ils/elles	**s'assiéraient**

PRESENT PARTICIPLE

s'asseyant

PAST PARTICIPLE

assis

IMPERATIVE

assieds-toi / asseyons-nous / asseyez-vous

EXAMPLE PHRASES

Assieds-toi, Nicole.   Sit down Nicole.
Asseyez-vous, les enfants.   Sit down children.
Je peux **m'assoir**?   May I sit down?
Je **me suis assise** sur un chewing-gum!   I've sat on some chewing gum!

je/j' = I **tu** = you **il** = he/it **elle** = she/it **on** = we/one **nous** = we **vous** = you **ils/elles** = they

avoir (to have)

PRESENT

j'	**ai**
tu	**as**
il/elle/on	**a**
nous	**avons**
vous	**avez**
ils/elles	**ont**

PRESENT SUBJUNCTIVE

j'	**aie**
tu	**aies**
il/elle/on	**ait**
nous	**ayons**
vous	**ayez**
ils/elles	**aient**

PERFECT

j'	**ai eu**
tu	**as eu**
il/elle/on	**a eu**
nous	**avons eu**
vous	**avez eu**
ils/elles	**ont eu**

IMPERFECT

j'	**avais**
tu	**avais**
il/elle/on	**avait**
nous	**avions**
vous	**aviez**
ils/elles	**avaient**

FUTURE

j'	**aurai**
tu	**auras**
il/elle/on	**aura**
nous	**aurons**
vous	**aurez**
ils/elles	**auront**

CONDITIONAL

j'	**aurais**
tu	**aurais**
il/elle/on	**aurait**
nous	**aurions**
vous	**auriez**
ils/elles	**auraient**

PRESENT PARTICIPLE

ayant

PAST PARTICIPLE

eu

IMPERATIVE

aie / ayons / ayez

EXAMPLE PHRASES

Il **a** les yeux bleus.   He's got blue eyes.
Quel âge **as**-tu?   How old are you?
Il **a eu** un accident.   He's had an accident.
J'**avais** faim.   I was hungry.
Il y **a** beaucoup de monde.   There are lots of people.

---

je/j' = I **tu** = you **il** = he/it **elle** = she/it **on** = we/one **nous** = we **vous** = you **ils/elles** = they

croire (to believe)

PRESENT

je	**crois**
tu	**crois**
il/elle/on	**croit**
nous	**croyons**
vous	**croyez**
ils/elles	**croient**

PRESENT SUBJUNCTIVE

je	**croie**
tu	**croies**
il/elle/on	**croie**
nous	**croyions**
vous	**croyiez**
ils/elles	**croient**

PERFECT

j'	**ai cru**
tu	**as cru**
il/elle/on	**a cru**
nous	**avons cru**
vous	**avez cru**
ils/elles	**ont cru**

IMPERFECT

je	**croyais**
tu	**croyais**
il/elle/on	**croyait**
nous	**croyions**
vous	**croyiez**
ils/elles	**croyaient**

FUTURE

je	**croirai**
tu	**croiras**
il/elle/on	**croira**
nous	**croirons**
vous	**croirez**
ils/elles	**croiront**

CONDITIONAL

je	**croirais**
tu	**croirais**
il/elle/on	**croirait**
nous	**croirions**
vous	**croiriez**
ils/elles	**croiraient**

PRESENT PARTICIPLE

croyant

PAST PARTICIPLE

cru

IMPERATIVE

crois / croyons / croyez

EXAMPLE PHRASES

Je ne te **crois** pas.   I don't believe you.
J'**ai cru** que tu n'allais pas venir.   I thought you weren't going to come.
Elle **croyait** encore au père Noël.   She still believed in Santa.

je/j' = I **tu** = you **il** = he/it **elle** = she/it **on** = we/one **nous** = we **vous** = you **ils/elles** = they

devoir (to have to; to owe)

PRESENT

je	**dois**
tu	**dois**
il/elle/on	**doit**
nous	**devons**
vous	**devez**
ils/elles	**doivent**

PRESENT SUBJUNCTIVE

je	**doive**
tu	**doives**
il/elle/on	**doive**
nous	**devions**
vous	**deviez**
ils/elles	**doivent**

PERFECT

j'	**ai dû**
tu	**as dû**
il/elle/on	**a dû**
nous	**avons dû**
vous	**avez dû**
ils/elles	**ont dû**

IMPERFECT

je	**devais**
tu	**devais**
il/elle/on	**devait**
nous	**devions**
vous	**deviez**
ils/elles	**devaient**

FUTURE

je	**devrai**
tu	**devras**
il/elle/on	**devra**
nous	**devrons**
vous	**devrez**
ils/elles	**devront**

CONDITIONAL

je	**devrais**
tu	**devrais**
il/elle/on	**devrait**
nous	**devrions**
vous	**devriez**
ils/elles	**devraient**

PRESENT PARTICIPLE

devant

PAST PARTICIPLE

dû (*NB*: **due, dus, dues**)

IMPERATIVE

dois / devons / devez

EXAMPLE PHRASES

Je **dois** aller faire les courses ce matin.   I have to do the shopping this morning.
À quelle heure est-ce que tu **dois** partir?   What time do you have to leave?
Il **a dû** faire ses devoirs hier soir.   He had to do his homework last night.
Il **devait** prendre le train pour aller travailler.   He had to go to work by train.

je/j' = I **tu** = you **il** = he/it **elle** = she/it **on** = we/one **nous** = we **vous** = you **ils/elles** = they

dire (to say)

	PRESENT			PRESENT SUBJUNCTIVE
je	**dis**		je	**dise**
tu	**dis**		tu	**dises**
il/elle/on	**dit**		il/elle/on	**dise**
nous	**disons**		nous	**disions**
vous	**dites**		vous	**disiez**
ils/elles	**disent**		ils/elles	**disent**

	PERFECT			IMPERFECT
j'	**ai dit**		je	**disais**
tu	**as dit**		tu	**disais**
il/elle/on	**a dit**		il/elle/on	**disait**
nous	**avons dit**		nous	**disions**
vous	**avez dit**		vous	**disiez**
ils/elles	**ont dit**		ils/elles	**disaient**

	FUTURE			CONDITIONAL
je	**dirai**		je	**dirais**
tu	**diras**		tu	**dirais**
il/elle/on	**dira**		il/elle/on	**dirait**
nous	**dirons**		nous	**dirions**
vous	**direz**		vous	**diriez**
ils/elles	**diront**		ils/elles	**diraient**

PRESENT PARTICIPLE

disant

PAST PARTICIPLE

dit

IMPERATIVE

dis / disons / dites

EXAMPLE PHRASES

Qu'est-ce qu'elle **dit**?   What is she saying?
"Bonjour!", **a**-t-il **dit**.   "Hello!" he said.
Ils m'**ont dit** que le film était nul.   They told me that the film was rubbish.
Comment ça **se dit** en anglais?   How do you say that in English?

je/j' = I **tu** = you **il** = he/it **elle** = she/it **on** = we/one **nous** = we **vous** = you **ils/elles** = they

donner (to give)

PRESENT

je	**donne**
tu	**donnes**
il/elle/on	**donne**
nous	**donnons**
vous	**donnez**
ils/elles	**donnent**

PRESENT SUBJUNCTIVE

je	**donne**
tu	**donnes**
il/elle/on	**donne**
nous	**donnions**
vous	**donniez**
ils/elles	**donnent**

PERFECT

j'	**ai donné**
tu	**as donné**
il/elle/on	**a donné**
nous	**avons donné**
vous	**avez donné**
ils/elles	**ont donné**

IMPERFECT

je	**donnais**
tu	**donnais**
il/elle/on	**donnait**
nous	**donnions**
vous	**donniez**
ils/elles	**donnaient**

FUTURE

je	**donnerai**
tu	**donneras**
il/elle/on	**donnera**
nous	**donnerons**
vous	**donnerez**
ils/elles	**donneront**

CONDITIONAL

je	**donnerais**
tu	**donnerais**
il/elle/on	**donnerait**
nous	**donnerions**
vous	**donneriez**
ils/elles	**donneraient**

PRESENT PARTICIPLE

donnant

PAST PARTICIPLE

donné

IMPERATIVE

donne / donnons / donnez

EXAMPLE PHRASES

Donne-moi la main.   Give me your hand.
Est-ce que je t'**ai donné** mon adresse?   Did I give you my address?
L'appartement **donne** sur la place.   The flat overlooks the square.

je/j' = I **tu** = you **il** = he/it **elle** = she/it **on** = we/one **nous** = we **vous** = you **ils/elles** = they

être (to be)

	PRESENT		**PRESENT SUBJUNCTIVE**
je	**suis**	je	**sois**
tu	**es**	tu	**sois**
il/elle/on	**est**	il/elle/on	**soit**
nous	**sommes**	nous	**soyons**
vous	**êtes**	vous	**soyez**
ils/elles	**sont**	ils/elles	**soient**

	PERFECT		**IMPERFECT**
j'	**ai été**	j'	**étais**
tu	**as été**	tu	**étais**
il/elle/on	**a été**	il/elle/on	**était**
nous	**avons été**	nous	**étions**
vous	**avez été**	vous	**étiez**
ils/elles	**ont été**	ils/elles	**étaient**

	FUTURE		**CONDITIONAL**
je	**serai**	je	**serais**
tu	**seras**	tu	**serais**
il/elle/on	**sera**	il/elle/on	**serait**
nous	**serons**	nous	**serions**
vous	**serez**	vous	**seriez**
ils/elles	**seront**	ils/elles	**seraient**

PRESENT PARTICIPLE
étant

PAST PARTICIPLE
été

IMPERATIVE
sois / soyons / soyez

EXAMPLE PHRASES

Mon père **est** professeur.   My father's a teacher.
Quelle heure **est**-il? – Il **est** dix heures.   What time is it? – It's 10 o'clock.
Ils ne **sont** pas encore arrivés.   They haven't arrived yet.

je/j' = I **tu** = you **il** = he/it **elle** = she/it **on** = we/one **nous** = we **vous** = you **ils/elles** = they

faire (to do; to make)

PRESENT

je	**fais**
tu	**fais**
il/elle/on	**fait**
nous	**faisons**
vous	**faites**
ils/elles	**font**

PRESENT SUBJUNCTIVE

je	**fasse**
tu	**fasses**
il/elle/on	**fasse**
nous	**fassions**
vous	**fassiez**
ils/elles	**fassent**

PERFECT

j'	**ai fait**
tu	**as fait**
il/elle/on	**a fait**
nous	**avons fait**
vous	**avez fait**
ils/elles	**ont fait**

IMPERFECT

je	**faisais**
tu	**faisais**
il/elle/on	**faisait**
nous	**faisions**
vous	**faisiez**
ils/elles	**faisaient**

FUTURE

je	**ferai**
tu	**feras**
il/elle/on	**fera**
nous	**ferons**
vous	**ferez**
ils/elles	**feront**

CONDITIONAL

je	**ferais**
tu	**ferais**
il/elle/on	**ferait**
nous	**ferions**
vous	**feriez**
ils/elles	**feraient**

PRESENT PARTICIPLE

faisant

PAST PARTICIPLE

fait

IMPERATIVE

fais / faisons / faites

EXAMPLE PHRASES

Qu'est-ce que tu **fais**?   What are you doing?
Qu'est-ce qu'il **a fait**?   What has he done? *or* What did he do?
J'**ai fait** un gâteau.   I've made a cake *or* I made a cake.
Il **s'est fait** couper les cheveux.   He's had his hair cut.

je/j' = I **tu** = you **il** = he/it **elle** = she/it **on** = we/one **nous** = we **vous** = you **ils/elles** = they

17

finir (to finish)

PRESENT

je	**finis**
tu	**finis**
il/elle/on	**finit**
nous	**finissons**
vous	**finissez**
ils/elles	**finissent**

PRESENT SUBJUNCTIVE

je	**finisse**
tu	**finisses**
il/elle/on	**finisse**
nous	**finissions**
vous	**finissiez**
ils/elles	**finissent**

PERFECT

j'	**ai fini**
tu	**as fini**
il/elle/on	**a fini**
nous	**avons fini**
vous	**avez fini**
ils/elles	**ont fini**

IMPERFECT

je	**finissais**
tu	**finissais**
il/elle/on	**finissait**
nous	**finissions**
vous	**finissiez**
ils/elles	**finissaient**

FUTURE

je	**finirai**
tu	**finiras**
il/elle/on	**finira**
nous	**finirons**
vous	**finirez**
ils/elles	**finiront**

CONDITIONAL

je	**finirais**
tu	**finirais**
il/elle/on	**finirait**
nous	**finirions**
vous	**finiriez**
ils/elles	**finiraient**

PRESENT PARTICIPLE

finissant

PAST PARTICIPLE

fini

IMPERATIVE

finis / finissons / finissez

EXAMPLE PHRASES

Finis ta soupe!   Finish your soup!
J'ai **fini**!   I've finished!
Je **finirai** mes devoirs demain.   I'll finish my homework tomorrow.

je/j' = I **tu** = you **il** = he/it **elle** = she/it **on** = we/one **nous** = we **vous** = you **ils/elles** = they

mettre (to put)

PRESENT

je	**mets**
tu	**mets**
il/elle/on	**met**
nous	**mettons**
vous	**mettez**
ils/elles	**mettent**

PRESENT SUBJUNCTIVE

je	**mette**
tu	**mettes**
il/elle/on	**mette**
nous	**mettions**
vous	**mettiez**
ils/elles	**mettent**

PERFECT

j'	**ai mis**
tu	**as mis**
il/elle/on	**a mis**
nous	**avons mis**
vous	**avez mis**
ils/elles	**ont mis**

IMPERFECT

je	**mettais**
tu	**mettais**
il/elle/on	**mettait**
nous	**mettions**
vous	**mettiez**
ils/elles	**mettaient**

FUTURE

je	**mettrai**
tu	**mettras**
il/elle/on	**mettra**
nous	**mettrons**
vous	**mettrez**
ils/elles	**mettront**

CONDITIONAL

je	**mettrais**
tu	**mettrais**
il/elle/on	**mettrait**
nous	**mettrions**
vous	**mettriez**
ils/elles	**mettraient**

PRESENT PARTICIPLE

mettant

PAST PARTICIPLE

mis

IMPERATIVE

mets / mettons / mettez

EXAMPLE PHRASES

Mets ton manteau! Put your coat on!
Où est-ce que tu **as mis** les clés? Where have you put the keys?
J'**ai mis** le livre sur la table. I put the book on the table.
Elle **s'est mise** à pleurer. She started crying.

je/j' = I **tu** = you **il** = he/it **elle** = she/it **on** = we/one **nous** = we **vous** = you **ils/elles** = they

ouvrir (to open)

	PRESENT		**PRESENT SUBJUNCTIVE**
j'	**ouvre**	j'	**ouvre**
tu	**ouvres**	tu	**ouvres**
il/elle/on	**ouvre**	il/elle/on	**ouvre**
nous	**ouvrons**	nous	**ouvrions**
vous	**ouvrez**	vous	**ouvriez**
ils/elles	**ouvrent**	ils/elles	**ouvrent**

	PERFECT		**IMPERFECT**
j'	**ai ouvert**	j'	**ouvrais**
tu	**as ouvert**	tu	**ouvrais**
il/elle/on	**a ouvert**	il/elle/on	**ouvrait**
nous	**avons ouvert**	nous	**ouvrions**
vous	**avez ouvert**	vous	**ouvriez**
ils/elles	**ont ouvert**	ils/elles	**ouvraient**

	FUTURE		**CONDITIONAL**
j'	**ouvrirai**	j'	**ouvrirais**
tu	**ouvriras**	tu	**ouvrirais**
il/elle/on	**ouvrira**	il/elle/on	**ouvrirait**
nous	**ouvrirons**	nous	**ouvririons**
vous	**ouvrirez**	vous	**ouvririez**
ils/elles	**ouvriront**	ils/elles	**ouvriraient**

PRESENT PARTICIPLE

ouvrant

PAST PARTICIPLE

ouvert

IMPERATIVE

ouvre / ouvrons / ouvrez

EXAMPLE PHRASES

Elle **a ouvert** la porte.   She opened the door.
Est-ce que tu pourrais **ouvrir** la fenêtre?   Could you open the window?
Je me suis coupé en **ouvrant** une boîte de conserve.   I cut myself opening a tin.
La porte **s'est ouverte**.   The door opened.

je/j' = I **tu** = you **il** = he/it **elle** = she/it **on** = we/one **nous** = we **vous** = you **ils/elles** = they

20

pouvoir (to be able)

PRESENT

je	**peux**
tu	**peux**
il/elle/on	**peut**
nous	**pouvons**
vous	**pouvez**
ils/elles	**peuvent**

PRESENT SUBJUNCTIVE

je	**puisse**
tu	**puisses**
il/elle/on	**puisse**
nous	**puissions**
vous	**puissiez**
ils/elles	**puissent**

PERFECT

j'	**ai pu**
tu	**as pu**
il/elle/on	**a pu**
nous	**avons pu**
vous	**avez pu**
ils/elles	**ont pu**

IMPERFECT

je	**pouvais**
tu	**pouvais**
il/elle/on	**pouvait**
nous	**pouvions**
vous	**pouviez**
ils/elles	**pouvaient**

FUTURE

je	**pourrai**
tu	**pourras**
il/elle/on	**pourra**
nous	**pourrons**
vous	**pourrez**
ils/elles	**pourront**

CONDITIONAL

je	**pourrais**
tu	**pourrais**
il/elle/on	**pourrait**
nous	**pourrions**
vous	**pourriez**
ils/elles	**pourraient**

PRESENT PARTICIPLE

pouvant

PAST PARTICIPLE

pu

IMPERATIVE

not used

EXAMPLE PHRASES

Je **peux** t'aider, si tu veux.   I can help you if you like.
J'ai fait tout ce que j'**ai pu**.   I did all I could.
Je ne **pourrai** pas venir samedi.   I won't be able to come on Saturday.

je/j' = I **tu** = you **il** = he/it **elle** = she/it **on** = we/one **nous** = we **vous** = you **ils/elles** = they

savoir (to know)

PRESENT

je	**sais**
tu	**sais**
il/elle/on	**sait**
nous	**savons**
vous	**savez**
ils/elles	**savent**

PRESENT SUBJUNCTIVE

je	**sache**
tu	**saches**
il/elle/on	**sache**
nous	**sachions**
vous	**sachiez**
ils/elles	**sachent**

PERFECT

j'	**ai su**
tu	**as su**
il/elle/on	**a su**
nous	**avons su**
vous	**avez su**
ils/elles	**ont su**

IMPERFECT

je	**savais**
tu	**savais**
il/elle/on	**savait**
nous	**savions**
vous	**saviez**
ils/elles	**savaient**

FUTURE

je	**saurai**
tu	**sauras**
il/elle/on	**saura**
nous	**saurons**
vous	**saurez**
ils/elles	**sauront**

CONDITIONAL

je	**saurais**
tu	**saurais**
il/elle/on	**saurait**
nous	**saurions**
vous	**sauriez**
ils/elles	**sauraient**

PRESENT PARTICIPLE

sachant

PAST PARTICIPLE

su

IMPERATIVE

sache / sachons / sachez

EXAMPLE PHRASES

Tu **sais** ce que tu vas faire l'année prochaine?   Do you know what you're doing next year?

Je ne **sais** pas.   I don't know.

Elle ne **sait** pas nager.   She can't swim.

Tu **savais** que son père était pakistanais?   Did you know her father was Pakistani?

je/j' = I **tu** = you **il** = he/it **elle** = she/it **on** = we/one **nous** = we **vous** = you **ils/elles** = they

sentir (to smell; to feel)

	PRESENT		PRESENT SUBJUNCTIVE
je	sens	je	sente
tu	sens	tu	sentes
il/elle/on	sent	il/elle/on	sente
nous	sentons	nous	sentions
vous	sentez	vous	sentiez
ils/elles	sentent	ils/elles	sentent

	PERFECT		IMPERFECT
j'	ai senti	je	sentais
tu	as senti	tu	sentais
il/elle/on	a senti	il/elle/on	sentait
nous	avons senti	nous	sentions
vous	avez senti	vous	sentiez
ils/elles	ont senti	ils/elles	sentaient

	FUTURE		CONDITIONAL
je	sentirai	je	sentirais
tu	sentiras	tu	sentirais
il/elle/on	sentira	il/elle/on	sentirait
nous	sentirons	nous	sentirions
vous	sentirez	vous	sentiriez
ils/elles	sentiront	ils/elles	sentiraient

PRESENT PARTICIPLE

sentant

PAST PARTICIPLE

senti

IMPERATIVE

sens / sentons / sentez

....

EXAMPLE PHRASES

Ça **sentait** mauvais. It smelt bad.
Je n'**ai** rien **senti**. I didn't feel a thing.
Elle ne **se sent** pas bien. She's not feeling well.

je/j' = I **tu** = you **il** = he/it **elle** = she/it **on** = we/one **nous** = we **vous** = you **ils/elles** = they

se taire (to stop talking)

PRESENT

je	**me tais**
tu	**te tais**
il/elle/on	**se tait**
nous	**nous taisons**
vous	**vous taisez**
ils/elles	**se taisent**

PRESENT SUBJUNCTIVE

je	**me taise**
tu	**te taises**
il/elle/on	**se taise**
nous	**nous taisions**
vous	**vous taisiez**
ils/elles	**se taisent**

PERFECT

je	**me suis tu(e)**
tu	**t'es tu(e)**
il/elle/on	**s'est tu(e)**
nous	**nous sommes tu(e)s**
vous	**vous êtes tu(e)(s)**
ils/elles	**se sont tu(e)s**

IMPERFECT

je	**me taisais**
tu	**te taisais**
il/elle/on	**se taisait**
nous	**nous taisions**
vous	**vous taisiez**
ils/elles	**se taisaient**

FUTURE

je	**me tairai**
tu	**te tairas**
il/elle/on	**se taira**
nous	**nous tairons**
vous	**vous tairez**
ils/elles	**se tairont**

CONDITIONAL

je	**me tairais**
tu	**te tairais**
il/elle/on	**se tairait**
nous	**nous tairions**
vous	**vous tairiez**
ils/elles	**se tairaient**

PRESENT PARTICIPLE

se taisant

PAST PARTICIPLE

tu

IMPERATIVE

tais-toi / taisons-nous / taisez-vous

EXAMPLE PHRASES

Il **s'est tu**.   He stopped talking.
Taisez-vous!   Be quiet!
Sophie, **tais-toi**!   Be quiet Sophie!

je/j' = I **tu** = you **il** = he/it **elle** = she/it **on** = we/one **nous** = we **vous** = you **ils/elles** = they

vendre (to sell)

PRESENT

je	**vends**
tu	**vends**
il/elle/on	**vend**
nous	**vendons**
vous	**vendez**
ils/elles	**vendent**

PRESENT SUBJUNCTIVE

je	**vende**
tu	**vendes**
il/elle/on	**vende**
nous	**vendions**
vous	**vendiez**
ils/elles	**vendent**

PERFECT

j'	**ai vendu**
tu	**as vendu**
il/elle/on	**a vendu**
nous	**avons vendu**
vous	**avez vendu**
ils/elles	**ont vendu**

IMPERFECT

je	**vendais**
tu	**vendais**
il/elle/on	**vendait**
nous	**vendions**
vous	**vendiez**
ils/elles	**vendaient**

FUTURE

je	**vendrai**
tu	**vendras**
il/elle/on	**vendra**
nous	**vendrons**
vous	**vendrez**
ils/elles	**vendront**

CONDITIONAL

je	**vendrais**
tu	**vendrais**
il/elle/on	**vendrait**
nous	**vendrions**
vous	**vendriez**
ils/elles	**vendraient**

PRESENT PARTICIPLE

vendant

PAST PARTICIPLE

vendu

IMPERATIVE

vends / vendons / vendez

EXAMPLE PHRASES

Il m'**a vendu** son vélo pour 50 euros.   He sold me his bike for 50 euros.
Est-ce que vous **vendez** des piles?   Do you sell batteries?
Elle voudrait **vendre** sa voiture.   She would like to sell her car.

je/j' = I **tu** = you **il** = he/it **elle** = she/it **on** = we/one **nous** = we **vous** = you **ils/elles** = they

venir (to come)

PRESENT

je	**viens**
tu	**viens**
il/elle/on	**vient**
nous	**venons**
vous	**venez**
ils/elles	**viennent**

PRESENT SUBJUNCTIVE

je	**vienne**
tu	**viennes**
il/elle/on	**vienne**
nous	**venions**
vous	**veniez**
ils/elles	**viennent**

PERFECT

je	**suis venu(e)**
tu	**es venu(e)**
il/elle/on	**est venu(e)**
nous	**sommes venu(e)s**
vous	**êtes venu(e)(s)**
ils/elles	**sont venu(e)s**

IMPERFECT

je	**venais**
tu	**venais**
il/elle/on	**venait**
nous	**venions**
vous	**veniez**
ils/elles	**venaient**

FUTURE

je	**viendrai**
tu	**viendras**
il/elle/on	**viendra**
nous	**viendrons**
vous	**viendrez**
ils/elles	**viendront**

CONDITIONAL

je	**viendrais**
tu	**viendrais**
il/elle/on	**viendrait**
nous	**viendrions**
vous	**viendriez**
ils/elles	**viendraient**

PRESENT PARTICIPLE

venant

PAST PARTICIPLE

venu

IMPERATIVE

viens / venons / venez

EXAMPLE PHRASES

Elle ne **viendra** pas cette année.   She won't be coming this year.
Fatou et Malik **viennent** du Sénégal.   Fatou and Malik come from Senegal.
Je **viens** de manger.   I've just eaten.

je/j' = I **tu** = you **il** = he/it **elle** = she/it **on** = we/one **nous** = we **vous** = you **ils/elles** = they

26

voir (to see)

PRESENT

je	**vois**
tu	**vois**
il/elle/on	**voit**
nous	**voyons**
vous	**voyez**
ils/elles	**voient**

PRESENT SUBJUNCTIVE

je	**voie**
tu	**voies**
il/elle/on	**voie**
nous	**voyions**
vous	**voyiez**
ils/elles	**voient**

PERFECT

j'	**ai vu**
tu	**as vu**
il/elle/on	**a vu**
nous	**avons vu**
vous	**avez vu**
ils/elles	**ont vu**

IMPERFECT

je	**voyais**
tu	**voyais**
il/elle/on	**voyait**
nous	**voyions**
vous	**voyiez**
ils/elles	**voyaient**

FUTURE

je	**verrai**
tu	**verras**
il/elle/on	**verra**
nous	**verrons**
vous	**verrez**
ils/elles	**verront**

CONDITIONAL

je	**verrais**
tu	**verrais**
il/elle/on	**verrait**
nous	**verrions**
vous	**verriez**
ils/elles	**verraient**

PRESENT PARTICIPLE

voyant

PAST PARTICIPLE

vu

IMPERATIVE

vois / voyons / voyez

EXAMPLE PHRASES

Venez me **voir** quand vous serez à Paris. Come and see me when you're in Paris.
Je ne **vois** rien sans mes lunettes. I can't see anything without my glasses.
Est-ce que tu l'**as vu**? Did you see him? *or* Have you seen him?
Est-ce que cette tache **se voit**? Does that stain show?

je/j' = I **tu** = you **il** = he/it **elle** = she/it **on** = we/one **nous** = we **vous** = you **ils/elles** = they

vouloir (to want)

PRESENT

je	**veux**
tu	**veux**
il/elle/on	**veut**
nous	**voulons**
vous	**voulez**
ils/elles	**veulent**

PRESENT SUBJUNCTIVE

je	**veuille**
tu	**veuilles**
il/elle/on	**veuille**
nous	**voulions**
vous	**vouliez**
ils/elles	**veuillent**

PERFECT

j'	**ai voulu**
tu	**as voulu**
il/elle/on	**a voulu**
nous	**avons voulu**
vous	**avez voulu**
ils/elles	**ont voulu**

IMPERFECT

je	**voulais**
tu	**voulais**
il/elle/on	**voulait**
nous	**voulions**
vous	**vouliez**
ils/elles	**voulaient**

FUTURE

je	**voudrai**
tu	**voudras**
il/elle/on	**voudra**
nous	**voudrons**
vous	**voudrez**
ils/elles	**voudront**

CONDITIONAL

je	**voudrais**
tu	**voudrais**
il/elle/on	**voudrait**
nous	**voudrions**
vous	**voudriez**
ils/elles	**voudraient**

PRESENT PARTICIPLE

voulant

PAST PARTICIPLE

voulu

IMPERATIVE

veuille / veuillons / veuillez

EXAMPLE PHRASES

Elle **veut** un vélo pour Noël.   She wants a bike for Christmas.
Ils **voulaient** aller au cinéma.   They wanted to go to the cinema.
Tu **voudrais** une tasse de thé?   Would you like a cup of tea?

je/j' = I **tu** = you **il** = he/it **elle** = she/it **on** = we/one **nous** = we **vous** = you **ils/elles** = they

28